# WOMEN IN NEW RELIGIONS

*Also by Elizabeth Puttick*

WOMEN AS TEACHERS AND DISCIPLES IN TRADITIONAL AND NEW RELIGIONS (*co-editor with Peter Clarke*)

# Women in New Religions

## In Search of Community, Sexuality and Spiritual Power

Elizabeth Puttick

Foreword by Ursula King

Consultant Editor: Jo Campling

St. Martin's Press
New York

WOMEN IN NEW RELIGIONS
Text copyright © 1997 by Elizabeth Puttick
Foreword copyright © 1997 by Ursula King

St. Martin's Press, Scholarly and Reference Division,
175 Fifth Avenue, New York, N.Y. 10010

First published in the United States of America in 1997

This book is printed on paper suitable for recycling and
made from fully managed and sustained forest sources.

Printed in Great Britain

ISBN 0–312–17259–1 (cloth)
ISBN 0–312–17260–5 (paperback)

Library of Congress Cataloging-in-Publication Data
Puttick, Elizabeth, 1952–
Women in new religions : in search of community, sexuality
and spiritual power / Elizabeth Puttick.
p.   cm.
Includes bibliographical references and index.
ISBN 0–312–17259–1 (cloth).— ISBN 0–312–17260–5 (pbk.)
1. Women and religion.   2. Sects—History—20th century.
3. Cults—History—20th century.   I. Title.
BL458.P88   1997
291'.046'082—dc21                                    96–46619
                                                        CIP

Unto the woman he said, I will greatly multiply thy sorrow and thy conception; in sorrow thou shall bring forth children; and thy desire shall be thy husband, and he shall rule over thee.

Genesis

A woman is not only capable of giving birth to children, she is also capable of giving birth to herself as a seeker of truth.

Osho

The importance of the Goddess symbol for women cannot be overstressed. The image of the Goddess inspires women to see ourselves as divine, our bodies as sacred, the changing phases of our lives as holy, our aggression as healthy, our anger as purifying, and our power to nurture and create, but also to limit and destroy when necessary, as the very force that sustains all life. Through the Goddess, we can discover our strength, enlighten our minds, own our bodies, and celebrate our emotions. We can move beyond narrow, constricting roles and become whole.

Starhawk

# Contents

# Acknowledgements

A number of people have helped me during the course of researching and writing this book. Warmest thanks to my academic supervisor, Peter Clarke, for his support and encouragement throughout the doctoral research that formed the basis for this book. Special thanks to Harriet Crabtree, Susan Greenwood, Stephen and Martine Batchelor for reading drafts, for illuminating, constructive criticisms and suggestions. Many people encouraged me through stimulating  discussion, helpful suggestions, and information. I would like to thank in particular Michael York, Elisabeth Arweck, Susan Palmer, Vivianne Crowley, Nina Coltart, Cari Shay, Anne Geraghty, and Guy Claxton. I am particularly grateful to all my respondents, for giving their time to be interviewed and for the authenticity and quality of their responses, which form the basis and heart of this book. Warmest thanks to Ursula King for her foreword; also to Jo Campling, consultant editor, and Annabelle Buckley, my commissioning editor at Macmillan, and my copy-editor Robyn Marsack. And finally, a most heartfelt thank-you to my husband Robin, for his unstinting support and interest, and for our ongoing lively and stimulating discussions.

# Foreword

Many publications deal with either women and religion or with new religious movements, but there are few which focus specifically on women in new religious movements. Elizabeth Puttick has provided us with just such a book which asks searching questions about women's participation and leadership roles in new religions. Most importantly, do these new movements empower, liberate or oppress women? Do they meet women's own spiritual needs at the present time, when traditional images and roles are being discarded and new ones have to be experimented with?

It has long been evident that it is not women alone but Western society as a whole that is experiencing a profound crisis of cultural and religious identity. This is all the more true the nearer we move towards a new millennium which presents us with urgent questions about the future of human life at both the personal and social level. New religious movements, though usually small in the total number of their adherents, are thriving in their attempts to give purpose, direction and meaning to the lives of disciples and seekers. Many of these movements have strong countercultural or revivalist tendencies; others are innovative and syncretistic, and quite a few are explicitly grounded in traditions derived from Eastern religions and cultures. There can be no doubt that in our postmodern age, when all certainties are doubted and differences are celebrated, the free and open-ended quest for a life-affirming and life-enhancing spirituality is undertaken more than ever before. It is also the first time in human history that women have taken such an active, public part in this quest and in the creative search for spiritual meaning.

Drawing on current theoretical and empirical work in sociology, psychology and religious studies, Elizabeth Puttick has used her first-hand knowledge of the Osho movement to critically discuss its remarkable experience of women in religious leadership roles. This discussion is greatly enhanced by comparing women in the Osho movement with those in many other movements, both present and past. The combination of these different perspectives leads to insightful discussions about leadership and its special charisma. Is the path of discipleship particularly congenial to women's spirituality, and how good are women at being disciples? Or by taking this path of spiritual discipleship, do women again become simply dependent and victims? What are the complex connections between sexuality, spirituality and power for both men and women?

In this context the question about the importance of asceticism and sexual abstinence is raised. How far can asceticism in the world religions be correlated with misogyny? Do the new religions fare any better here than the old ones? The image and experience of motherhood is also something new religious movements have to wrestle with if they do not simply wish to adhere to traditional models of womanhood. Elizabeth Puttick also addresses a theme which is hardly ever mentioned: what is the role of children on the spiritual path to enlightenment? This surely is a very important topic which deserves much fuller attention, especially if female religious leadership becomes more prominent in the future.

But is there a specifically female style of leadership? What is the experience of women leaders in religious movements founded by men – and that means all traditional religions and almost all new ones too. This book points to the ambiguities and tensions, the ambivalence of spiritual equality between women and men which is rarely ever satisfactorily resolved.

The penultimate chapter discusses Goddess spirituality as a modern alternative for women, and it judges Paganism as the most vital and most interesting new religious movement for women. Another valuable aspect of this study is the typology of new religious movements with which it concludes, based on a hierarchy of human needs from those of survival and security to esteem, love and self-actualization.

This book throws light on the current transformation of traditional gender stereotypes, the new thinking and social organization experimented with in communes, the search for new identities, the suffering and doubt of individuals on their inner quest, and the endemic sexism of many religious institutions, including some of the more conservative new religious movements. The relationship between women and new religious movements is a many-sided, complex story, but one of much vitality, new vigour and fresh approaches. To me at least, this story also shows the growing importance and participation of women in spirituality, a contribution which I judge both essential and indispensable for a healthy, balanced future of human society on this planet.

URSULA KING,
*Professor of Theology and Religious Studies*
*University of Bristol*

# List of Abbreviations

| | |
|---|---|
| ACM | Anti-Cult Movement |
| BK | Brahma Kumaris |
| COG | Children of God |
| CUT | Church Universal and Triumphant |
| FWBO | Friends of the Western Buddhist Order |
| HPM | Human Potential Movement |
| ISKCON | International Society for Krishna Consciousness |
| NRM | New Religious Movement |
| *OTI* | *Osho Times International* |
| TM | Transcendental Meditation |

# Introduction

## Women and Religion

Women have always been the biggest 'consumers' of religion, but on the whole have been badly served, disparaged and oppressed by the religions themselves. In most organized religions, to be born a woman is viewed as a punishment, either for misdeeds in a previous life or for the sin of the first woman: the original Evil Temptress. In the first case, the only recourse is to become a well-behaved, submissive wife and mother in order to be reborn as a man. In the second case, redemption is possible through suffering and sacrifice: endlessly bringing forth babies in sorrow. Although such misogyny is rare in contemporary Western religion, some fundamentalist sects and new religions do display it. Furthermore, millennia of misogyny and sexism are not easily eradicated, and their effects still subtly pervade the religions, particularly at doctrinal level. Marx and Freud contend that father/phallus worship in the form of organized religion keeps women in a state of childlike submission and oppression. Feminists have tended to agree. During the second wave of feminism in the 1970s, religion was right off the agenda, perceived as irrelevant and irredeemably patriarchal. In a secular world in which religion was overshadowed by science, it was deemed better to ignore it, let it wither and rot of its own accord, and get on with the 'real' political work.

However, religion and religiosity did not disappear. Out in the 'real world', women were storming barriers in campaigns for political and economic rights, but the citadels of the religions remained relatively untouched. In the meantime, many women wanted to reclaim their spiritual heritage; they felt a deep calling to be rabbis, priests and ministers, yet were discriminated against or barred from their vocation. Nevertheless, some women remained in their Jewish or Christian religion of birth, questioning and challenging the theological and structural underpinnings, in particular the male gender of the deity and the exclusion of women from the priesthood. Others rejected organized religion not just on account of its sexism but

1

because they found its dogmas, rituals and outlook dry, dead, meaningless and outmoded. Instead they turned to Eastern mysticism, the remains of pre-Christian Paganism, and a plethora of other new religious movements, seeking alternatives that would acknowledge and affirm female spirituality, and empower women as full participants, priests and leaders.

## New Religious Movements (NRMs)[1]

Mainstream society may be seen as a relatively static, stable conglomeration of individuals, groups and institutions that throws up more dynamic, deviant groups on its margins covering all fields including politics, science, health, gender, the arts and religion. The margin may also be the leading edge, whose experiments create the future. New religious movements (NRMs) are marginal groups in society, but have an impact and influence beyond the numbers of people involved.[2] This is partly owing to the dramatic scandals and tragedies sometimes associated with them, which make front-page news. Certain NRMs hit the headlines continually, such as Scientology, the Unification Church ('Moonies'), Children of God (now known as the Family), ISKCON ('Hare Krishna'), and the Osho movement. Even less well known NRMs can create a major impact when tragedy strikes, as demonstrated by the Branch Davidians, Solar Temple, and Aum Shunrikyo.

On the other hand, long-term changes in ideas, attitudes and practices can sometimes be traced at least partly to the influence of NRMs, such as the widespread belief in reincarnation, the fast increasing use of complementary medicine and health approaches, vegetarianism, meditation, body-positive spirituality and sacred sex. 'Personal development' originated in a psychospiritual context but has now become a fundamental concept in mainstream society, including the new business philosophy with its growing emphasis on empowerment, human values and ethics. Other ideas have a reciprocal influence, emerging in secular form but developing a sacred dimension in alternative religion. For example, ecology has transmuted from a scientific discipline into sociopolitical activism and then into ecospirituality. In this form it influenced the new religions, particularly Paganism, but then became a major force in mainstream religions.

It has been widely noted that NRMs flourish during periods of rapid social change, arising as vehicles of protest, deviation and challenge. They are responses to but also agents of transformation, experimenting with new ideas and practices, often in sealed-off communities, isolated from the norms, conventions and restrictions of society. In this respect they function as laboratories, crucibles for new experiments of which the more successful are taken up – usually in a more diluted, digestible form – by mainstream society. They offer a critique of family and society as well as established religion. In NRMs sexual and family relationships tend to take second place, break up, or be renounced altogether. On the other hand they may also be entered into in order to stabilize relationships and social structures, or to provide viable alternatives to the dysfunctional nuclear families into which many participants were born. NRMs may provide *gemeinschaft*, an alternative family and community. They may also provide women with an alternative destiny to motherhood or career in the form of a spiritual path.

Not all NRMs are on the cutting edge. Just as they may be perceived as either a threat or a hope for the future, so they themselves tend to adopt one of two responses to social change. Some see it as an opportunity for growth, experimentation and rebellion against old norms and paradigms, as with left-wing political and social protest groups, new artistic movements, and millennialist sects. In contemporary religion, this trend is exemplified by the Eastern-based counter-cultural NRMs of the 1970s and the current New Age and Pagan revival. However, another response to change is a fear of instability and chaos, which is resisted by reverting to tradition. Such groups are likely to be more conservative, rigid and reactionary than the mainstream, as with right-wing political groups and 'back to roots' movements in the social sphere. The conservative NRMs of the 1970s (mostly Christian but some Eastern) and the current rise of evangelicalism in world religions are examples of this trend. Yet within these broad categories they present an enormous range and variety of belief, practice, social structure and style of expression – a complexity that defies classification yet within which trends and patterns may be discerned.[3] This book is in part an attempt to interpret and shape these into a meaningful typology.

## The Osho Movement

The main focus of this book is on the Osho movement, partly because it is the one of which I have the most intimate, in-depth knowledge – initially as a member, later as a researcher. My own 'conversion career' was fairly typical of people who joined this and other counter-cultural NRMs in the 1970s. As a student I identified with the 'alternative society', experimenting freely with social activism and self-exploration. I went on political demonstrations, joined a feminist CR group, lived in country communes and urban squats. My vacations were spent on an organic market garden in the depths of the English country-side, run by an Indian yoga teacher, where I learned about the environmental crisis and consequently became a vegetarian.

At the same time, I was becoming more and more drawn into inner-directed 'growth', learning TM and participating in encounter groups and enlightenment intensives. India was the most fashionable destination, land of yogis, sadhus and gurus, but like many pragmatic English people I was initially sceptical about gurus. I preferred to search in my own way, shopping in the ever-expanding spiritual supermarket. However, in the mid-1970s I finally visited India, where I became a disciple of the controversial Bhagwan Shree Rajneesh (later known as Osho). Eventually I left, but look back at those five years as one of the most intense, exuberant, challenging and 'growthful' periods of my life.

I have also chosen to focus on the Osho movement because it is one of the best known post-war NRMs and the most rep-resentative of the counter-culture. East–West relations are still a global concern on many fronts, including religion, and one of Osho's main aims was to create a model of psychospiritual development grounded in a synthesis between Western human-istic psychology and Eastern meditation. This has now been widely adopted and adapted in the Human Potential Move-ment and transpersonal psychology, within other NRMs and the wider New Age and Pagan revival, and even within some world religions that previously disdained psychotherapy, such as Buddhism and Christianity.

Osho is also interesting as a pure type charismatic leader in his self-legitimated status as guru of the New Age. One of the most contentious aspects of NRMs is the master–disciple relationship; they are often led by immensely charismatic men, who claim to derive their authority by divine appointment or the possession of esoteric knowledge. They offer to pass their enlightenment on to their followers, but the price is total surrender. This phenomenon has aroused concern among academics, priests, teachers, psychiatrists, the media, and the parents of members, some of whom have formed the Anti-Cult Movement (ACM) in response to the perceived threat to democratic liberties. There is also widespread concern in the women's movement about NRMs and their potential for the abuse of power, particularly the sexual abuse by male leaders of their female followers. As in the public and political spheres, sexual scandals have been erupting in old and new religions, including Christianity and Buddhism. One bizarre result is that in some cases an unlikely alliance between fundamentalists and feminists has been formed, as sometimes happens in secular debates around birth control and pornography.

## Women in NRMs

This book focuses mainly on the experience of women in NRMs. It asks why well-educated young women with the potential for successful careers and happy home lives within society chose to relegate themselves to the margins in pursuit of spiritual quests. Was their search fulfilled, both in personal and social terms? Did they find or create any improvements over both older religions and secular society? These questions are also explored in the context of a feminization of society that is happening in all spheres, in the family and workplace as well as in religion. The main feminist issue in the study of NRMs is gender roles, and the extent to which these movements suppress or liberate women, both spiritually and socially. Most of the existing research suggests that women are subordinated and exploited in old and new religions, but there is growing evidence that in some NRMs women may be empowered. This book looks at what forms of religion empower women, and what different needs are fulfilled.

The Osho movement is one of the most interesting NRMs in terms of gender issues. Osho's gender ideology was based on Jungian concepts of sexual polarity and balance, which led to a strong emphasis on androgyny, whereby women and men aimed to explore and develop their opposite-sex attributes, and ultimately to transcend gender altogether. However, he perceived feminine attributes as superior to masculine and believed women were more spiritual and made better disciples than men. He therefore promoted women and gave them many opportunities to hold power. It is an issue as to how far women may be empowered in the context of absolute surrender to a male master.

Other NRMs were exploring these issues in similar and different ways, and I bring them in for comparison and contrast. Throughout the focus is more on the counter-cultural movements, the conservative ones being used more for contrast. This is because the former seem to me (and to many other commentators) to be of more interest and relevance to the future in their experimental and syncretic approach. In many ways the counter-cultural NRMs of the 1970s prepared the way for the New Age and Pagan NRMs of the 1990s, which are attempting to create Westernized, democratized, feminized forms of spirituality.

## Methodological and Gender Issues

Some years after I left the Osho movement, I ended up studying and researching the movement with which I'd been so intimately involved. This was initially a most disorienting experience, doubly so as a woman researching women's experience: insider turned outsider, going native in reverse. Yet this is now becoming an increasingly common situation, resulting in the blurring of boundaries between the subjects and objects of study. As new religions are becoming more integrated into mainstream society, they appeal more than ever to professionals and even academics, who may therefore cross the line out of personal interest. At the same time members of NRMs are becoming less anti-intellectual, perceiving the value of certain academic disciplines for understanding religion, and joining the ranks of academia as students and teachers. This trend presents a challenge to traditional notions of objectivity and the subject/object duality, which are the basis of scientific methodology, requiring a rigorous exclusion or 'bracketing out' of personal beliefs and values.

My ambiguous status as ex-insider found some support from

Weber's methodology of *Verstehen*, which places primary value on understanding the inner experience and self-interpretation of practitioners. Weber moves on from his definition to state the classic ethnographic position: 'Only if he [*sic*] can gain some apprehension of what it means to be a believer can he say anything useful about the religious movement he studies; and yet, in gaining that understanding, he must not actually become a believer' (1982, 13). This precarious balance between empathy and objectivity is the aim of social science, but with a greater emphasis on scientific objectivity. Value freeness is the aim, but there is an inherent gender bias at work here in the greater respectability of the more 'masculine' approach of quantitative research over the more 'feminine' values of qualitative research.

Gender itself is a vexed concept, as is the terminology surrounding it. I am using the term in its most widely used sense among sociologists and feminist researchers: as social construction rather than biological manifestation.[4] Feminist theology has also challenged prevailing concepts of gender as spiritually and ethically inadequate and offensive, and tends to prefer social definitions.[5] I use the terms masculine and feminine to describe those aspects and attributes of gender that are widely agreed to be socialized, constructed or imposed, while reserving the terms male and female for psychobiological functions. However, there is intense disagreement on the differences and boundaries even where the basic definition is accepted – and often it is not – so my respondents as well as the writers I quote sometimes use these terms in contradictory ways.[6] I have aimed for as much consistency as possible in my own usage. This book contains frequent references to sexism and misogyny. These are value-loaded, polemical terms, but they have a literal meaning and only too potent relevance in the lives of many women. I use sexism as referring to attitudes and behaviour by men towards women (and sometimes vice versa) based on prejudice regarding gender differences and the values ascribed to them. Sexism may be unconscious, an internalization of early socialization without malicious intent though potentially harmful in its consequences. Misogyny literally means hatred of women, and I use it in instances where anti-women attitudes seem to originate in more intense, violently negative feelings and issue in more destructive behaviour.

Gender bias was one of the first allegations to challenge the supremacy and attainability of scientific objectivity, along with the critiques of other minority groups exposing class and racial bias, all masked by the assumed universalism of the white, middle-class, male perspective. Its claims and hegemony were also undermined by the discoveries of quantum mechanics, including the observer effect, chaos theory, and Eisenberg's uncertainty principle, which demonstrate the impossibility of perfect objectivity, even if personal value judgements and social bias are avoided. As a result of these various critiques, it has now become allowable though still contentious to take an ideological stance. Despite the backlash again political correctness, it may be legitimated in the interests of presenting the experience and views of previously ignored minorities, thus presenting a more complete and comprehensive record of historical events and social phenomena.

Feminist research is in line with Weber's methodology, but politicizes it in order to challenge the relations of dominance. In the words of the feminist theologian Emily Culpepper: 'feminists must develop our own methods for recognizing and researching women's direct, positive efforts to create the Self and the world that are not patriarchal' (1978, 8).[7] The aim is to replace objective scientific research with conscious partiality, which may lead to even more actively partisan approaches such as Lather's 'emancipatory social science' and Fiorenza's 'action–research oriented approach and methodology', which aim to liberate the women whose lives they research by bringing them to awareness of their oppression. This is in line with Marxist principles, though neo-Marxists have pointed out the dangers of relying solely on participants' perceptions, which may be clouded with false consciousness and ideological mystification. It is also a somewhat patronizing position. Foucault has also warned of 'the violence of a position that sides against those who are happy in their ignorance, against the effective illusions by which humanity protects itself'.[8]

I personally believe that to admit one's personal position is more valid and illuminating than hiding behind the defence of scientific objectivity, which is anyway unattainable. But it is equally unhelpful to turn the quest for truth into a crusade. Academic research entails a particular responsibility to the people whose lives and innermost thoughts and feelings we are investigating: to present these in as empathetic, fair and accurate a form as possible. In addition, we are accountable to the multi-level complexity of 'truth': to present as complete and comprehensive an interpretation as possible in the context of broader social and spiritual trends.

My research is based in a three-aspected perspective: a) as a practitioner, with 25 years' experience in a range of human potential groups, Eastern philosophy and meditation, including eight years in an Eastern-based new religion, and various New Age and shamanic practices; b) as a feminist sociologist of religion, trying to understand these movements and phenomena from a more detached academic perspective within a broader social context; c) as a professional, a former publisher of books on personal development and spirituality, which gave me a broad overview of the whole field of contemporary spirituality accompanied by a keen awareness of current and emerging trends. The resulting book is based on my experience as a participant and a participant-observer (very different perspectives), and on formal, recorded interviews and informal conversations with many women and a few men from a range of new religious movements. Much insight has come through the work of other scholars and researchers from various fields, to whom I refer in the course of the book. The Internet has also been an invaluable resource for information, news and views on NRMs and related issues. I have therefore added a list of Internet addresses to the bibliography of sites referenced in the book and other sites of interest, for anyone wanting more detailed information, updates, or contact with the groups via e-mail.

# 1 New Religions and the Counter-Culture

## The Counter-Culture of the 1960s

The 1960s marked the beginning of a period of rapid social change, which is transforming the world radically and fundamentally. These changes correlate with the millennialist visions of many old and new religions, but are also perceived by political leaders such as Vaclav Havel:

> There are good reasons for suggesting that the modern age has ended. Many things indicate that we are going through a transitional period, when it seems that something is on the way out and something else is painfully being born. It is as if something were crumbling, decaying and exhausting itself, while something else, still indistinct, were arising from the rubble.[1]

This transformation of the world and of consciousness is sometimes termed a 'paradigm shift'.[2] The causes of the shift are complex and multidimensional and can be traced back at least as far as the eighteenth-century Romantic movement.[3] However, the explosion of rebellious creativity in the 1960s seemed both at the time and in retrospect to be a turning point. This was partly because it followed a period of particularly staid conservatism in the 1950s; partly because rather than remaining a fringe subculture it grew to have enormous impact on all aspects of society: politics, social and political activism, the arts, literature, fashion, health, gender, sexuality and spirituality. Those creating and participating in it called it the alternative society, while sociologists labelled it the counter-culture.

The counter-culture arose partly as a rebellion against the materialism and 'technocracy' of the post-war climate. An entire generation of young people – well fed and well educated – rejected their parents' goals of wealth, success and status in favour of the search for meaning and fulfilment. It was sometimes castigated by social commentators and moralists as an escapist flight into sex, drugs and rock 'n' roll – the aspect that was given the most media attention. As much as escapism, however, it was an active rejection of scientific developments and socio-political values that had been invalidated – if not annihilated – by two world wars, and most immediately by the pointless destruction of the Vietnam War. Those who looked deeper perceived it as also 'a reaction against the "disenchantment of the world", and the loss of magic, mystery, prophecy and the sacred. A search to find one's "real self" amidst the multiplicity of roles and selves we are made to act out' (Mullan 1983, 17).[4]

The counter-culture was also a 'rebellion against reason': the arid intellectualism of Western philosophy and theology with its over-reliance on 'left-brain' thinking. Polytechnics were replaced by Polytantrics, and the 1968 Antiuniversity of London aspired to transform Western Man through such sources as Artaud, Zimmer, Gurdjieff, Reich, Marx, Gnostic, Sufi and Tantric texts, autobiographical accounts of madness and ecstatic states of consciousness – all synthesized into a 'free-wheeling succession of open-ended situations'. One of the main chroniclers of the counter-culture, Theodore Roszak, summarized this trend:

> One can discern, then, a continuum of thought and experience among the young which links together the New Left sociology of Mills, the Freudian Marxism of Herbert Marcuse, the Gestalt-therapy anarchism of Paul Goodman, the apocalyptic body mysticism of Norman Brown, the Zen-based psychotherapy of Alan Watts, and finally Timothy Leary's impenetrably occult narcissism. (1968, 64)

**The Human Potential Movement**

With its enthusiastic explorations of self and society, its questioning of values and overturning of conventions, the counter-culture paved the way for a spiritual revival on the broadest possible front: seeking to integrate the dualities of society and religion, psyche and soma, masculine and feminine, East and West. Since the Judaeo-Christian tradition had no developed tradition or methodology for the inner quest, the tools were provided by the relatively new science of psychology.

The Human Potential Movement (HPM) was the psycho-spiritual wing of the counter-culture. It was largely an outgrowth of humanistic psychology, which was developed by Abraham Maslow in response to the limitations of psychoanalysis and behaviourism. Maslow's main influence on the HPM was his concept of the 'self-actualized' human being: one who is fully alive and responsive, having solved the basic survival needs and psychological problems; who has ecstatic 'peak experiences' and is therefore able to explore all the realms of human potential, including mysticism. Maslow thus paved the way for the later spiritualization of psychotherapy, although the HPM was originally more secular in its aims.[5]

The primary goal of the HPM was to explore the realms of feelings and relationships, a taboo area in British society at the time. The militarization of two world wars had encouraged a rigidity and repression that Wilhelm Reich (1968) called 'character armour', and identified as the cause of neurosis, many psychosomatic disorders and sociopolitical problems, including fascism. Psychotherapy for the populace was integral to the socialist utopia proposed by Reich as the only effective antidote to fascism.[6] In this austere climate the Roman virtues of discipline, duty, gravity, firmness, tenacity, hard work and frugality restrained the softer virtues and the spontaneous expression of affection. So the children of the post-war period grew up economically privileged but emotionally and spiritually deprived.

This phenomenon can also be interpreted in gender terms: hard, military, 'masculine' values subjugating the softer 'feminine' values: relationship, feeling, nurturing, tenderness, intuition. These repressed virtues were rediscovered and affirmed by the HPM, with the aid of Eastern spirituality. Mysticism has partly been neglected and disparaged in the West on account of its perceived associations with femininity – not just by soldiers but by philosophers, including Nietzsche. The former philosopher Osho saw the East–West dichotomy partly in genderized terms: 'The West represents the male mind, aggressive, intellectual. The East represents the female mind, receptive, intuitive' (1981, 7).

The exploration and development of these issues and values by the HPM in the 1970s was also the precursor of the now widespread interest in personal development, the quality of relationships and emotional literacy; human values in the work-place; and the replacement of hard political causes with softer issues such as environmentalism and animal rights. Our outlook has been affected to the point where even philosophy may be interpreted in terms of the philosopher's emotional problems, as with the latest biography of Bertrand Russell.[7] A new organ-ization called Antidote has been set up by a group of British psychotherapists including Susie Orbach to re-engage the emo-tional and psychological dimensions of life with the political process, although it may have a struggle to contend with the 'stiff upper lip' attitude that still dominates the Conservative party, as expressed by the MP Nicholas Soames, grandson of Winston Churchill:

> This terrible counselling thing has grown up in Britain. Whatever you do wrong it's somebody else's fault, or your mother hit you. I think that's all balls. It's ghastly political correctness. People need to pull themselves together. I'm not a great believer in blubbing in your tent. I do get melan-choly now and again, but you go to bed, sleep well and wake up pawing the ground like a horse in the morning.[8]

The psyche was also the 'forbidden zone' of Christianity. Although psychoanalysis had been thriving in America for nearly 50 years, many Christians distrusted it because of the apparent contradtion between the therapeutic goal of personal development and the Christian ideal of self-abasement through service and sacrifice. Even within psychology this tension was apparent, as expressed by a psychologist of religion: 'Self-love is perhaps the most crippling of the cravings from which the per-son on the contemplative path needs to be liberated' (Thouless 1971, 123). Although Christianity itself is being influenced by the HPM, the antagonism continues at both academic and popular levels, as exemplified by a recent book review in a national newspaper:

> Wander into the 'spiritual uplift' section (or whatever it's called) of a modern bookshop and amuse yourself at the ridiculous attempts contemporary authors make to help you convince yourself that you are wonderful. Compare with à Kempis: 'The highest and most profitable form of study is to understand one's inmost nature and despise it.' This is why

*The Imitation of Christ* has been in print for 500 years, and *I'm
OK, You're OK* won't be.[9]

This puritanism was echoed by social commentators such as
Schur (1976) and Lasch (1978) who castigated the movement
for its narcissistic selfishness, self-indulgence, and lack of
social conscience. Tom Wolfe, who labelled this period the
'Me Decade', commented: 'The new alchemical dream is:
changing one's personality – remaking, remodeling, elevating,
and polishing one's very *self*. . . and observing, studying, and
doting on it' (1976, 143). However, this somewhat cynical
and reductionist view is countered by Patricia Lowe (formerly
Poonam), one of the leading psychotherapists of the time,
with a grander vision: 'It became clear that the only thing that
had any real value was the discovery of ourselves, our beings,
our spiritual beings, and of God.' The version of God believed
in by this psychotherapist exemplifies one of the most profound and significant religious changes taking place at this
time and still continuing: a replacement of the old monotheistic, transcendent, autocratic, male God by a monistic, immanent, androgynous God/dess.[10]
Despite the tremendous creativity and experimentation in
the HPM at this time, it hit a barrier around the early 1970s.[11]
There was a widespread feeling that the full potential implied
in self-actualization had not been realized: self-improvement
had indeed happened, but not radical transformation. One
woman, who later became a Rajneesh therapist, summarizes
the mood of the time: 'By now I'd been doing groups for two
years very intensively, and I began to feel there was something
more. All this looking inside and emoting all these feelings,
behind that was something deeper, but I had no idea how to
reach it.' Many people shared this experience, and started
looking for the 'something deeper' in spiritual transformation, including Eastern forms of meditation.

## The Influence of Eastern Spirituality on Western Psychotherapy

The influence of Eastern mysticism on the counter-culture has
been well documented.[12] India has long exerted a magnetic
attraction on Westerners. This can be traced back at least to

Voltaire, who believed that 'Our religion was hidden deep in India' and 'incontestably comes to us from the brahmins' (Batchelor 1994, 252). The discovery and translation of ancient Buddhist scriptures by European scholars in the nineteenth century revealed the quality and sophistication of this religion, and led to the founding of the Buddhist Society in London in 1907 and the spread of Theravada teachings. In America the influx of Chinese and Japanese immigration during this period inspired a fascination with Zen Buddhism, leading to the foundation of many Zen monasteries. The Chinese seizure of power in Tibet in 1959 brought an influx of Tibetan lamas to the West, who set up many meditation centres. Out of these developments arose a minority but increasingly influential belief in the superiority of Eastern religion, as expressed by the renowned Indologist Conze: 'For 3000 years Asia alone has been creative of spiritual ideas and methods. The Europeans have in these matters borrowed from Asia, have adapted Asiatic ideas, and, often coarsened them' (1951, 11).

Psychologists from Jung onwards have found a natural correlation between psychology and Buddhist philosophy. Jung had been very interested in Eastern mysticism and symbolism, though his interpretations have been criticized by Indians and Westerners.[13] Fromm and Maslow had made theoretical connections between psychoanalysis and Zen Buddhism in the 1950s, but until the 1970s psychotherapy and meditation were perceived as different, mutually exclusive paths. Fitzgerald argues that it was Alan Watts 'who constructed the intellectual bridge between the therapists and Bhagwan Shree Rajneesh' by interpreting the Eastern mystical traditions as being closer to psychotherapy than to philosophy or religion (1986, 286). He thus influenced many people to travel to India to discover meditation.

Until the 1960s, interest in Eastern religion had been largely intellectual, confined to an élite group of scholars and psychologists. However, the ground had been prepared for a more experiential, mystical approach by the American Transcendentalists, the Theosophical Society and the teachings of Krishnamurti (originally trained by the Theosophists), as well as by the visits of other Indian sages such as Vivekananda and Yogananda. After the Second World War, Western seekers began to go on pilgrimage to India. A lone trail was blazed by

Sangharakshita, but it was not until the visits of Allen Ginsberg and other Beat poets in the 1960s that the 'hippie trail' began in earnest.[14] It was a two-way traffic, accompanied and inspired by an influx of Asian teachers: gurus from India, lamas from Tibet, and Zen monks from Japan. The writings and teachings of the Asians and some of their Western followers became disseminated to a whole generation of spiritual seekers. Whether they approved, censured or simply noted, commentators agreed that the influence of Asian religions was 'one of the most striking characteristics of the counterculture'.[15]

**The Rise of Indian Gurus**

The Human Potential Movement arose partly in response to widespread disillusion with on the one hand the Judaeo-Christian tradition, on the other hand scientific materialism. When it in turn failed to fulfil participants' spiritual aspirations, they were drawn to Indian gurus who offered a highly developed, ancient tradition of teachings and practices, grounded in meditation. Out of these informal gatherings of gurus and initiates arose the NRMs of the 1970s.

The first guru to popularize meditation was Maharishi Mahesh Yogi. He brought Transcendental Meditation (TM) to the West in 1958, and captured the public imagination in the 1960s when the Beatles, Mia Farrow and other celebrities visited his ashram in Rishikesh. For a small fee, people were given a mantra to be used in a simple, twice-daily, twenty-minute meditation. 'Easy is right' was the continual message, and the accompanying idea of instant enlightenment held tremendous appeal. It is claimed that millions of Westerners have learned TM over the last 30 years. The Spiritual Regeneration Movement, as it is now called, has grown into a worldwide, highly lucrative chain of organizations including meditation centres, corporate development programmes, and an International University that has conducted and motivated extensive scientific research to demonstrate and measure the benefits of meditation. Despite its popularity, most practitioners did not become involved in TM full-time. Indeed its appeal lay in its ability to be slotted into a busy working life without renouncing material comfort or retiring to a monastery. TM therefore did not take off as a religious movement on the scale of some other NRMs, but many seekers acquired their first experience of meditation through it and then moved on to other teachers.

Next on the scene was the International Society for Krishna Consciousness (ISKCON), popularly known as the Hare Krishna movement. It was founded in New York in 1966 by Swami Prabhupada, and soon reached Britain, again becoming famous via the Beatles who used Hare Krishna chants in their music. George Harrison eventually became a devotee and donated a large house which became the British headquarters, Bhaktivedanta Manor. The saffron-robed devotees were a colourful sight on street corners throughout the West, chanting the Hare Krishna mantra. Membership required an austere, traditional Hindu regime that begins at 3 a.m. with a cold shower and a schedule of rigorous devotions, and demands the renunciation of meat, alcohol, drugs and sex. This asceticism was in stark contrast to the hedonism of the counter-culture, but constituted its appeal for some members. ISKCON rejects the label NRM, seeing itself as a continuation of Vaishnava Hinduism. Its social organization has been adapted and Westernized in many ways, but it was the provision of a coherent, traditional system of doctrine and practice that attracted so many Westerners to become full-time members. These have also enabled it to survive various scandals and crises, including the death of its founder and the departure or expulsion of half the gurus initiated by Prabhupada.

The third most popular guru in the early 1970s was Maharaji, 'boy guru' of the Divine Light Mission (later known as Elan Vital) that had been founded by his father, Shri Hans Ji Maharaj. Maharaji first visited Britain in 1971, aged 13, and shortly afterwards established his headquarters in America. His devotees, called 'premies', were taught a system of self-realization called 'Knowledge'. Hundreds of thousands of followers were claimed, though numbers fell dramatically after Maharaji fell out with his mother, who denounced him, took over the movement in India, and eventually set up his brother as head of the Indian branch. As with Prabhupada and other Indian gurus who attracted Western followers, such as Muktananda and Satya Sai Baba, Maharaji offered a teaching and practice closely based on traditional Hinduism. Westerners were attracted by the exoticism, by the differences from Christianity, by the heart-centred devotionalism, and by a spiritual practice based in meditation and self-development.

## The Osho Movement

The problem with the teachings of the Indian gurus was that they had no organic connection with Western spiritual and cultural traditions. This uprootedness was the main criticism made by philosophers and theologians such as Jacob Needleman (1977) and Harvey Cox (1979), although many members of NRMs claimed to feel more 'at home' in them than in their religion of birth. Still, a marriage between East and West was required. Psychology had made theoretical connections, but it was within the practical, experiential approach of psychotherapy that a living synthesis was created. Therapists of the HPM were utilizing meditation as an adjunct to 'growth' and experimenting with it in their groups, particularly at Esalen in California. The first 'growth centre' in Britain was Quaesitor, founded in London in 1970 by Paul and Patricia Lowe (later Teertha and Poonam), and it was here that these experiments were brought to fruition. At first their main focus was on psychotherapy, but as they and their clients began to meditate, a natural integration started. Clare Soloway (formerly Patricia) describes the process:

> There isn't a point where therapy ends and transformation begins; it's a continuation. We were laying the groundwork for that at that time. We were involved with meditation, because it's a process of self-awareness. We were continuously looking for the new, always looking for the next person who would come, and who could shine a light from that angle. We were on the path of searching very consciously. So there wasn't a time when anything began, we were already in that process of finding ourselves very consciously.

In 1972 the Lowes discovered Dynamic Meditation, a cathartic, neo-Reichian meditation technique, invented by an Indian guru, Bhagwan Shree Rajneesh.[17] Patricia Lowe was 'blown out by it, very impressed. I felt it was a really powerful tool.' The rationale for this departure from static, silent meditations such as *vipassana*, was that the complexity and stress of contemporary life, with its frenzied activity and emotional repression, make it hard for Westerners to sit in meditation for long periods.

As one Buddhist convert expressed it: 'I've been sitting zazen for years and I still don't like it particularly. It makes me mad. I shake, sometimes very violently' (Needleman 1977, 48). This was a problem described by some of my own respondents who had previously been Buddhists, which was resolved by the 'Dynamic': an active meditation featuring breathing, but chaotic rather than the controlled techniques of Eastern meditations. Breath is perceived as the bridge between body and soul, and the Dynamic meditation became a bridge between East and West.

Shortly after this discovery, the Lowes went to India to meet Bhagwan, and became two of his first Western disciples. His first Western disciples were drawn from hippies and seekers travelling round India, but the Lowes inspired other key HPM therapists to join. His following then grew very fast from their clientele. Wallis summarizes the phenomenon: 'Rajneesh's tantrism overlapped extensively with the principal ideological elements of Human Potential Movement, but offered something far more, a path to Enlightenment' (1986, 197). By the mid-1970s the Osho movement had become the most fashionable and fastest growing NRM in the West. Its popularity was at least partly the result of its praxis, a programme of psycho-spiritual development known as Rajneesh therapy. This began with body-based, cathartic methods and progressed to more subtle Buddhist meditations, as summarized by Osho:

> When Western people come to me, I put them into the groups. That is good for them. They should start with what is easier for them. Then by and by, slowly I change. First they go into cathartic groups like encounter, primal therapy, and then I start putting them into intensive enlightenment, then vipassana. Vipassana is a witnessing. From encounter to vipassana there is a great synthesis. When you move from encounter to vipassana, you are moving from West to East. (1977, 170)

Osho began his career as a professor of philosophy at Jabalpur University. In 1966, having become 'enlightened', he resigned his professorship and began travelling round India speaking to huge crowds on controversial subjects such as politics and sex. His contentiousness was part of his appeal to the rebels, drop-outs and jaded intellectuals who comprised his early following, and it is one of the aspects of his teaching that distinguishes him from other Asian gurus of the time. In 1970 he settled in Bombay, where his teachings and meditation camps started attracting Westerners to 'take sannyas'. In traditional Hinduism, sannyas is the fourth and last stage of a man's life in which the world and its pleasures are renounced. Osho gave sannyas to Westerners of all ages and both sexes, and redefined it as a life-affirmative spirituality. The initiation process involved four conditions: taking a new name, wearing orange, wearing a *mala* (a necklace of wooden beads with a locket containing Osho's photo), and doing at least one meditation daily. These conditions were not arduous, though sometimes caused difficulties with friends and family and in the workplace. The orange robes often caused sannyasins to be mistaken for Hare Krishna devotees, to the annoyance of both groups. By 1974 his following had grown to such a size that he set up his own ashram in Poona, which soon become a mecca for spiritual seekers all over the world. At the height of the movement's success in the late 1970s, there were about 250 000 sannyasins worldwide, of whom about 3000 were permanently based in Poona. As inevitably happens with successful movements, growth led to routinization, and the relaxed countercultural modes of the early days gave way to ever tighter organization. This phase is now referred to as 'Poona I' in distinction from 'Poona II', the return to India after the American phase.

The movement now expanded so rapidly that in 1981, after failing to find larger premises elsewhere in India, it moved to America and built a commune called Rajneeshpuram in Oregon. America has always represented a land of hope, freedom and boundless opportunity for religious communities, and since the first World Parliament of Religions at Chicago in 1893, Indian teachers have been visiting and sometimes settling in America. Rajneeshpuram became incorporated as a city and began to 'green the desert' with an assortment of agricultural and environmental projects. Great advances were made, for which the community won great admiration. However, their building projects ran up against the strict land use and planning laws of the state of Oregon. Legal battles and opposition from neighbours provoked hostility from the commune and a series of defence strategies including the stockpiling of weapons, combined with an increasingly harsh, authoritarian work regime. Rajneeshpuram collapsed in 1985 after the government brought a case with an array of charges including tax evasion, embezzlement, wire-tapping and immigration offences. Osho was deported and three of his chief administrators were arrested.[18]

In 1986 Osho returned to Poona, where he lived uneventfully until his death in 1990. The Osho movement has quietly flourished ever since, becoming more inner-directed and less controversial. After a big drop in membership post-Rajneeshpuram, numbers are claimed to be rising again, though in Britain and America the movement is fairly quiescent.

The after-effects of Rajneeshpuram linger on, the latest episode being the trial of two former sannyasins, Sally Anne Croft and Susan Hagan, for conspiring to murder a US attorney in Oregon. The case provoked a storm of protest in Britain, partly owing to the perceived injustice of the case, which was based on the American practice of plea-bargaining, whereby their accomplices lightened their sentences by agreeing to give evidence against the two women. Since the alleged plot took place ten years ago, was never carried out, and no harm came to the intended victim, it was widely felt to be a mockery of justice. The result was a swing of public sympathy towards the women, notwithstanding the almost universal denunciations of the movement five years previously, accompanied by strong public and parliamentary support. A campaign was launched on their behalf in 1990, with the Labour leader Tony Blair and the Liberal-Democrat leader Paddy Ashdown among their defenders. However, after a four-year struggle to avoid extradition, they were finally extradited to America where they received a five-year prison sentence.

The demise of Rajneeshpuram is one incident in a history of scandals involving NRMs and their leaders – although it should be remembered that many mainstream Western religious leaders such as televangelists and Catholic priests have also fallen into disrepute. But the gurus inspired a particularly strong devotion, owing to their undoubted charisma, which was attributed by their followers to their enlightened state. As a result, many thousands of young women and men flocked to Indian ashrams, often giving up well-paid jobs, sometimes leaving behind partners and children, occasionally donating large sums of money. One of the interesting phenomena arising out of the counter-culture is the transformation of large numbers of rebellious individualists into surrendered devotees sitting at the feet of their gurus.

# 2 The Making of the Master–Disciple Relationship

The most contentious issue regarding NRMs concerns the power of 'cult leaders' over their followers. Since the tragedy of Jonestown in 1978 there have been a series of catastrophes that have fuelled public fears concerning NRMs, featuring the Branch Davidians, the Solar Temple, and Aum Shunrikyo. All these groups had powerful charismatic leaders, as do most NRMs. When tragedy strikes, therefore, questions are asked about the nature of the relationship between the leaders of NRMs and their followers and how it is connected or gives rise to such calamities.

Research on the master–disciple relationship has been mainly based on Weber's theory of charismatic authority. He classified authority into three types: rational–legal authority, based on social customs, rules and legal norms, as in constitutions and democracies; traditional authority, based on time-honoured tradition, dynasties and lineage, as in monarchies; and charismatic authority, derived from a charismatic leader:

> The term 'charisma' will be applied to a certain quality of an individual personality by virtue of which he is set apart from ordinary men and treated as endowed with supernatural, superhuman, or at least specifically exceptional powers or qualities. These are such as are not accessible to the ordinary person, but are regarded as of divine origin or as exemplary, and on the basis of them the individual concerned is treated as a leader. (1964, 358–9)

Weber's ideal type construct is still widely adhered to, as the most useful theoretical framework for understanding power and leadership issues in NRMs, although it has been adapted to emphasize the social construction of charismatic authority rather than the personality attributes.[1] Weber's theory is useful in explaining the master–disciple relationship in terms of group dynamics and social structures, but fails to wholly account for the depth of devotion experienced by disciples and their claims of self-transformation. Practitioners therefore tend to reject the concept, as Tipton found studying a Zen monastery: 'Students usually object to the use of the ideas of authority and accepting authority to interpret their relationship to this exemplary figure' (1982, 131).

On the other hand, the presence of a powerful leader may be an important or the main element in attracting a potential member, but this is by no means always the case. Some members 'fall in love' gradually, or not at all, while others are 'struck by lightning' (which may parallel different styles of falling in love with a partner). Even where there is a powerful initial attraction, the evidence shows that this is not the result of brainwashing or hypnosis, although some people have strong psychic experiences around gurus.

## Why People Join NRMs

What makes a spiritual seeker is a mystery that can never be fully plumbed and explained, although there have been many attempts at typologizing the elements of religious experience and conversion. The Pauline conversion is the most dramatic and often thought of as typical, but in my fieldwork I only came across one example of this. It seems to be more common in evangelical movements, typically producing a 'born again' convert. Much more common in my fieldwork was a diversity of factors, culminating eventually in the joining of an NRM.

Until recently, the favourite theory of why people join NRMs was deprivation: the belief that desperate times create extraordinary needs, for which an extremist religious group seems the solution. This explanation was convincing for movements composed of the poor and dispossessed for whom survival is primary, such as the medieval millennialist sects and modern 'cargo cults', but it failed to explain the appeal of post-war NRMs to the educated and privileged. A related explanation was social marginality, but again this status does not apply to most members, except temporarily as with students, and has also been discredited.[2] Furthermore, in the counter-culture marginality could be a voluntary status, and was celebrated by hippies and others who proudly bore the label of 'freak'. Osho also elevated marginality into the superiority of consciousness to truth:

The people who have gathered around me are all misfits in the rotten society. Any intelligent person is bound to be a misfit in a society which is dead, out of date, superstitious, based on belief systems. Only retarded people can be the fit ones . . . all the great names in the history of man were just misfits in their society. To be a misfit is a tremendously valuable quality. (1985, 413)

Deprivation theory was later extended to include ethical and psychic deprivation, more relevant categories to NRMs but still giving a negative slant that was often inappropriate. It was also adapted by psychologists characterizing converts as extraordinarily needy and helplessly dependent (Camic 1987). Nowadays it has largely lost credibility, mainly on the grounds of being too deterministic in its assumption of passive subjects. Psychiatrists also tend to pathologize the conversion process in terms of the dysfunctional childhoods of members or the coercive recruitment techniques of movements. Such methods are rarely used by NRMs, and nowadays 'brainwashing' as an explanation has been rejected academically, largely owing to Eileen Barker's (1984) study of the Unification Church, which demonstrated the importance of choice in the movement that most seemed to exemplify this crude model. However, more active, even coercive recruiting techniques have been used by this NRM and some others, particularly the more evangelical movements.

Psychologically, Maslow's theory of human motivation (1943; 1970a) is more relevant for explaining religious conversion. It is also derived largely from clinical experience and is thus more empirically reliable. Maslow identifies a 'hierarchy of needs', progressing from basic survival to self-actualization. An individual is fully human and healthy in so far as these needs are satisfied, but someone arrested at a lower developmental level will experience different motivations. 'Self-actualization' became a fundamental principle of humanistic psychology and the HPM, an antidote to the pathological emphasis of traditional psychology, legitimating the search for wholeness. In his later work Maslow related his findings to religious experience, arguing that 'affluence itself throws into the clearest, coldest light the spiritual, ethical, philosophical hunger of mankind' (1970b, 38). His theory is not only phenomenologically more

accurate but can also be used to link psychological and sociological explanations. It is flexible and multidimensional enough
to be adapted and applied as a typology of the differences
between NRMs and the people who join them (see Chapter 10).

Sociologists have proposed similar models, discovering that
people join movements that directly affirm their personal values, thus creating a 'cultic milieu'. They see the typical member of an NRM as an active, conscious seeker, pursuing personal
development, often through a series of experiments that could
be called a 'conversion career'. However, there are different
types of NRM and different types of people who join them.
Eastern-based meditation groups tend to be at the other end
of the recruitment spectrum from actively proselytizing groups
such as the Unification Church. Members of meditation groups
undergo a 'spiritual journey'; they 'leave the larger society of
their own volition . . . in order to participate in meditation and
other practices from the East' (Volinn 1985, 148–9).[3] Another,
related feature common to such groups, and also to New Age
and Pagan groups as well as healers and transpersonal psychologists, is continuity between earlier psychic and spiritual
experiences and later spiritual choices.

Many seekers reveal a predisposition for the spiritual life,
which may emerge very early in life. A surprising number of
people have described spiritual experiences and a sense of
seekership stemming from early childhood. Sometimes these
confirmed the tradition they were born into, such as a woman
I interviewed who wanted to become a nun at the age of six.
Another of my respondents had had serious aspirations to
sainthood as a child, practising mortifications and burning her
teddy bear to destroy her attachment to the material world. As
a result she had been revered as a holy child and asked to pray
for people. Others had experiences that contradicted their
religion, such as one who remembered 'having a very deep
sense that there's no God as such, and Jesus was not what the
church said. I felt my search really began at 7.' Many described
feeling alienated by the perceived hypocrisy, apathy, stupidity
and sterility of organized religion. Others, particularly from a
Catholic background, felt damaged by the 'terrible fear of
hell' and 'nightmares' that religious teaching had induced, the
'fear and terror that those very awful situations harrow out of
you'. Some of these found consolation and sometimes mystical

experiences through nature or the arts, especially music, which provided the emotional and aesthetic intensity lacking in formal religion.

People who join Christian-based NRMs tend, understandably, to have remained in the Christian fold prior to joining, although some have had atheist backgrounds or periods of atheism beforehand. Their conversion is often triggered by experiences of intense grief or trauma such as sickness, divorce or bereavement. Perhaps as a result, their experience is more likely to be of the Pauline type. Those who leave, particularly if assisted by 'deprogrammers' from the Anti-Cult Movement, tend to revert to Christianity, particularly of the more evangelical variety. Those who join Eastern-based or New Age movements have usually already left the Jewish or Christian religion into which they were born. Many members of Christian-identified NRMs such as the Unification Church and the Family (Children of God), which may be considered 'destructive cults' by mainstream Christians, are themselves Christians who may or may not be aware of the unorthodox beliefs of such groups when they join. They are typically less innovative and experimental, more concerned with security needs, than counter-cultural seekers.

Those who joined the Osho movement and other Eastern-based NRMs had usually rejected the Judaeo-Christian tradition and been associated with the counter-culture previously. The typical sannyasin is: '"middle-class", well educated, professionally qualified, has been divorced at least once, has suffered a "personal crisis", has been through mysticism, drugs, politics, feminism and is "thirtyish" – in short, the counter-culturalist brought up to date'.[4] My respondents referred to the vision and values of the counter-culture as an important influence. Many had already travelled to India and other exotic destinations. Most had experimented with drugs, often gaining significant spiritual experiences with their aid, as with this typical example:

> When I had this acid trip, I dissolved into the whole consciousness and became one with everything. I knew that everything contained God, and that I'm God, you're God, and everything was. It was so profound that nothing's ever been the same. My life totally changed.

The main focus of the counter-culture was on personal, inner experience. Members of the Osho movement had often had their most important growth experiences in the HPM prior to joining, so were attracted to Osho's development of psychotherapy for spiritual growth. Others were interested in social transformation through political action. They described themselves as 'rebels', often from an early age, and for a number of these, left-wing politics had been an outlet, but usually combined with some kind of spiritual or philosophical ideal. People read Marx, squatted in the East End of London ('a shopping mall of ideas'), joined revolutionary groups, and did voluntary work in the Third World. The ideal of the utopian community was important (see Chapter 6), and a number of people experimented with communal living before joining an NRM. Some women had joined radical feminist communes ('tougher than an Indian ashram'). One had worked in R.D. Laing's therapeutic commune, which she found supportive but uncreative, later recognizing the Rajneesh ashram as 'what I've been looking for my whole life: a place with people living, working, able to be themselves and let go in a sense I hadn't felt in Laing's group'.

## Women and Feminism

In general, research shows a predominance of women in religion, including NRMs.[5] It is generally believed that religion holds more appeal for women, particularly older women, who comprise the bulk of most church congregations. This has tended to be explained in Freudian terms: male Oedipal complexes leading to ambivalent feelings towards fathers and father figures, whereas women emerge with more positive feelings. However, sociological research does not bear this out, particularly given the large numbers of women now turning to goddess spirituality. Similarly discredited is the related theory of women's biologically based personality differences: higher measures of guilt, anxiety, passivity, dependence, submissiveness, etc. These differences may be encouraged in more conservative NRMs but not in the more counter-cultural or secularized movements where women are at the forefront of democratization.

Furthermore, the proportions of women to men vary between individual movements and in some, such as the Unification Church and ISKCON, men are in the majority. Significantly, these are also movements where women have lower status. However, in movements and groups with a strong emphasis on personal development, or where women are elevated and empowered, such as the Osho movement, the Brahma Kumaris and Paganism, women tend to predominate. This also reflects and correlates with the much greater number of women undergoing psychotherapy – which itself may be seen as promoting female values (see pp. 12–13).

Feminism was a significant influence on many of the women who joined the Osho movement, though sometimes as one strand among various alternative ideas. Nearly a quarter of the women I interviewed had been actively involved in the women's movement, three of them as founder members of the 1970s' revival. Yet despite their key roles, they downplayed the significance of feminism in their lives in favour of personal development. For some women, feminism had played this function: 'It was a revelation. It broadened my horizons, gave me permission to see myself differently, to mix with a different lot of people. It was incredibly strong.' Another described it as her 'new religion'. Feminism was a stronger influence upon American sannyasins, perhaps because there is less antagonism between political feminism and the women's spirituality movement in America.[6]

## Becoming a Disciple

The counter-culture may be seen as a halfway house between mainstream society and the fringe area of NRMs. The question is, why some people took the ultimate step of moving even further out, whereas others put away their bells, cut their hair and beards, and returned to the serious business of getting a job and raising a family. Whatever the deeper causes, often a more immediate trigger can be identified, although to classify these into a model of conversion is more problematic.[7]

Most members of NRMs are well-educated, and many have read widely among Western and Eastern mystical literature. Books were an important influence on many sannyasins, and reading Osho's books or listening to tapes of his discourses had a profound effect on their decision to join. They were 'overwhelmed', 'knocked out', and one woman went straight out to Poona as a result. One sannyasin contrasted Osho with a humanistic psychologist: 'Rogers made these phrases come alive, but [Osho] made them glow, made them incandescent with meaning and potential.' A Christian clergyman's wife took sannyas because: 'When I read his lectures on Jesus, it immediately clicked that here was a different Jesus, the Jesus we suspected was there, and we'd found him.' Books are also an important influence in other NRMs, but were particularly significant in the Osho movement, which had an intellectual cutting edge lacking in many other movements.

However, in the HPM and counter-culture, personal, mystical experience was valued over intellect. Books might spark off an intense emotional or psychic experience, but direct, spontaneous experience was the most powerful trigger. Many described past-life, out-of-body and other esoteric experiences, miracles, and enlightenment flashes that they sometimes compared to the Zen *satori*: 'I can feel it still, when suddenly everything was one, and I was part of it. I didn't know what it was, but it was a moment I've never forgotten, very special.' Such people had often had similar experiences earlier in their lives, which had been unexplained or even condemned by Christian priests. Their experiences were validated in Eastern NRMs that provide a context and interpretation. People also described precognitive experiences of the guru's face in visions and dreams. This happened with Osho and other gurus such as Maharishi Mahesh Yogi, Muktananda, Sathya Sai Baba and Maharaji.

It was atypical for people to jump straight into a high-commitment group such as the Osho movement without some prior experimentation. Most had shopped around in the 'spiritual supermarket', trying various groups and techniques before settling for long-term commitment. In particular, TM was many people's first experience of meditation but was later found superficial and over-commercialized. Others had joined Gurdjieff groups, but found Gurdjieff's successors unimpressive or the teachings too 'dry' without the presence of Gurdjieff. Many counter-cultural seekers became Buddhists, and those who found the discipline too arduous or ascetic, joined the

Osho movement instead. Conversely, some who left the Osho movement became Buddhists. Some joined NRMs casually, experimentally, but would usually leave soon unless their commitment and devotion were triggered fast. Others joined because their partner had already joined, but unless they themselves were able to make a strong personal commitment, the relationship would tend to break up and they would leave the movement.

Like most NRMs, the Osho movement did not employ coercive recruitment techniques, nor were converts misled or deceived as to the nature of the movement and its beliefs and practices. In the early days people usually joined in India, while doing the rounds of gurus and ashrams, or through the influence of friends who had joined in that way. After psychotherapy became the main praxis, many people joined as a result of participating in these groups, which could be compared to revivalist meetings in their generation of high arousal, even ecstasy. Some individual group leaders put emotional pressure on participants to take sannyas, but there was no organized strategy to use these groups for recruitment. One prominent psychotherapist described her motivation: 'I felt I had something there to share and to give, which was transforming my life and my energy. I wanted to share that with people.'

Many sannyasins and other seekers joined out of a combination of a number of the above factors that could not be separated in their own experience. However, a few generalizations can be made. Sannyasins were typical of most NRM members in being youngish, middle-class and well-educated. They were typically counter-cultural in being active, conscious seekers, experienced consumers in the spiritual supermarket. There is no evidence of members being gullible teenagers who joined out of inadequacy, weakness or fear of failure. On the contrary, many were successful in their careers and relationships, and those who were relatively marginal had chosen this status as an act of rebellion. These findings may appear to make it even more surprising that such people would choose to surrender their hard-won egos and powers of self-determination to a guru. The key point is that although they had experimented and searched widely, as yet nothing – and nobody – had satisfied their spiritual aspirations. The master–disciple relationship seemed to hold out the answers to their search.

## Becoming a Guru: The Fabrication of Charisma

It is not possible to understand the master–disciple relationship in the Osho movement and other NRMs without some knowledge of the Indian *bhakti* tradition, which provides an alternative theoretical framework and language to describe and interpret intrapsychic processes. *Bhakti* is an ancient spiritual path that can be traced back to the Upanishadic era, beginning at least several centuries BCE. Initially the guru's role was quite low key, comparable to the role of spiritual director in a Catholic monastery. His status gradually evolved, and peaked in the fifteenth century CE with Kabir and Nanak, who raised the guru's status above scriptures, sacred symbols, sometimes even God. Over the next 400–500 years this tradition was overshadowed by Islam and Christianity, whose monotheism prevented the identification of guru and God. However, the revival of Hindu monism at the end of the nineteenth century paved the way for the re-emergence of the most exalted idea of the guru.

There are very few studies of the master–disciple relationship available in English by Hindus, but Upadhyaya defines the guru's role in Indian religion:

A true Guru is said to be the manifest form of God. He comes to this world under God's command on a mission of mercy to take the individual souls back to God. A true Guru is thus essentially one with God. He only appears to be different in the outward form. God in His pure spiritual form is inaccessible to man in his physical form. He becomes accessible to man only when He assumes a human form and meets man at his level. It is this form of Divinity which is known as Guru. A Guru is thus God made man or man made God. (1983, 65)

The early years of a charismatic religious leader are important, and are often linked to prophecies of the coming of a messiah or avatar. The mythologizing process usually happens posthumously, but may take place in the leader's lifetime. In the case of the Osho movement, the myth-making began in Poona, when sannyas was proclaimed as the new world religion predicted by Nostradamus, and linked with Native American prophecies. The birth stories and childhoods of such leaders are often sacralized with reports of miracles and psychic powers. This also happens with Christian saints, but Indian gurus are additionally exalted via their previous incarnations. Such stories have proliferated around Sathya Sai Baba, Muktananda, Mother Meera and others. Osho was no exception in this respect:

> The birth of Rajneesh was not of an ordinary kind, for it was the birth of one who had walked on this earth before in search of Truth. He had traveled numerous paths before, through many schools and systems. His last birth was seven hundred years ago in the mountains where he had a mystic school that attracted disciples of many traditions and paths from faraway lands.[18]

The divinization process was encouraged by Osho himself, who often narrated 'myths' of his remarkable childhood and youth, which were widely believed by disciples and augmented with their own stories of his supernatural powers.

The next important stage in the story is an enlightenment experience, which serves as an initiation into the role of teacher or guru. Osho's enlightenment happened at the age of 21 under a tree – the traditional location for enlightenment since the Buddha. However, unlike most other Indian gurus, Osho did not legitimate his authority through a connection to a guru and a lineage but declared himself to be the sole source and authority for his teachings. This self-proclaimed authority is classically charismatic. His powers had already been successfully tested in his travels round India and his fiery orations on controversial subjects to huge crowds. He was now ready to work intensively with a smaller but growing band of committed disciples, first in Bombay and later in Poona.

After he began formally initiating disciples into sannyas, he changed his title from Acharya (teacher) to Bhagwan ('God'). Bhagwan is a title used by other Indian sages, but caused much annoyance and offence in India when he used it, mainly, it seems, because he and his followers did not conform to the ascetic, world-renouncing tradition of Hindu sannyas. Although less blasphemous within the context of monistic Hinduism than it would be in the monotheistic Western religions, it is still a big leap in status from the 'technical' expertise of the teacher to the 'charismatic' role of guru/godman: 'The word *bhagvan* is essentially an honorific but is also the word in common use for God . . . [it is] an honorific of far greater encomiastic potency than *acarya*' (Sharma 1985, 115).

It is relatively common for Indian gurus to change their names and titles, usually to mark changes in role and status. Osho dropped the title Bhagwan post-Rajneeshpuram, perhaps to distance himself from the scandals, and for a while tried calling himself Buddha, but eventually settled on the more modest Osho, a Japanese title for a Zen Buddhist priest. Other Indian gurus have also experimented with name changes. For example, Guru Maharaj Ji became simply Maharaji, hinting that he was the incarnation of various great leaders of the path, and allowing his disciples to identify him as Kalki the tenth incarnation of Vishnu, Buddha Maitreya, and the Second Coming of Christ. Sathya Sai Baba has not changed his name, but his status has risen from the incarnation of the nineteenth-century saint Shirdi Sai Baba, to avatar of Shiva, to universal God and ultimate receiver of all forms of devotion to other Godheads.

### Recognition: The Attributes of an Enlightened Master

Weber emphasized that the decisive factor for the validity of charisma was recognition by those subject to authority, usually through a miraculous sign. This results in devotion, hero worship and absolute trust in the leader. Bryan Wilson has suggested that 'In advanced Western society, it appears that claims to real charisma, if they are to succeed, must be supported by exotic provenance' (1975, 114). The majority of gurus have been Indian, and this was Osho's first qualification.

The Westerners who took sannyas in the early days of the movement had very few preconceptions of what a master was, though some of them were consciously looking for one. Most sannyasins had joined in search of spiritual growth. Even if they had not heard of enlightenment, this objective of Eastern mysticism soon became their primary goal. Most had no concept of this state beyond words, beyond the grasp of the rational mind, but the one universal, unquestionable sannyasin belief – the primary article of faith – was that Osho was enlightened.

At the time I didn't know what the word [enlightenment] meant, but looking at Osho I knew there was something –

self-realization, godhead, I don't know. But certainly it was a goal, something I desired. I was looking for peace, happiness, and for God.

There was a consensus that Osho's function was to get people enlightened, and that he did this primarily through his presence or charisma, and through example. In this sense he was what Weber called an 'exemplary prophet', as expressed by one sannyasin: 'It's the example. He's there all the time, so he can guide me back to the place I know exists.' An ex-sannyasin summarized how Osho exactly matched Western needs:

> He was life's gift to thousands of us, because we were looking for something. We were Western people lost in a materialist, consumerist society, struggling. We were the generation who had taken acid, we knew there was something else, but we didn't know how to get there. And life threw up this incredible gateway, which was like a magnet to thousands of us. And he had to be beautiful-looking, very clean, intelligent, articulate – who he was – or we wouldn't have gone there, because we were pretty sussed. And he also had to look perfect, because that was the hook.

A powerful element of his appeal was sensory. Many people mentioned his physical beauty and the hypnotic effect of his enormous, brilliantly dark eyes, 'radiating authority'. This is an impression often described regarding gurus, and may be empirically observed, sometimes even from photographs. His voice and oratorical skills were equally persuasive. In India, the oral tradition is still kept alive by highly accomplished village storytellers, who weave into the traditional myths stories of their grandmothers and political events. Osho may well have been nourished by this tradition,[9] and certainly polished his gift during his academic career and later travels. As a former professor, educated in Eastern and Western philosophy, he appealed to the minds of his more intellectual disciples, and this was supplemented by his later extensive reading within popular Western culture. The content of his discourses was highly rated, but it was his voice and performance that enthralled his audience: 'He speaks like a poet. He sings, he dances, he mesmerizes with his words. What he says, the Vedas have said, the Upanishads have said, the Bible, the Koran, the Gita have all said' (Bharti 1981, 178).

Despite these charismatic qualities, many sannyasins did not have an instant sense of his charisma – of his being their master or being enlightened – when they first met him, whether or not they had had a build-up previously. Osho would often claim to be 'just an ordinary man' as well as being enlightened, but the ordinariness that people experienced in the beginning was sometimes felt as a disappointment and let-down. This was particularly the case with two women who had taken sannyas after their husbands. On the other hand, a number of people spoke of their sense of 'homecoming' in meeting Osho, a sense of mutual recognition, acceptance and love that could sometimes be overwhelming: 'I remember waiting to meet him, and feeling I'd come home. I always felt he knew me in depth without knowing me – this kind of inner recognition.' The feeling of coming home is common to people joining all kinds of NRMs, sometimes instant, sometimes growing over time.

Once sannyasins had accepted Osho as their master, this 'recognition' was often augmented by perceptions of his power and wisdom. Many believed he possessed psychic abilities such as mind-reading, telepathy, and the ability to visit disciples at night in his astral body. Most sannyasins believed in reincarnation, and there are many accounts of past-life experiences, often connected with Osho. Again these beliefs and experiences are found throughout new and old religions. For example, Sai Baba is famous throughout the world for his apparent miraculous powers, most commonly the production of *vibhuti* (sacred ash), though these have been contested as conjuring tricks and imitated by professional magicians. His disciples believe he visits them in their dreams, and these experiences may form the basis of decisions taken by the movement's World Council. Possession of paranormal powers and miracle-working may be among the criteria for recognizing Catholic saints.

## The Routinization of Charisma

In Bombay and the first few years in Poona Osho's following was small and his relationships with his disciples were much more intimate, consisting of one-to-one or small-group meetings. This stage corresponded to Weber's 'pure type of charisma'. One of my respondents described how 'I used to sometimes walk in the garden with him alone, and that was quite a gift. I didn't see it as a gift. I was arguing with him all the time ... I'd often be very rude, I didn't follow any etiquette at that time. It was only later that I got awed by the whole thing, but it was such a group thing by then.' He also described how not only did the relationship offered by the master change, but different waves of disciples would arrive to receive it. 'If you look at what he used to say around 1975, it was all master–disciple stuff – the love of the master for the disciple, the love of the disciple for the master. It appealed to that group who wanted a one-to-one master–disciple relationship.' He felt that the next group saw it as an extension of the psychotherapy scene, and were more interested in the group experience, while those who took sannyas at Rajneeshpuram were more interested in the commune as social experiment.

This process corresponds to Weber's 'routinization of charisma', as the movement became more organized and access to the leader more difficult. Osho's appearances now became more public and ceremonial, emphasizing his difference and distance. This distancing is similar to the process in the Children of God, which Wallis interprets in terms of the preservation of charisma:

> Through distancing himself and milieu control, Berg was able to avoid the danger of familiarity incompatible with his sacred status. This tendency was encouraged too by his household who sought to protect Mo from intrusion to enable him to 'stay in the spirit', but also to enhance the prevailing conception of him as one in daily communication with God. (Wallis 1986a, 150)

In contrast to his orange-robed disciples, Osho would appear white-robed. In Rajneeshpuram, when sannyasins wore jeans and work-clothes, he would appear in sumptuous satins and velvets. His chair was specially made for him (officially because of his back condition), and two highly privileged sannyasins would carry it into discourse, under wraps, and place it upon a podium. His audience would await his entrance in strict silence, even coughing being prohibited. Even the expensive cars, in which he was driven the hundred yards to the lecture hall, were mainly understood by sannyasins as part of the ritual and as teaching devices. Religious organizations are experts in the fabrication of charisma through elaborate trappings and ritual, the Vatican being perhaps the supreme example. Other Asian gurus were also adepts at such effects, as this description of Chogyam Trungpa's organization by an ex-disciple demonstrates:

> I reflected on the means by which that feeling [of Trungpa's elevated status] was created: the throne, the ceremonies, the master's esoteric knowledge, the elaborate rituals that he knew and we wanted to learn, the forms of obeisance we accorded him, the luxuriant accommodations we always made every effort to provide him as a sign of our respect and devotion, his special robes and colors, his luxury automobile and chauffeur, his procession of attendants, the wall of secrecy that kept us from observing him too closely. It was all good theater – it created a willing suspension of disbelief, and projected us into a sacred atmosphere. (Butterfield 1994, 190)

The effect is magical, but the spell is dependent for its effect on the eye or ear of the recipient. Milne describes how when he first met Osho he was 'bowled over by the charisma, the power, the authority and the presence of the man' (1986, 16), and believed he was enlightened. Yet after dropping sannyas he attributed Osho's powers to hypnosis, or at best to mere psychic rather than spiritual powers. Co-dependence or collusion are likelier explanations. While the relationship lasts, master and disciple co-create a drama, whether sumptuous and spectacular or simple and spartan. As in a love affair where the lover wants to turn his beloved into a goddess, the disciple wants to put the master on a pedestal and worship him. The disciple wants to believe her master is the greatest – the World Teacher, Second Coming, or Maitreya. Disillusion when it comes is correspondingly bitter, as the glitter and magic vanish. The following two accounts of the same series of lectures demonstrate this difference of perception dramatically:

1) For about a year when he was talking about Zen, he just kept going up and up. To see such a masterly performance,

such a Zen sword – it was unsurpassable! And then it was surpassed by great leaps.

2) There was a feeling he wasn't taking it any further. It was the cup he'd first given me to drink when I'd first gone there, and I was being given the same cup over and over again.

There are clearly elements of manipulation in the creation of these effects. The problem with judging such contrivances is that masters themselves openly admit to the use of trickery and deception but for a higher end: a conscious strategy to get people enlightened. Even the master–disciple relationship was presented as a 'game' for this purpose. Sannyasins accepted the 'rules of the game' because it worked for them, and because they believed in its goal. One made the point quite explicitly, saying how much he enjoyed the morning discourse 'stage-managed and contrived though the whole thing was', because he felt the reality of what Osho represented. Everything that happened within the community was therefore interpreted as opportunities for growth and surrender, including Osho's inconsistencies and contradictions. In this respect he may be called a shaman or 'trickster guru':

> In personalities like those of Blavatsky, Gurdjieff, and many another luminary of counterspirituality, one observes qualities not only of the paradigmatic shaman and magus, but also of the trickster and 'ritual clown'. The trickster is that figure in many mythologies who cleverly outwits both gods and men and manages to establish a precarious immortality for himself on the tenuous boundary between heaven and human society. From that outsider's vantage point he laughs at the pomposity and gullibility of both realms. (Ellwood 1979, 56)

Even after Bharti 'dropped sannyas' (left the movement), she was still unable to explain away her experiences rationally. The phenomenon was too mysterious and sacred to be reduced in this way, and her summary illustrates the difficulties faced by academic researchers attempting to interpret these phenomena:

> Yet there was clearly something special about Bhagwan. He exuded love; his power and charisma was astounding;

something extraordinary happened to me whenever I was
with him. Fifteen years later I still don't know how to account for the stoned, blissed-out feelings he evoked in me
and thousands of others. To call it hypnosis is to miss the
point. Utterly at peace, more than myself, he seemed to
bring me up to his level till I felt as if I were enlightened,
too. (Franklin 1992, 29)

## When Prophecy Fails: Testing Charisma

Current educational and training theory favours an optimum
of 12–20 participants in a teaching group, and 200–300 in an
effectively functioning organization. After Osho's disciples grew
beyond a few dozen, formal appointments to see him were
introduced. When the movement grew above a few hundred,
structures were instituted, informal meetings were replaced by
lectures, and many powers and functions were delegated to
deputies. At Rajneeshpuram, Osho withdrew even more from
direct relationship with sannyasins, being in silence for three
years. This intensified his mystery and charisma, while allowing the organization to develop around him. Sannyasins'
energy was redirected from devotion and personal growth to
hard work. This was the beginning of a millennialist phase of
vision and commitment to building the New City for the New
Man (see Chapter 6). It was also where charisma began to turn
graceless. External hostilities with the commune's neighbours
were parallelled by mistreatment and abuse of power inside
the community.

Sooner or later, inevitably, the growth and success of an
NRM will be challenged by a crisis. This may come in the form
of opposition by rival religions, the state or the ACM; scandal
(usually sexual or financial); the failure of powers or prophecies;
the illness or death of the leader. There have been two crises
in sannyasin history, turning points that could have signified
the end of Osho's credibility as an enlightened master. The
first, and probably most serious, was after the departure of his
deputy, Sheela, when all her crimes were revealed. The resulting shock, pain and anger could have resulted in collapse, and
been turned against Osho. This was the time of the greatest
rate of defection from the Osho movement, though no statistics are available. Opinion among sannyasins and researchers

is divided as to Osho's own responsibility for events (see Chapter 7), though the evidence shows that he actively supported the regime. Yet what is interesting and perhaps surprising is how many sannyasins stayed loyal, or left temporarily and returned over the next few years. Some took events as evidence that he had somehow 'lost' his enlightenment, whereas others took them as confirmation of his greatness.

The Osho movement has partially succeeded in turning failure and disgrace into triumph, at least in their own view, partly through historical revisionism. The official version of events is that a spiritual utopia had been defeated by a conspiracy of red-necked Christian fundamentalists in league with a paranoid government which had tried to poison Osho in prison. This belief is an article of faith for sannyasins and was apocalyptically expressed by Osho: 'We created the first holy place in America. We created a new Kaaba . . . And the American government did everything illegal, criminal, to destroy the commune' (1987, 234).

The second crisis the movement has passed through was the death of Osho in January 1990. Osho had always been impressed by Christianity's success in turning the disgrace of its leader's death into a glorious badge of martyrdom. While always claiming that he would never seek a martyr's death, it is ironic that his death is now being presented as martyrdom: the delayed effects of the CIA poisoning. The titles of his later books emphasize the point: *Jesus Crucified Again, This Time in Ronald Reagan's America* and *Socrates Poisoned Again After 25 Centuries*. There was a wide range of responses to his death, but most people remained in the movement. The commonest response has been a spiritualization of the master–disciple relationship: 'In some way it doesn't make any difference. Rationally, if he is a master and can help and guide me, then he'll continue to do it. If he isn't, it doesn't make any difference because whatever's been carrying me through these last years will still be there.' It is exemplified by the replacement of the word 'died' with the phrase: 'He has left His body'. This is a common Indian usage heard also in the Brahma Kumaris and ISKCON, which emphasizes the continuity of the connection.

The main challenge facing an NRM that survives its founder's death without disintegrating into rival factions is to maintain

the original enthusiasm and freshness, resisting the final routinization into an organized religion. In the case of the Osho
movement this is particularly challenging since Osho did not
appoint a successor. Instead he formed a committee of 21
disciples (11 women, 10 men) to be responsible for the administration of the community. The spiritual responsibility was
given to sannyasins individually and as a group, to avoid the
dangers of a priesthood. As in Protestantism, the emphasis is
therefore on each sannyasin's unique, direct, inner communion
with Osho. Through relying on their own inner voice or light,
sannyasins claim to feel his presence or energy stronger than
ever, which also helps to preserve and even intensify the charisma: 'I experience him, since he's left the body, even stronger
than before. He feels totally available to me whenever I remember to tune in. It seems like a way of him pushing us into
acknowledging more than ever that it's here, within each one
of us.'

Whether charismatic leaders are 'really' what they claim to
be – enlightened masters, Buddhas, Messiahs, World Teachers
– is beyond the scope of empirical research or reason to determine. What is clear is that the master–disciple relationship
works best during the 'pure' stage of charisma, when the following is small enough for the guru to have an intimate, in-
depth relationship with each disciple. It becomes problematic
when the movement becomes too large for direct responsibility. Failure is therefore the result not just of routinization *per
se* but of the kind of abuses that any large organization is liable
to, such as delegation to unsuitable people. Nevertheless, the
impossibility of questioning, analysing or criticizing charismatic
authority, coupled with the demand for total surrender, renders
the master–disciple relationship particularly vulnerable to the
abuse of power.

# 3 Abuse of Power: The Shadow Side of Charismatic Authority

## Authority and Dependence: The Master as Father Figure

The guru is not only a spiritual guide but a supreme authority, demanding absolute surrender from the disciple as a prerequisite for spiritual growth. It is without doubt this requirement from charismatic religious leaders, and the attendant risks of childish dependence and exploitation, that gives rise to the widespread Western distrust of gurus:

> The concept of a Master is repugnant to most Westerners. The very word, especially when capitalized, implies a dominion over others that is threatening, and ugly, to people who see democracy and self-determination as preeminent values. Christians will agree that Jesus was a Master – he is spoken of in this way in the Gospels – but he was unique, 'the only begotten son of God.' Anyone who now claims a similar authority is angrily accused of heresy, pitied as insane, or scorned as a con man. (Gordon 1987, 35)

The master–disciple relationship arose within the authoritarian structure of Indian society, which requires unquestioning respect and obedience to the father. These virtues become easily transferred to the guru, who is a highly respected figure in Indian culture, and may even be seen as a rescuer, providing a 'happy slavery' for the devotee.[1]

It may be that Westerners, too, were looking for a father substitute. Berger sees this need as one of the symptoms of modernization and a contributory factor in campus rebellions: 'We find it quite erroneous to say that contemporary youth is rebelling against father figures. On the contrary, the rebellion is against the absence of paternal solicitude in the large bureaucratized structures. If anything, contemporary youth is in search of plausible father figures' (1974, 174).

43

Janet Jacobs perceives a similar process in NRMs: 'devotion to God-the-father in the form of the charismatic leader who assumes, for the devotees, the attributes of God on earth' (1987, 304). This theory was developed in her later book, where she postulates that 'converts were often drawn to religious movements whose structure and organization replicated the primary associations of the family and childhood relations' (1989, 2). Her theory is that this accounts largely for the appeal of these movements:

> In the new religious movements, the person of the charismatic leader represents a merging of the human paternal ideal with the all-powerful god father . . . The rise of charismatic religious movements can thus be understood as the desire to experience both the ideal family and the fathering of a protective and loving male authority figure. (1989, 5)

The master is 'a father figure who is internalized as both a symbol of love and power'. This is expressed by 'merging with the leader' in a three-stage process, progressing from the father–child relationship to 'mystical union with the charismatic figure' (76–7). Jacobs's interpretive context for this model is a shift from 'mother consciousness' – the 'female-centered spiritual tradition' now being rediscovered by the goddess spirituality movement (see Chapter 9) – to 'father consciousness' and patriarchy. This accounts for the apparent contradiction whereby 'symbiosis . . . as a desire for reunification with the feminine' (80) becomes projected onto a male figure. Most of Jacobs's accounts of mystical merging were given by her male respondents. The relationship offers men fulfilment 'within the parameters of male bonding with a patriarchal god figure. The spiritual father offers the male devotee an affirmation of self and at the same time provides a role model on which to project the ego ideal.' She argues that merging is harder for women, who 'have more difficulty projecting the ego ideal onto a masculine love object' (86–7).

In focusing on a single type of master–disciple relationship, Jacobs reaches a significant but limited conclusion:

> [R]eligious experience in patriarchal traditions is derived from identification of father with son, as the notion of the Trilogy implies, a social construction of spirituality that

creates barriers rather than opportunities for female transcendence. (88)

In Hinduism, the master may sometimes be perceived as a mother figure, soft and accepting, nurturing his disciples' spiritual development. Osho on occasions would emphasize his maternal function: 'Let my hand be just your mother's hand, or your father's hand. The moment you are ready, I will be the first to withdraw my hand' (1979c, 361). However, on the whole the father image predominated. Some sannyasins denied that he was a father figure and provided an alternative explanation of his role:

> He's not a father figure at all, he's just someone I trust, because I see in him my own potential, and I see that he's managed to remember his enlightenment, to let go of his illusions. That makes my own intuition not just a fairy story but a reality. He's the living proof.

On the other hand this disciple also said that after years of shopping around 'it was a relief that I didn't have to decide or choose anything', which suggests a paternal dependence. People's experiences were often complex and inconsistent in this way. Similarly, another woman described how after her mother's death Osho became a replacement parent, a 'being greater than me', protecting her with his power and energy. Another woman admitted that he was partly a father figure but more importantly a spiritual guide: 'My father wasn't very present in my life, so in some ways it's possible that he was father and mother, but I always saw it in the spiritual context.'

Some who completely accepted him as a father figure found it a positive, healing experience, particularly in contrast to lack of love from their own fathers.[2] Often the issues were confronted in the therapy groups and meditations. One sannyasin gave a particularly articulate account of the psychospiritual dimension of this 'spiritual fathering':

> He was a father figure, but I was in touch with that. I knew enough about myself that I knew if I was looking at him in a particular way, like give me answers, that the child was talking to daddy, and if I was looking to him to make things better for me, he was a mother figure for me. . . . But while this psychological stuff was going on, there was a whole other

dimension of relating happening that was not verbal, which is about consciousness, trust, going deeper. It was not something I could control any more. There was another part of me, my higher self or whatever, awakening, coming to life, and this began to create changes in my way of being. . . . That was much deeper, realer to me than the part of me that was projecting a father onto him. And I was always aware when that was going on, which gave me the space to observe the process. I didn't need to do anything about it, they were just projections. And in that process of coming alive, the trust in him began to grow enormously, a real feeling of wanting to surrender.

However, as well as representing the ideal father, Osho could manifest the negative, authoritarian attributes of fatherhood. At Rajneeshpuram many of the abuses latent in a situation of absolute power were manifested – though not always interpreted as abusive by sannyasins. Many sannyasins who spoke up were silenced or expelled, or left of their own accord. One ex-sannyasin talked about needing to 'take back the power' she had given to him, after she left the movement. Another ex-sannyasin who had been in the movement since 1972, and had also been something of a charismatic leader in her own right, found many present sannyasins 'childish and immature', and felt they 'want to belong to the group and are rather scared of standing alone'. Asked if she felt he was primarily a father figure, she replied:

> Well, of course he was, for me as well. But then any charismatic figure like that is. It's human nature. And it can be used for good, as it was, and it can be used for power, as it was. It seemed to me like a nursery school play-ground. I think it had the potential to move into something that was what it had always promised to be, and somewhere something went wrong. He couldn't quite handle it.

Much of the confusion was caused by the unclear balance between authority and responsibility, which tacitly shifted after the demise of Rajneeshpuram. In Poona the model of the master–disciple relationship had clearly required absolute, childlike trust and obedience. However, after Sheela's departure, Osho shifted much of the blame for events onto rank-and-file sannyasins for their failure to grow up, take responsibility and exercise their own judgement (see Chapter 7). There seems to have been an innate paradox, if not contradiction, between the goal of therapy (responsible maturity) and the path of Eastern mysticism (childlike innocence and trust). This may be an endemic, insoluble problem at the heart of the master–disciple relationship.

And yet, despite the dangers, it may be that it is time to reevaluate the negative connotations that the father figure concept has acquired in Western society. In this post-Freudian age it is taken as read that maturity – particularly for men but increasingly for women – involves overcoming one's 'Oedipal complex' and childish dependencies, becoming an autonomous, self-determining individual. It is acceptable to have mentors in adolescence, but in adulthood any reliance on another person beyond professional guidance is considered a sign of immaturity. Jacobs's critique of the charismatic leader *qua* father figure in the context of patriarchy carries great force and conviction, particularly with regard to more traditional religious movements, but it also risks rejecting the positive aspects. The men's movement is a vanguard in this respect, blaming many of society's ills on absent fathers, particularly the resulting lack of a father–son bond and of appreciation for older men as mentors. Although there has been a strong feminist critique of the sexism and misogyny implicit in some aspects of the men's movement, it does expose how many of the evils of patriarchy stem from negative fathering and male role models rather than fathering *per se*.

## Surrendering to Nobody: The Master as Mirror

There were two important reasons why people were prepared to give up the hard-won humanistic ideals of self-determination and individuation to surrender to a master. Firstly, the rewards of spiritual growth and enlightenment were seen as well worth the cost. Secondly, they learned a positive Eastern concept of surrender, very different from Western associations with defeat. Hugh Milne, in his obituary, remembered the banner that used to float above Osho in his lectures, with the message: 'Surrender to me and I will transform you, that is my promise.' The Eastern style of surrender entailed giving up the ego, the personal identity, sense of selfhood – which is understood as the ultimate illusion – and merging with the greater whole through the master. This is an accepted, time-honoured spiritual path in Eastern religion, though initially hard for Westerners to understand. For many, surrender was a gradual learning process, accompanied by doubts and resistance. Yet few admitted to giving up all personal autonomy, to blind trust and mindless obedience. One sannyasin felt that the term 'surrender' was a misnomer responsible for the misunderstanding:

> Surrender's such a rotten term anyway, it doesn't really mean very much. When the old boy used to talk of surrender I think that was the nearest he could get to it. Surrender suggests you're absolved of all responsiblity, which as far as I can see is not the case. Surrender suggests you give everything to the other without any intelligence, consciousness, awareness. I don't think that's what it meant at all. Surrender suggests a trust that doesn't allow doubt, whereas the Ranch showed we'd become too trusting, stupidly doubting. . . .
>
> It's a paradox to be with a master, basically. You are surrendering something which you don't possess anyway. You're getting something which he's not giving, you've already got it. It's a total paradox.

One of the key differences between the concept of obedience in Western monasticism and the monistic Eastern concept of surrender, which are close in some respects, is the metaphor of the master as mirror. The key to surrender was trust, and people were helped in this process by the oft-used mirror metaphor. It signifies that he is not there as an ego to obstruct, manipulate, exploit; he is simply an emptiness mirroring the disciple back to herself. This concept has no equivalent in Western religion, but it fits with the psychological theory of projection: our mind projects images from our unconscious onto an outer person or situation, preventing us seeing the reality. Another person does the same to us; hence the difficulties of communication. Psychologically, an enlightened person no longer has an unconscious to project, hence sees reality in itself. If disciples can withdraw their projections, they can see their own divinity mirrored in the master. The metaphor was sometimes psychologized in this way by Westerners, such as a student of the Tibetan teacher Akong Rinpoche at Samye Ling: 'He's more like a blank screen. If you talk with him, your own projections are reflected back at you.'

The mirror metaphor is widespread in Hindu, Buddhist and Sufi mysticism, and is often encountered in NRMs based on these traditions, such as Elan Vital, Tibetan Buddhist groups, the Friends of the Western Buddhist Order (FWBO) and the Sufi teacher Irina Tweedie. It was much used by Osho, and was internalized by many sannyasins, who understood him as saying 'I am merely a mirror to show you what you have within yourself. I am here to show you that you're no different from me. This is the potential of humanity.' It also functioned to ease the process of surrender:

> You cannot trust existence, but you can trust a master because he's a mirror of yourself. But finally you need to trust everything. It's not just trusting in him or what he's going to do, or whether he's going to keep all his promises. It's a much more overall trust, that even if the promises aren't fulfilled that's good too, that's the way it should be as well.

Sannyasins usually felt that in some sense surrendering to a master was not giving up one's autonomy to another person, an authority. This was partly because they perceived Osho as a mirror and partly the corollary experience that they were surrendering to their own essential self:

> It's not like giving away your authority, it's more like a recognition of something sacred in yourself, and a commitment to it, and a desire to just let go and merge with it. Bhagwan was an embodiment of that inner divinity, symbolically surrendering to him was like surrendering to that inside yourself. So it's like wanting to connect inside yourself with who you really are.

The metaphor of the mirror expresses a high-level spiritual truth, but depends for its efficacy on an honouring of the master–disciple bond. Within this symbol system the master is seen as pure, enlightened, empty of ego. The disciple aspires to become equally purified; any ugliness or evil is interpreted as the result of one's own ignorance and impurity. These ideas are developed in Tibetan Buddhism as the doctrine of 'pure perception', particularly in the Rigpa Foundation founded by

Sogyal Rinpoche. However, they do contain the potential for abuse, particularly in relationships between male masters and female disciples.

## Sexual Abuse in Religion

In recent years there has been a growing awareness of the problem of sexual abuse throughout society including religion, within the context of the patriarchal abuse of power. It is the shadow side of the master–disciple relationship, which has darkened the reputations of a number of NRMs and the lives of their members. Much of the evidence is in the form of un-substantiated allegations, since very few cases have come to court and even fewer of the alleged perpetrators have admitted to misdemeanours. However, there is enough evidence from reliable sources to comprise a serious case.

In the past sexual abuse has often been perceived as a prob-lem of Asian gurus encountering more permissive Western societies. This chapter is focused largely on Buddhism, which reflects not necessarily the greater prevalence but the greater openness and willingness to publicize and look at the problem within Buddhist groups. However, the problem is widespread within new and old religions, including Christianity. Within the last ten years, Christianity's moral hegemony has been under-mined by a series of scandals regarding the love affairs of evangelical preachers, most notoriously Revd Jimmy Swaggart, and between priests and their parishioners, who have often been abandoned when pregnant while the priest is moved on to a new parish.[3] The abuse of children by priests and choir-masters is so widespread that it is now acknowledged as a problem even within the churches. These violations have been exposed worldwide but particularly in America and Ireland.

The most recent of these Christian scandals in Britain fea-tured Chris Brain, vicar and former leader of the 9 O'Clock Service in Sheffield. In November 1995 he admitted having had improper sexual relations with 20 of his female parish-ioners, as a result of which he resigned. His ministry had for-merly been greatly admired by the Anglican establishment, who had therefore speeded up his ordination. He had also been endorsed by the well-known American religious teacher and writer Matthew Fox, whose Creation Spirituality rituals he had adapted in his own services. Women who complained to their local bishop were dismissed as troublemakers, and 'rubbished very effectively' by Brain and his staff. Following his exposure he was condemned as a 'cult leader'. He had a team of beautiful young women whom he called 'nuns' but who were dubbed by disgruntled parishioners the 'Lycra Lovelies'. Their 'duties' were to put him to bed and massage him, and they were also sexually fondled by him during the healing services. After the event, the women displayed the symptoms of abuse such as depression, not eating or sleeping, sickness, suicidal tendencies, and described their experiences in those terms: 'I felt in some way he owned my body, and that disgusts me'; 'He was the first person to be sexual with me, which I found abusive.' Brain's theological justification for his behaviour was original and contemporary: 'discovering a post-modern definition of sexuality in the church'.[4]

Women complied in the belief that 'to displease Chris was to displease God'. This identification of leader with God is intrinsic to charismatic authority and one of its most dangerous beliefs. It was also voiced by victims of Brother Julius Schacknow of the Worldwide Church of God in America, who told the teenagers he slept with: 'This is your way to get close to God', which followers took on board: 'I believed in the Lord, so of course that's God's will.' David Koresh, the 'Sinful Messiah' of the Branch Davidians, drank, smoke and 'fornicated' while dissolving the marriages of his followers and prescribing celibacy for them. He took their wives and daughters to be his own 'wives' because God had instructed him to father many children, which the women and men accepted because they were consecrated to doing God's will.

The most widescale example of sexual abuse in an NRM is another Christian movement, the Children of God (now the Family). David Berg, the leader, abandoned his wife for another, younger follower, and then had multiple sexual relationships with other female followers. The practice for which the movement is most notorious is 'Flirty Fishing' (FFing), a recruitment technique by which women brought in potential converts through prostitution, as a result of which they were dubbed 'Hookers for Jesus'. It began with Berg's experiment using his new wife, which worked, so he then set up an ambitious social experiment. In 1974 Berg wrote a letter to his followers requiring them to express their own, and God's, love for lonely men (the 'fish') using sexual allure to the point of kissing them and letting them fall in love. Later this was extended to include sexual intercourse:

> The fish can't understand crucifixion, they can't understand Jesus. But they can understand the ultimate creation of God, a woman. . . . Everyone of you girls who spreads out your arms and your legs on the bed for those men are just like Jesus, exactly like Jesus![5]

Some attempts were made at extending FFing to men, but abandoned on the grounds that women are better at prostitution. Originally their services were free, but soon money began to be requested as a 'gift for the work' in exchange for the 'gift of love'. Eventually the recruitment function receded in favour of straight fundraising, and the women got jobs in escort agencies and as callgirls to 'make it pay'. At the peak of this phase, 1978–82, the practice spread throughout the movement's international communes, and women were working two to five nights a week. By the mid-1980s FFing was in decline because of the spread of sexually transmitted diseases, combined with the strain on family life and the increasing demands of childcare. Berg then advocated a less sexualized approach moving on quickly to salvationary tactics, which were found to be much more successful in winning recruits. In 1987 the practice was stopped altogether on account of AIDS.

Feminist research raises further issues about the presentation and interpretation of such contentious material. One concern is the 'sexual objectification' that results from the imposition of so-called value-free, scientific methodology. Janet Jacobs particularly highlights Wallis's research on the Family as typifying 'those studies that fail to question the norms of patriarchal control that lead to the sexual exploitation of female devotees'. She accuses him of dehumanizing them by describing them as the group's 'sexual resources' and not investigating or even acknowledging their responses (1991, 351–2).

Jacobs herself has undertaken the most extensive research on the abuse of women by male religious leaders, involving 17 women who had left various NRMs, mainly charismatic Christian or traditional Eastern-based movements. She sees the problem as stemming from the affective dimension: 'the link between love and religious commitment' (1984, 155). In most of the NRMs she studied, 'sexual intimacy with the guru or teacher was often held out as a reward or privilege, the means by which the female devotee could become quite literally one with the god figure or deity'. This confusion between sexual and spiritual fulfilment led to exploitation: 'those women who became disillusioned and left the movement were rarely those followers who remained intimate with the leaders, but those who had been rejected by the guru or denied access to his bed' (161).

Jacobs describes this dynamic as an 'economy of love', a process of affiliation in which 'the female devotee develops a deep emotional commitment which is expressed through submission, devotion, and obedience to a male hierarchy. In return for this commitment, the devotee hopes to receive love and the emotional support that has been promised by the spiritual leaders.' Thus, the guru becomes a variant of the fairy tale stereotype, 'the knight in spiritual armor, a hero who will save the female devotee from her own weakness and feminine liabilities' (166–7). Unfortunately, this dynamic works to the disadvantage of the devotee, who is more emotionally involved. Continuing the economic metaphor, Jacobs argues:

> This disadvantage is further enhanced by the effects of supply and demand on the love economy. The demand for the leader's love is great and yet it is a limited commodity, allocated sparingly and only to those who are deemed worthy. The value placed on the leader's love is therefore very high, while the value placed on the devotee's love is much less significant because of the availability of this emotional resource among the group members. The inequality of power relations is therefore a function of the emotional exchange. Accordingly, it provides a basis for increasing the demands made on the female devotees. (168)

The 'economy of love' breaks down when the devotee perceives that she is no longer receiving a fair exchange. Rejection, abuse or coercion lead to loss of trust, then to a sense of betrayal, then to a questioning of commitment, and finally to a painful severing of the emotional bond with the male leadership. This creates a 'new social reality [which] in part replaces notions of romantic idealism with notions of female exploitation. Devotees often describe this stage in terms of new self awareness and a heightened feminist consciousness' (169). But the break with the leader is the hardest part, whatever the provocation. In a later article Jacobs concluded that 'A willingness to exonerate the leader from any wrongdoing or questionable behavior was perhaps the most consistent theme that apeared throughout the accounts of conversion and disaffection' (1987, 299).

A psychological account and explanation of this kind of relationship is given by Peter Rutter in his seminal work, *Sex in the Forbidden Zone*. He focused mainly on psychotherapists and their female clients but included other situations including the master–disciple relationship:

> Religious cults in which the guru or spiritual leader has sexual relationships with many of his female congregants are more blatant examples of this phenomenon. The leader exploits the trust and value of the spiritual relationship in the same way that therapists, lawyers, teachers, and mentors do in the privacy of their offices. (1990, 28)

Rutter sees it as 'an epidemic mainstream problem that reenacts in the professional relationship a wider cultural power-imbalance between men and women' (1990, 2). The central factor is 'the existence of a relationship of trust that was betrayed through sexual behavior . . . betrayal of what had been a *nonsexual* relationship with a man who had been centrally important to a woman's development' (13). The betrayal is compounded since the relationship generates a double-edged energy, with the power to heal as well as harm: 'when a man who has power over and intimate access to a woman maintains complete respect for her sexual boundaries, the healing promise of relationships of trust between men and women can be fulfilled' (21). His book explores the dynamics of this situation in all its psychological (though not organizational) ramifications: the 'wounds' in women and men that encourage it, the ways it develops, the damage it inflicts, and how to prevent it. He is adamant throughout that no matter what the provocation, it is always harmful: 'When it occurs in the forbidden zone with a man who has a responsibility not to let it happen, a woman inevitably leaves the sexual relationship with more damage than when she entered it' (124).

Teachers of any kind are vulnerable to such temptation,

particularly in the affective domain.[6] Above all it applies to religious teachers, priests and gurus, where the spiritual dimension introduces a higher authority, but also a special intimacy combined with a sacred bond of trust. To complicate such a sensitive, subtle relationship by bringing in the raw, powerful, irrational energies of sexuality is always dangerous and sometimes disastrous.

Rutter highlights the *in loco parentis* responsibility of male authority figures in sensitive positions, which applies even more significantly to the master–disciple relationship, as already discussed. This responsibility is generally accepted in the pastoral relationship, as symbolized by the widespread convention of addressing priests and teachers as Father or Mother and the ways this imagery is developed within the traditions. Correspondingly the student or disciple is cast in the child role. In return for cultivating trust and innocence, they expect their vulnerability to be honoured.

> A man in this position of trust and authority becomes unavoidably a parent figure and is charged with the ethical responsibilities of the parenting role. Violations of these boundaries are, psychologically speaking, not only rapes but also acts of incest. (88)

Katherine Webster, who carried out an in-depth investigation into allegations of sexual abuse against the Indian teacher Swami Rama, asserts an equivalent to this moral stance in Asian religion: 'Sex with a guru is a form of spiritual incest. In the mythology of the ashram, the guru is the all-powerful, all-knowing father and the disciples are his spiritual children' (1990, 60). She interviewed another Indian swami, Pandit Arya, who confirmed that such activity would be 'very terrible, a violation of the teaching that says one should treat all women as daughters' (ibid., 66). Within NRMs it may be seen as the failure of the teacher's responsibility as both father figure and mirror: whereby the father commits incest with his daughters, and the mirror reflects not purity but corruption.

## Tantra: Crazy Wisdom or Abuse?

There is a minority view, particularly in Eastern-based NRMs with Tantric influences, that sexual relations between guru and disciple can be part of spiritual growth, a means for the guru to transmit energy that can provoke an enlightenment experience. For example, Irina Tweedie's guru described four possible variations of the master–disciple relationship, including lover and beloved (literally), as practised in Tantra Yoga, but warned that in their system it 'would be considered an obstacle' (Tweedie 1979, 78).

Tantra is an esoteric Hindu tradition whose texts go back to around the fourth century CE. It is an umbrella term, covering an enormous range of rituals and techniques, of which only a tiny minority involve sex, collectively known as the 'left-hand path'. Some of the practices were taken over and further developed within Buddhism, through which they spread to other countries, notably Tibet.

Tantra is a life-affirmative, body-positive path on which sexual passion is seen not as an obstruction but as our most powerful natural energy, which may be explored and transmuted into the Great Bliss of Liberation. It is non-dualistic, immanentist: 'nirvana is samsara; the passions themselves constitute enlightenment'. Historically, Tantra has been dedicated to the female principle, and Tantric myths and icons depict the erotic goddess as a life-giving force.

> Women are seen as earthly, or bodily, manifestations of goddesses, and this identity is reinforced by the patterning of male–female relationships upon the relationship between a devotee and a deity. The man's divinity is an accepted premise of Tantric metaphysics, but it is not given the same range of concrete expressions as the woman's divinity in this gynocentric context. (Shaw 1994, 69)

Women are worshipped, the male principle being complementary but subordinate: 'The female element is an embodiment of *prajna*, transcendental wisdom; the woman's *yoni* is the abode of pure bliss' (Stevens 1990, 63).

The main feminist debate around Tantra is whether the woman in a Tantric relationship was primarily a sex object for the *man's* enlightenment, or whether she was an equal partner. Padmasambhava, who brought Tantra from India to Tibet, taught that although there was no great difference between male and female bodies, 'if she develops the mind bent on enlightenment, the woman's body is better'. It is believed that at this time women were at least consorts in a Tantric relationship; sometimes they became teachers, as with Padmasambhava's own disciple Tsogyel. Miranda Shaw's detailed, meticulously researched book presents a convincing case for the empowerment of women not only as equal partners but often as superior, more skilled and capable, hence teachers to the male initiates:

> Seeing one's partner as divine is the key to this form of worship. Having seen one's partner as a god or goddess, one naturally feels a sense of devotion. . . . Although the man and woman recognize one another's divinity, implying complete reciprocity, the man is required to respond to the woman's divinity with numerous expressions of devotion, physical acts of homage, and a reverential, suppliant attitude. (1994, 153)

Other writers, however, argue that women were marginalized, oppressed and exploited in Tantra. Shaw attributes the disparagement of women in the research to distorted interpretation governed by misogyny, but even some feminist researchers support this view. June Campbell (1996) argues in her study of female identity in Tibetan Buddhism that although historically women have sometimes been admitted as Tantrikas in India and very rarely as tulkus in Tibet, over the last 500 years 'there has been a degeneration of the teachings in general, which has resulted in women losing touch with their own powers and knowledge as Tantric lineage-holders'.[7] As a result the status of women has declined dramatically. She writes from personal experience of how the problems are exacerbated in the case of lamas who outwardly maintain celibacy but secretly maintain a *songhyum* (sexual partner) who is sworn to secrecy and threatened with all manner of punishments for indiscretion in this world and the next. It is only the Nyingma school of Tibetan Buddhism, in which the lamas are usually married, that the importance of women practitioners is acknowledged. Although many lamas have had consorts, there is no lineage of women teachers, and no women with any position of power. The very few women who are publicly recognized as possessing high spiritual qualities are the wives, mothers or sisters of lamas.

Anthony and Wilber, both experienced meditators as well as

academics, censure attempts to legitimate sexual exploitation through Tantra: 'Tantric Freudianism can serve as a rationalization for flamboyant acting-out and impulsivity' (1987, 67). They ask the question: 'Does a master's sexual behavior have implications regarding the master's level of spiritual realization and trustworthiness?' (89), and conclude:

> Actual experience shows that the chances of deception and self-deception in this matter are so great as to be almost a guarantee that a master's sexual advances constitute not authentic Tantric mysticism . . . but spiritual fraudulence and exploitation. Most female disciples who describe the effects of sexual intercourse with a master report not inner spiritual progress but deep psychological wounds and spiritual disillusionment and derailment. (90)

Yet Tantra is the commonest legitimation for these relationships, whether conducted in the name of crazy wisdom, divine love, or tantric enlightenment. Such practices do appear to have worked in the past, but within a highly disciplined context in which the rules and aims were understood by both parties – thus permitting the equality essential to success. Buddhism also contains moral strictures against sexual misconduct, including the doctrine that animalistic or 'evil-minded' sex leads to hell; to achieve enlightenment one must act as a *bodhisattva*, that is, with the highest sanctity. There have been complaints that Westerners misunderstand and misuse the sacred principles of Tantra, but some of the Asian gurus have contributed to this confusion by ignoring or distorting the moral sanctions. It may well be that within modern groups these rituals are replicated successfully in some instances, such as sacred sexuality groups where sexual activity is carefully regulated and takes place only between participants, not with therapists. These conditions do not appear to have applied in any of the groups accused of abuse.

### Buddist Consorts and *Dakinis*

Buddhism is generally considered respectable in the West, though not always in Asia, where in some countries monks have been considered highly lecherous, among other faults.

This view appears to be borne out in Thailand, where a number of monks have been exposed, including the most popular teacher Phra Yantra, who had devotees in the government, army and royal family as well as in 20 other countries. His exploits included regular visits to the Wild Orchid Escort Lounge in New Zealand, where his partners called him Batman because he kept on his robes during sex.

Boucher (1985) devotes a chapter to 'the problem of the male teacher', revealing how widespread it is in American Buddhism, including some of the most famous teachers such as Chogyam Trungpa, Richard Baker and Soen Sa Nim. Like Rutter, she makes the comparison with other professional relationships involving sexual/power abuse, 'thus removing Buddhist teachers' misdeeds from spiritual or otherworldly justifications' (213). She quotes one woman who felt that 'sexual power abuse was the most insidious and at the core of the others' (237), though 'related to larger issues in the spiritual or Buddhist community concerning power, authority, and the relationships between women and men' (239). Most of the women she interviewed expressed tremendous pain and confusion regarding their experiences and the implications for their practice, except for Chogyam Trungpa's students, who 'had usually gone through an internal process to move from disapproval and dis–ease to acceptance of their teacher's actions' (240). However, asked if they were distressed by Trungpa's sexual liaisons, some of the replies seemed a bit confused, and certainly take a lot on trust:

> I did [feel distressed], but as I practice more and get into more of the Tantric practices I have begun to realize that his manifestation is totally brilliant. Not that I understand it, but that I understand not–understanding. . . . I accept him as a totally enlightened vajra master, and so it makes sense to me that he does what he does. (241)

Trungpa was notorious for his many sexual partners, called 'consorts', as well as his alcoholism and generally excessive behaviour. He had been a monk in Tibet, where he had fathered a child before leaving holy orders. He advocated the Tantric practice of 'drinking the poison' of sex, alcohol and so on, to transform them into vehicles of *dharma*. He coined the term 'crazy wisdom' for these practices, an adaptation of an existing Tibetan term to which he gave a currency and level of significance disproportionate to its meaning in Tibet. He believed in the necessity of training in order to successfully practise such dangerous techniques, but chose as his *dharma* heir Osel Tendzin, who died of AIDS, having allegedly infected his many partners without telling them. Tendzin claimed Trungpa had authorized him in this behaviour, on the basis that if he did his purification practice his partners would not be infected, which is plausible given the Tibetan belief in miracles and the abilities of lamas to intervene in nature. The results were disastrous, and almost destroyed his community Vajradhatu. Tendzin was seen as 'the cult guru who seduces his students into self-destruction. Trungpa's entire organization was splitting apart over the issue. Almost overnight, devotion to gurus became politically incorrect, a way of enabling the drunken elephant in the shrine room' (Butterfield 1994, 6).

Butterfield himself is an interesting example of the confusion and double standards that may affect even intelligent and normally compassionate people in these situations. In an article written for the leading Buddhist publication *Tricycle*, he produced a vindication of Trungpa despite admitting the problems of disparity of power and the need for extensive preparation for the goal of union with the guru's mind (not body). He achieves his defence partly by disparagement of the body (and by implication the women whose bodies are involved): 'From this nondual perspective, the friction of body parts is a nonissue.' He continues:

Let us assume that a student, of either gender, who sleeps with a spiritual teacher feels afterward that she or he has been diminished, alienated from self, abandoned, treated as an object, or used to enhance the teacher's power. These feelings have a twofold character; they may reflect insight into the real nature of the teacher's attitude, but insofar as they center on defending the self, they are also the ego-responses that Buddhist practice seeks to illuminate and undermine. An ethic forbidding the teacher to elicit such responses in a student assumes that self-clinging ought to be sheltered and protected. This ethic is ultimately demeaning to the student; it turns the student into a kind of ward: 'Yes, the teacher really is more powerful than you; because you are not adult enough to make your own decisions, you should be put into protective custody.'

He argues that such questions as Am I being violated? 'are lyrics in the everlasting song of *me*' arising from insecurity. 'A good teacher would not force a trauma of self-exposure on an unprepared student', but his job is 'to help the student take off the suit of armor. If we think no private parts ought to be exposed in this process, we are living in a Disneyworld.' This defence raises a number of questions, such as whether this teaching is a vehicle for *dharma* – or *karma*; whether the ego is such a bad thing that the student should be grateful to a teacher for demolishing it even at the cost of abuse; whether it accords with Buddhist compassion to rip it open violently, or rather to let it ripen naturally.

Trungpa and his students were at least open about his drinking and sexuality, thus avoiding the problems of secrecy (see below). This was not the case with his protégé Sogyal Rinpoche, founder of the Rigpa Foundation. He is now the best known Tibetan lama in the West apart from the Dalai Lama, with a worldwide following and a best-selling book, *The Tibetan Book of Living and Dying*. He was generally considered a model of propriety until he was sued for $10 million by an American ex-devotee claiming sexual and physical abuse. The woman, known by the pseudonym of Janice Doe, claimed that Sogyal took advantage of her confusion following her father's death to seduce her, claiming she would be healed and strengthened by having sex with him – an oft-used justification by Buddhist teachers. She decided to press charges partly as a result of many other allegations from current and former students. The case was finally settled out of court, partly because none of the other women involved would agree to stand up in court.

Sogyal's female disciples were called *dakinis*, which means 'sky dancer' or 'traveller in space' in Tibetan. In the scriptures, these women were wild and powerful beings who were often instrumental in bringing the masters to enlightenment. *Dakinis* embody wisdom and the uncompromising, fearless encounter with truth. However at Rigpa, it is claimed, this meaning was confined to mythology and not allowed to be embodied in practice. Sogyal's *dakinis* had two functions, as explained by a former devotee (based on firsthand observation and accounts given to her by the women involved):

> There was a split between women who were seen as sexual beings – the sexual consorts who were usually rather glamorous, beautiful women – and the worker women who were mother types, beavering away behind the scenes working all hours. . . . Sexual *dakinis* would also serve by offering sex on demand, staying up all hours of the day and night to cook the lama a meal or do whatever was required. They all got very thin because they didn't have time to eat. Some favourites didn't have to work that hard but most got exhausted, the sensual ones as much as the office ones.

There are many stories and allegations circulating concerning Sogyal's exploits, though no proven evidence. For example, it has also been claimed that it was usual for Sogyal to invite women to come and make him a cup of tea, lock the door and tell them to take their clothes off and have sex. They would be told they were special, would become his consort, even marry him. They would then be ushered out and meet another woman coming down the corridor. This might happen six or seven times in one night. It appears that he had very little respect for the women concerned and would boss them around and humiliate them in public. Neither group of *dakinis* had as high status as the male disciples, who were thanked for their services, seen as more devoted, worthy servants, and considered better teachers. I was not able to interview any current devotees (many have now left, including most of the senior British students), so the *dakini* model may work for some, but a woman who has counselled many ex-members reported:

> People spoke to me of distress, disappointment, confusion, pain, so I don't have any evidence that people reached an enlightened state. Some women would ask for an experience of enlightenment [in exchange for their sexual services] so would be given some meditation exercises. They would then feel guilty, like a prostitute, for having sex with him in return for special teachings. But the sex itself was not enlightening.

## Sannyas as a 'Love Affair': Ecstasy or Exploitation?

Osho was popularly known as the 'sex guru' on account of his Tantric teachings on the integration of sexuality and spirituality, and his encouragement of experimentation among his disciples. There have been some accusations that he had sexual relationships with his female disciples, mainly by anti-cultists and ex-members.[8] Franklin discussed the issue frankly in a book written while still a sannyasin and approved by the ashram, concluding that there might be some truth in the rumours but that a) such incidents happened only in the Bombay phase when the movement was much smaller and more experimental; b) it was irrelevant, since sannyasins were 'outgrowing sex as a need', hence 'obviously the same must be true for Bhagwan' (Bharti 1981, 115). In a later book she went into more detail, reporting that her roommate had been instructed by Osho to spread rumours about his sexual exploits in order to 'give my Indian ladies something to gossip about' (Franklin 1992, 32). Her main impression was that Osho's interest in the sexuality of his disciples was 'as impersonal as if he were a doctor taking my pulse' (33).

This is also Gordon's impression. He spoke to a few women who claimed to have had sexual experiences with Osho and used similar language: 'rewiring my circuits', 'orchestrating their energies' (1987, 79–80). Most sannyasins believed he was celibate, having 'transcended sex'. If they had heard rumours, they tended to either disbelieve them, relegating them to the past, or justify them in Tantric terms. The only woman I interviewed with firsthand experience described how when she first met Osho in Bombay he had asked her to take off her clothes. She had felt his interest in her was more voyeuristic than sexual, but had not responded: 'I didn't get turned on by it, though I think some women did, and I don't know what would have happened if I had. But I was still a good Catholic girl, so I retreated.'

The confusion was exacerbated by Osho's repeated declaration: 'Sannyas is a love affair', though this was intended metaphorically (see Chapter 4). Most sannyasins displayed a strong resistance to a literal sexualization of the master–disciple relationship. One of my respondents described Osho as being behind a 'veil' of people's projections, including the lover image, but asked if she had this fantasy replied: 'Absolutely not! It totally shocked me. Lots of people say they had fantasies of making love to Osho, but I was much too puritanical.' For another woman it was a temporary phase: 'In the early days I did have sexual fantasies about what it would be like to make love with an enlightened being, in particular Osho, but now he's just a very precious being.'

From the conflicting evidence, it seems likely that there were some sexual relationships between Osho and his female disciples, at least in the early days, but that they were not regarded as exploitative or abusive. However, one of Osho's former disciples, Michael Barnett, has been accused of exploitative sexual relationships with his group of female followers. One of Barnett's disciples who was not in his 'harem' felt very angry about his activities, even though she had no evidence of anyone 'damaged' by them:

> Michael was a man, and all the games that men and women play together were there. He had his little bevy of female followers, and I found it very difficult to fit into the role of female follower with such an obviously potent male teacher. It feels that because of his position he can ask women to sleep with him, and they will.

Other leaders of NRMs against whom unsubstantiated allegations of sexual abuse have been made include Maharishi Mahesh Yogi, Munindra, Sri Chinmoy, Da Avabhasa, Swami Prem Paramahansa and Muktananda. There is currently an 'open letter' about Siddha Yoga on the Internet, endorsing claims made in a 1994 *New Yorker* article regarding the sexual abuse and exploitation of young women, including minors, by Muktananda, which were justified as having a 'divine purpose'. These claims have been confirmed by senior ex-members, but are not accepted by the Siddha Yoga organization.

### Colluders, Co-dependents or Victims?

So far the emphasis has been on the misdemeanours of the perpetrators, but it has to be asked what role the women played in these activities. Some are under-age teenagers, but most are adult women consenting to sex. So are they victims or colluders? Why did they do it and what, if anything, did they hope to gain?

It is difficult to determine how far an apparently oppressive relationship that is voluntarily, even joyfully entered into, can be termed exploitation. Feminist research has made a powerful case for a shift of emphasis from victimization to empowerment. In the words of the feminist theologian Emily Culpepper: 'Feminists must develop our own methods for recognizing and researching women's direct, positive efforts to create the Self and the world that are not patriarchal. Women have not been only, nor should we see ourselves exclusively as, victims' (1987, 8). On the other hand, anti-cultists who denounce abuse and masochism in new religions may exonerate and even glorify such behaviour in Christianity. Martyrdom still has a strong hold on the Christian imagination, especially in Catholicism.

Maitland castigates the 'sado-masochistic relationship with God' that many Christian women have, and the role of imagery in encouraging this process, including cannibalism, necrophilia, incest and rape. She sees this tendency as best exemplified in Christianity's 'ecstatic lust for martyrdom which can formally be described as masochistic'. Women, being identified with nature and the body and therefore more 'sinful', were also perceived to need punishment more, so were made to inflict martyrdom on themselves through extreme asceticism. The Bride of Christ image is the final perversion:

> [Women must also be wedded to Jesus] To Jesus who suffered for them, who suffers still because they are not good enough, who restrains his loving hands from the punishment they deserve and he desires. . . .
>
> I have called this spiritual disease sado-masochism precisely because the woman so afflicted acts out both roles herself. She has internalized the sadist who is her beloved other, her own projection and her one hope of salvation. He is the lover who loves her pain and she offers it to him humbly and ecstatically. (Maitland 1987, 135–7)

Yet women continue to present experiences of suffering gladly embraced for the sake of spiritual growth, which cannot always be dismissed as masochism. Bougaud wrote of a French saint: 'Often the assaults of the divine love reduced her almost to the point of death. She used tenderly to complain of this to God. "I cannot support it," she used to say. "Bear gently with my weakness, or I shall expire under the violence of your love"' (James 1960, 275). As a contemporary example, Tweedie took ten years to edit her diaries because of the remembered suffering: 'The slow grinding down of the personality is a painful process.' But she went through the process bravely, because she believed in and achieved its purpose: 'It is the task of the Teacher to set the heart aflame with an unquenchable fire of longing; it is his duty to keep it burning until it is reduced to ashes. For only a heart which has burned itself empty is capable of love' (1979, 7). The book records her daily sufferings at the hands of her Sufi master, which often sound unbearably harsh, yet she vindicates him totally – and also experiences ecstasy and illumination. In other words, what might appear to the 'objective' outsider as a brutally abusive relationship within a patriarchal system could equally be viewed as a triumphant achievement of spiritual development within a venerable religious tradition.

Women often fall in love with their gurus, partly owing to the attraction of power, partly because the gurus may be genuinely charismatic, but also because devotional love is often fundamental to such relationships (see Chapter 4). But romantic love is a dangerous energy at the best of times, even more so when combined with the intensity of a spiritual relationship. As one of Boucher's respondents expressed it:

> In serious Zen study, the teacher and student meet alone in the interview room several times a week for ten years or more, in the most intense and intimate study imaginable. In koan study the student plunges into and becomes all aspects of existence and nonexistence: anger, love, hate, death, birth, emptiness, animal realms, male, female. The teacher continually strips away anything the student is clinging to, using any technique which works. The process is frightening, exhilarating, frustrating, horrible, and wonderful. The student and teacher become extremely close during this process, like people who have been through a war together. I think it's no wonder that this closeness sometimes takes a physical form, not that it *should*, but that it does. (1988, 216–17)

It may even work, as a serious love relationship. But like all such relationships, only more so, it is painful and disruptive for the individual and the community when it goes wrong – as it usually does eventually. One woman described a 'psychic merging' with her teacher whereby she became 'so close to this person that I was really fused with him in a way that my identity was submerged. That's part of Dharma transmission, to become one with your teacher so that you can see through their eyes.' However, after the affair finished, 'I realized, "No, I really now need to unmerge and become myself again." That's actually what Zen practice is about, is to become more and more yourself' (Boucher 1988, 218–19).[9]

Whether or not sexual abuse takes place, a further question is whether the devotional love felt by devotees for their master is exploited. Sociological research tends to focus on sexual abuse, which is easier to identify, but emotional and power abuse can cause even greater suffering. As Secunda puts it: 'Psychological abuse is at the heart of all maltreatment' (1993, 95). Jacobs, despite her emphasis on sexuality and status, concluded: 'This final acknowledgment, that the devotee will never be loved by the teacher, is perhaps the most painful realization of all, the turning point from hopefulness to disillusionment' (1987, 302).

If the woman has not been loved in return, she will experience feelings of intense bitterness and betrayal and will probably leave the community, as happened with Jacobs's respondents. Some of the women who have left Tibetan lamas in such circumstances have also left the religion, unable to dissociate the practice from the flawed practitioner, and may take years to renew their practice. One criticism Westerners have of Tantra is its dissociation from the affective domain. Even Stevens, who commends it so highly, contrasts it with Zen where the teachers might fall in love with their partners: 'In Tantric sex, there is always a sense of detachment, an emphasis on transcending the physical form of one's partner and focusing on his or her impersonal, universal aspects' (1990, 101). Western teachers of sacred sex take a more emotionally centred approach: 'I introduce intimacy as a subtle set of skills, an art that has to be developed before sexual union should be considered. From this perspective sex happens as the crowning act of intimacy' (Anand 1989, 94). Shaw believes devotion to one's partner is integral to Tantra, which believes that 'men and women together can create relationships that are non-exploitative, noncoercive, and mutually enlightening' (1994, 195). Unfortunately, there is little evidence of this attitude in NRMs, where the women are more likely to be treated as sexual resources than true consorts.

Finally and above all, a spiritual justification is often made for these relationships whereby the women honoured with such attentions expect to receive special teachings or transmissions of energy through the sexual act. It may happen. One of Sogyal Rinpoche's *dakinis* has allegedly claimed that the sex was not up to much but it was worth it for the teachings. Teachers often offer strength through sex, which may derive from the Asian belief in the magical powers of semen (according to the Vedas, one drop can dispel 3200 diseases). One woman commented of Soen Sa Nim: 'He said that he slept with this woman because ... sleeping with him helped make her strong. ... It took *five years* to make her strong!' (Boucher 1988, 228).

The evidence suggests that these sexual relationships usually arise out of the psychological woundedness of both perpetrators and victims. The men are wounded, and require sexual healing from the equally wounded women, as Peter Rutter explains it, thus perpetuating a negative cycle involving secrecy, lies, deceit, hypocrisy, denial and fear. Women in such relationships are usually instructed to conceal their existence, and are sometimes threatened with punishment and damnation if they reveal the truth. This secrecy is partly in line with a highly esoteric tradition, but also protects the reputations of teachers and lamas who often claim to be celibate and reject the importance of female power and influence to their attainment. Campbell claims that secrecy also allowed lamas 'to *maintain control over the women* who became involved so that any decision-making which should concern both of them regarding the duration of the relationship, and the conditions under which it was perpetuated, were all made by the lama himself' (1996, 106; her italics). In practice, as these relationships are known about by senior disciples, hypocrisy is also required, sometimes further disguised as 'pure perception':

> The traditional teachings say any partner of the lama is equal, a source of inspiration who should be respected. One is

encouraged to have pure perception of the lama, see him as a Buddha, therefore his partner must be equally elevated. So if one noticed the lama was having girlfriends, and in the next breath was giving high spiritual teachings, one would assume his girlfriend must be a very special person, although one knew at the same time there seemed to be a lot of girlfriends.

There are lies to the women about the number and extent of other relationships, to rank-and-file students and to the outside world. A pattern of denial serves to hold the 'family' together against the outside world at all costs. The motivation is to protect the teacher and other students, to preserve the positive aspects of the teaching and community, but the cost is great. Any victim who complains is liable to ridicule and rejection within the community and sometimes even by higher religious authorities. Fear and tension are generated, and confusion, pain and bitterness follow.

It has been pointed out by therapists and some participants that several of these communities mirrored the dynamic of the alcoholic family, in which family members deny that there is a problem and protect the alcoholic father, while covertly encouraging his behavior. Such an addictive system requires dishonesty and promotes confusion and abnormal thinking processes. (Boucher 1988, 212)

Thus the women become co-dependents, and have difficulty in either exposing the misdemeanours or leaving.[10] Many members of NRMs come from dysfunctional families and some may even be incest survivors, which helps explain how the dynamic is replicated but intensifies the problems.[11] In terms of emotional health, one of the worst problems is around personal boundaries, which are weakest in survivors of abuse, who are therefore further disadvantaged in an environment that rejects all boundaries in favour of the chaos of 'crazy wisdom'. It is the lack of respect for people's vulnerability that produces such contorted vindications as that for Trungpa quoted above (p.59). As a Buddhist woman seduced by a roshi at the age of 16 asked, 'What do you do when God makes a pass at you?'

Some commentators take a harshly moralistic line towards the women, as does Victoria Gillick regarding priests' lovers:

'They know exactly what they are doing when they set their cap at a priest. It's a variation on adultery. Then they turn round and say it's not fair. They can't say that because what they've done is wrong. If you do something wrong, you're going to hurt and suffer.'[12] Gillick is an avowedly anti-feminist campaigner, but even Jacobs acknowledges collusion:

> While some of the former devotees look on this aspect of commitment as coercion, the majority of women involved with these groups expressed a strong willingness, even desire, to engage in sexual relations with the spiritual teacher. This willingness seemed to arise partially out of the desire to be intimate with the men in power, partially out of a deep feeling of love for the teacher, and partially out of the belief . . . that the promise of enlightenment might be that much closer if one were to have a physical relationship with a godly being. (1984, 162)

All these motivations are expressed to varying degrees by the women involved. Regarding the goal of power: just as men see sex as the reward of power (see above), women see it as the means to power, with much historical justification. But there is a price. Jacobs argues that 'women are often objectified . . . by a bartering system in which their only access to power is through relationships to high-status men in the movement' (1989, 62). This was certainly the case in the Family, where women had to go through a lengthy process of approval to participate in FFing, and complained about 'the reluctance of some leaders to give more than a few women permission to engage in flirty fishing' (Melton 1994). Within Tibetan Buddhism, June Campbell admits that the role of *songhyum* does confer prestige on the woman, despite her sufferings and indignities. The status is ambivalent: she interprets it as basically abusive from a contemporary feminist perspective. Another Buddhist woman, however, insisted that she had misunderstood the spiritual honour of the position, and that gratitude would have been a more appropriate response. Some women boasted about sleeping with Trungpa, believing it gave them status, but power and status gained in this way may well prove illusory; since there are many rivals for the guru's favours, the chosen one is liable to be rejected summarily at any moment or discover she is not alone in her position.

When this pattern is built into the structure and dynamics of an organization it is hard to avoid: 'The class hierarchy of Trungpa's mandala carried over into the pattern of its love affairs. As it does in the samsaric world, passion flowed toward those who had power' (Butterfield 1994, 114). Another consequence is the example set by the teacher to his male disciples, in a situation where they are encouraged to emulate and compete with the 'top baboon', hence should not be encouraged in spiritual practice. The men advance in order to gain access to sex, the women advance through sex. In Buddhism power is an attribute of the ego which is meant to be renounced. Sex as the reward of spiritual service might well be deemed *vajra* hell!

There are ways of using religious ritual to heal the effects of abuse, which have been created within the women's spirituality movement and Paganism. Dolores Ashcroft-Nowicki has a ritual for rape victims, which has been widely and successfully used inside and outside her tradition.[13] Susan Greenwood (forthcoming) has described how survivors of childhood abuse may be attracted to magic as a form of self-empowerment, though some may find it works negatively:

> One witch I knew, who had been abused as a child, felt empowered by being in charge of a ritual circle. She controlled the energy of the group and drew power from this. Another gained much from the positive value given to female genitalia as a symbol of displaying and empowering that which had been kept a secret. However, one woman had decided to leave her witchcraft coven after four years because she said it did not feel right to practice anymore . . . she did not want a secret part of her life anymore because it reminded her of being abused as a child.

Altogether the evidence suggests that when the powerful energy of sexuality is harnessed to the drive for power and the search for enlightenment, a strong ego and stable personality are prerequisites. The worst problems arise within the most hierachical and 'dysfunctional' NRMs, particularly when lip-service is paid to decorum and morality, to celibacy or monogamy. Such leaders are also 'having it both ways': the kudos of the monk's or lama's robe combined with the rewards of profligacy. A more antinomian environment will be less hypocritical, but creates worse problems around boundaries.

Nevertheless, even when there is some justification of love and spirituality, these motives are so easily mixed with power and woundedness that the Tantric path is probably best avoided unless set up with the utmost care, compassion and expertise. The spiritual teacher Andrew Cohen was recently asked a question on the Tantric rationale for these relationships, and replied: 'Isn't it interesting how it's always the youngest and prettiest women who are chosen?' The Dalai Lama has said that the true Tantric master is capable of drinking urine or alcohol with complete equanimity, but that the path is so difficult and demanding that he knew of no one capable of practising it. It seems that in most cases the great spiritual tradition of Tantra is exploited and trivialized as an excuse for philandery.

## Solutions

What the West now terms sexual abuse is a deeply entrenched cultural phenomenon in Asia, even though there are many scriptural strictures against such misconduct.[14] The leaders of Eastern-based NRMs are distanced from their peers; they lack the institutional support structures, the system of checks and balances built into their own society and religion. On the other hand they are no longer in the position of feudal lords, accountable to nobody, and now encounter the norms of modern democracy. It might seem preferable to acknowledge the problems than to allow the teaching to fall into disrepute.

It is clearly essential to establish some form of accountability, perhaps in the form of guidelines for assessing these practices, or even a voluntary code of ethics. The Network for Western Buddhist Teachers has issued such a code, which the Dalai Lama appears to support but not officially, although he has said that misbehaviour should be publicized. Neither Vajradhatu nor Rigpa have signed the code, which they see as moral policing.

Training would also help: 'we have to be trained so we are aware that the problem might arise, just the way psychotherapists are trained about the transference phenomenon with their patients and the risk of physical intimacy' (Boucher 1988, 217). Outside counselling and therapeutic back-up should also be available. Psychotherapy has been disparaged in Buddhism in the past, but is becoming more acceptable within the Westernization process. One goal of therapy is 'owning the shadow', which is made darker through the denial of sexuality but may be integrated through openness and consciousness. Psychologizing deviant groups as dysfunctional families seems preferable to demonizing them as cults.

It is also important that behaviour considered abusive should be labelled, acknowledged as such. Preferably it should be dealt with privately, at source, but if the organizational politics preclude this, it should be publicly exposed. Chris Brain was exposed after a group of his women parishioners had agreed: 'This is not just a sex scandal, but an abuse of religious power.' Similarly, Richard Baker was thrown out of San Francisco Zen Center following a mass rebellion after he was discovered to be sleeping with a trustee's wife. On a wider scale, public awareness of the extent of abuse within Buddhism emerged following the first conference on Women and Buddhism in America in 1983.

The problem is hard to deal with legally, though there are precedents such as sexual harassment cases. As discussed, there are strong arguments for viewing such 'forbidden zone' misconduct within a spiritual community even more seriously. If it does take place, and cannot be dealt with internally, it needs to be brought to court in the same way as other sexual crimes. The Sogyal Rinpoche case is significant because even though it did not come to trial, it established a precedent for legal action.

Above all, there is a need for teachers not to exploit their position. Doctors not only take the Hippocratic oath but tend to maintain a social distance with their patients. There is a case for the maintenance of such boundaries in the much higher-risk master–disciple relationship. Likewise, there is an onus on women to empower themselves, and to listen to their bodies, instincts and feelings. As a former Buddhist nun expressed it: 'I think it's important for each person to use their own discriminating wisdom and common sense. If something doesn't make sense, look into it. If a monk asks you to go to bed with him say no, even if he says it will get you enlightened!'

# 4 Devotion: The Path of Feminine Spirituality?

## Bhakti Yoga: The Path of Devotion

Historically sannyas in India has been confined almost exclusively to men, although the occasional post-menopausal widow might be allowed to live at an ashram. *Moksha* (liberation) was not possible in a female body; at best a woman could hope for rebirth into a male body in order to pursue the spiritual path.[1] Yet within *bhakti* yoga, the most popular branch of Hinduism which arose in southern India in the sixth century CE, women have had a religious role, albeit mainly confined to domestic rituals while men dominated the priestly and teaching roles. Nevertheless, gender ideology in *bhakti* was more liberal than in Brahminism. It produced a number of female saints, some of them famous, such as the sixteenth-century Mirabai, and re-established female lineages. These developments may be connected to the fact that *bhakti* means 'devotion' and can be viewed as a feminine path.[2]

One of the most significant developments of *bhakti* is 'marriage mysticism'. Sexual imagery is traditional in mystical writing, partly owing to the inadequacy of language to describe such experiences. Hood and Hall note that 'Even a casual perusal of this literature reveals a consistent utilization of sexual and erotic descriptive phrases in both Western and Eastern traditions to characterize the mystical experience' (1980, 195). Sometimes these experiences may be developed to the point where sexuality and spirituality fuse ecstatically, as described by Irina Tweedie's guru:

> When I was young with my first wife, I rarely had intercourse with her. Every night I merged into my Revered Guru Maharaj. There can be no greater bliss imaginable than when two Souls are merging into one with love. Sometimes the body is also merged. How is it done? The body partakes of it, is included in it, by reflection, so to say. And no bliss in the world is greater than this: when you are one with your Teacher. (1979, 55)

74

Osho's use of sexual imagery and his oft-repeated declaration: 'Sannyas is a love affair' may be understood in this context. It was a concept he explored and developed extensively: 'The disciple and teacher must become deep lovers. Only then can the higher, the beyond, be expressed' (1974, 5). He used images of dancing, ecstasy, melting and merging, sometimes explicitly sexual, particularly in his 'seduction' of new recruits: 'without becoming a sannyasin you will never come close to me, you will never have that orgasmic experience that is possible by feeling deep empathy with me' (1979, 178).

Such experiences are occasionally encountered in Christian mystical literature. Both the Old and New Testament contain nuptial imagery, which was developed into the 'sacred marriage' of Gnostic writings. In the mid-twelfth century Bernard of Clairvaux developed a form of nuptial mysticism in which the image of Christ the Groom of the Church as Bride became extended to the monks as brides. The vocabulary of courtly love fused romance and sexuality, and was later adopted by the Cathars and other Christian mystics to express spiritual experience.[3] Mystical love poetry also provides examples, playing with the etymological and experiential relationship between rapture and rape.[4] An interesting example is John Donne, who in his earlier, erotic poetry depicts himself as a masterful philanderer but whose later, religious verse describes ecstatic self-abnegation:

> Take mee to you, imprison mee, for I
> Except you'enthrall mee, never shall be free,
> Nor ever chast, except you ravish mee.[5]

All these examples show the poet or mystic casting himself in the role of a woman, in relation to a God invariably perceived as male. Since this devotional love is paradigmatically expressed by a man to a male god or guru, an interesting paradox arises, which has been resolved in Indian mysticism:

> Because of the male–female attraction, we find, at least for some of the bhakti traditions, that a woman was paradigmatic as devotee when the supreme deity was male. Thus, for a male devotee to enter into 'marriage mysticism' with a male god, he had to assume the psychology of a woman in love. (Young 1987, 77)

O'Flaherty takes this insight further: 'The devotee visualizes himself as a woman not merely because god is male but because in the Hindu view the stance of the ideal devotee is identical with the stance of the ideal woman' (1980, 88).

Transvestism is an accepted devotional expression in India historically and in the present. For example, Leslie describes how the famous nineteenth-century mystic Ramakrishna 'spent six months in systematic devotion as a woman to Krsna. He dressed as a woman . . . and used feminine gestures with such effect that village women accepted him as one of themselves' (1983, 103). Similarly in ancient Greece in the cult of Dionysus, himself an androgynous figure, men donned the ritual clothing of women in his worship. Yet there is something paradoxical if not perverse in a religious path that is so feminine in style, yet so limiting of women's roles, thus constraining men to enact the female role literally.

ISKCON can be seen as a transitional movement in this respect, in that Prabhupada allowed women disciples but was ambivalent about their status, alternating between a mystical concept of spiritual equality with male disciples and a conservative Hindu belief in female inferiority. Krishna Consciousness itself is 'a feminine approach to spirituality' in that it consists of 'surrender and service to others', and ultimately to Krishna, who represents the masculine polarity (Knott 1995). Women are better socialized to practise this path, but the misogyny sometimes displayed by Prabhupada and by the male leadership has resulted in lower status for women.

Osho was clearly drawing on the *bhakti* tradition, taking the next logical step: if 'feminine' devotion to a male god is the primary characteristic of devotional religion, it is easier, more natural, for women to be devotees of a male god – or male master: 'The master–disciple relationship is a man–woman relationship. The greatest disciples have always been women' (1978, 44). Osho elaborated, in words that echo the above comments on *bhakti* yoga: 'The disciple needs receptivity; he has to receive. Even the male disciple has to function almost in a feminine way. . . . Hence the woman proves to be the perfect disciple' (1983a, 266).

In this discourse and elsewhere he described the Indian mystic Mirabai, Mary Magdalene and Jesus's other female disciples, as the prototype, far superior to the male disciples.[6] He often described his model of discipleship as a 'path of the heart', an approach derived also from Sufi mysticism, which influenced *bhakti* following the Muslim invasion of India. Most of my respondents considered themselves on this path. They found it hard to describe but distinguished it from sexuality, romance and 'emotions as normally understood'. Several women used the phrase 'falling in love' with the master, as if the experience were an apotheosis of a love affair. The appeal might derive from disillusion with the failure of romantic love. These longings are then transmuted into a spiritualized love affair with a guru or god: the ultimate love object who won't let you down. Thus the perfection of first love – for the father, for teenage idols – may be recaptured; but then as now such love depends on distance. If the god comes too close, he may reveal feet of clay, as evidenced by the sexual abuse discussed in the last chapter. But lovers in this ultimate love affair of the master–disciple relationship all emphasized its spiritual dimension:

> Once I'd made the commitment to stay forever . . . then I think I allowed all the love, whatever love I'd been sitting on, to pour out and go into him. It grew all the time. Nothing he did or said ever detracted from it, it just got vaster and vaster. And when I was going every night to *darshan*, it was one peak to another. It was interesting because it maintained that peak of love for him in his physical body, while I would just be gone.

> I think it's a very mysterious relationship. I'm sure that's why he put so much emphasis on love, because you do need to fall in love with a master in order to enter into that mystery. We all accept that love doesn't make sense, and trust comes from allowing what doesn't make sense to wash over you; not being able to figure things out, just letting things happen. Love's always been a bit of a wishy-washy word that's always been tricky to use, but it has a meaning that we understand when we feel it, and I don't know that it could work without it, because it allows for the completely mysterious.

## Jung's Theories of Gender

One of the strongest influences on counter-cultural and New Age religions, including their gender ideologies, is Jungian psychology. Jung's theory of anima and animus was the first significant reversal of sexism in the psychospiritual dimensions by granting women a spiritual nature, albeit different from men and still riddled with sexist assumptions:

> I find the scholastic question *Habet mulier animam?* especially interesting, since in my view it is an intelligent one inasmuch as the doubt seems justified. Woman has no anima, no soul, but she has an *animus*. The anima has an erotic, emotional character, the animus a rationalizing one. Hence most of what men say about feminine eroticism, and particularly about the emotional life of women, is derived from their own anima projections and distorted accordingly. On the other hand, the astonishing assumptions and fantasies that women make about men come from the activity of the animus, who produces an inexhaustible supply of illogical arguments and false explanations. (1982, 50)

Jung believed firmly in difference: 'A man should live as a man and a woman as a woman' (ibid., 60), and the differences are spelt out in terms that today we would castigate as sexist: 'Personal relations are as a rule more important and interesting to her than objective facts and their interconnections. The wide fields of commerce, politics, technology, and science, the whole realm of the applied masculine mind, she relegates to the penumbra of consciousness' (ibid., 95). These ideas were sanctified in his theory of Eros (the principle of relatedness, most developed in women) versus Logos (the principle of objective thought, the male prerogative). This idea, combined with his demonization of the animus-possessed woman, has sometimes led him into misogyny:

> No matter how friendly and obliging a woman's Eros may be, no logic on earth can shake her if she is ridden by the animus. Often the man has the feeling – and he is not altogether wrong – that only seduction or a beating or rape would have the necessary power of persuasion. (ibid., 172)

Jung has many disciples, male and female psychologists who have developed his theories into one of the most powerful and influential schools of psychology, particularly for alternative and New Age seekers. On the other hand, unsurprisingly, he has been widely criticized and condemned by feminists, particularly feminist theologians, since his theories have the status and authority of religion in some quarters.[7] This is the problem:

> Patriarchal religion has been accepted as transcendent and revealed, and thus as above human criticism. Patriarchal science has stood on the principle of empirical investigation, without scientists' awareness of the possibility of gender assumptions influencing the choice of data, the method of investigation, and the results. Because Jung's psychology partakes of the status of both religion and psychology, even though it also suffers loss of credibility by being associated with both, his pronouncements about the nature of the 'feminine' and women can stand on practically unassailable grounds – 'sacred' on the one hand, and 'empirical' on the other. (Wehr, 1988, 75)

Wehr gives a particularly astute and trenchant critique of the flaws, confusions and inconsistencies in Jung's ideas, which were distorted by his own androcentrism and misogyny, and serve to reinforce women's internalized oppression. Although many women feel validated by his vindication of certain feminine qualities, particularly receptivity, it is ultimately a pseudo-empowerment, identified in relation to men and failing to address the gap between men's perceptions of women (via their anima) as enormously powerful and the reality of women's powerlessness. Furthermore, his negative theories compound the problem:

> Jung's term 'animus-possessed woman' is analogous to Freud's labeling of certain women as 'castrating'. It serves the same purpose, which is to keep women subdued, 'feminine', and unempowered except through whatever indirect channels for empowerment they can find in being 'feminine'. (ibid., 120)

## Celebrating Femininity in the Osho Movement

Jungian psychology combined with traditional *bhakti* to form the basis of Osho's model of gender and discipleship, although he was highly critical of Jung, as are many Indians (see Chapter

1). Osho adapted a reversed gender polarity: 'The qualities that are thought to be weak are all the feminine qualities. And it is a strange fact that all the great qualities come into that category. What is left are only the brutal qualities, animal qualities.' Therefore femininity should be celebrated: 'Rejoice in your feminine qualities, make a poetry of your feminine qualities. . . . I would like the whole world to be full of feminine qualities' (1987b, 29–31). 'Feminine qualities' were understood quite specifically by Osho and sannyasins, and relate mainly to the affective domain; words chosen included: caring, nurturing, loving, devotional, intuitive, soft, warm, receptive. On the other hand, intellectual attributes were almost unanimously perceived as masculine, by both sexes. His teaching was ambiguous and inconsistent as to the correspondence between femininity and women, masculinity and men. Often they are correlated, but sometimes he would emphasize that a man could be a feminine type and vice versa, or that both men and women could shift between modes:

> In some moments a woman is more of a man than a woman, and so is the case with a man . . . there are soft moments and there are hard moments, there are aggressive moments and there are receptive moments. . . . Sometimes in a rage a woman becomes more dangerous than a man, and sometimes in soft moments a man is more loving than any woman – and these moments go on changing. This duality is part of nature. (1978d, 198–9)

Like most religious teachers, Osho equated femininity with an emphasis on body and emotion, opposed to a masculine identification with mind, but unusually he believed spirituality could arise more easily out of body and feelings than mind. His methodology of enlightenment began with body-based meditations and therapies, which drew strongly on Reichian therapy. It is therefore unsurprising that many people were attracted to sannyas who felt that the body was an important element in spirituality. Contradicting Durkheim's theory of sacred versus profane, 'earthy' was a much-used term of approbation, linked to purity: 'I like Bhagwan's view that because women are so earthy, they're truly spiritual. They're not just in the mind, they're real. I see them as more valuable.'[8]
Most women expressed a holistic sense of their femaleness

closely connected with their belief in embodied spirituality, and often with their sexuality (see next chapter). Ursula King has warned against the dangers of idealizing and narrowing down women's experience 'in terms of a uniqueness grounded in female bodily existence' (1989, 79), but for sannyasins it was a basis and bridge connecting them to what is sometimes dualistically referred to as the spiritual. As one put it succinctly: 'One of the things I liked very much was the getting into your body. I could feel my body so much in a way I never had before, and that helped me to feel my whole self more, which also put me in touch with my feelings.' The most extensive and articulate articulation came from one of the ashram's massage therapists, who preferred massaging women, and had found massage a spiritual path in itself, integrating body and soul:

Women are much more open to touch and less afraid of it corresponding to something sexual. Women seem to be naturally sensual. . . .

When I started doing massage – and I do consider that being given massage [as a job] was the greatest gift I got from Bhagwan – my body changed completely in shape. It suddenly looked like a woman's body. I think I'd been very disconnected from myself and how I presented myself as a woman. I really moved into my sexuality, began to enjoy my sexual relationships. . . .

This whole thing I'd had all my life about devotion, wanting to serve, all this love in my heart – it was overflowing and bursting. Massage really became a channel for that. I felt much more giving. I had an outlet for it, but an outlet that was very creative and constructive. So all those things contributed to my development as a woman, and I started to feel myself as a rich woman.

Several women mentioned the importance of dance in their spiritual practice and their sense of self. One of Osho's meditations consisted almost entirely of dancing, and freeform dancing was part of the ashram's daily activities. It was seen as an appropriate female practice, as opposed to yoga which was seen as harmful and masculinizing for women. Dance was a way of both celebrating and transcending the body, uniting body and soul.

Through doing a lot of meditations, especially the dynamic and *kundalini,* people's bodies became very loose, and there was this encouragement not to perform in the dance, but simply to disappear, to dissolve. Consequently some of the dancing that happened was supernatural – I can't think of a better word to explain it. It was just beyond this world, magical. And because it was something that happened every day, I felt it never got explained or even mentioned.

Dance is central in many native traditions such as Candomblé, Santería and Voodoo, where women are priestesses. In these religions, dance is a means for women to express themselves and to mediate the spiritual message by going into trance states. In Candomblé it is believed that men (apart from homosexuals) are incapable of attaining the deep spiritual experience bestowed by dance, which is why only women are priests: 'In effect the only truly valid priest and medium was a woman on the grounds of her natural innate disposition qua woman to express in dance that deep inner awareness of the self as divine and to act a a channel for the communication of the spiritual, sacred, transcendent form of life to others' (Clarke 1993, 103). In ancient Pagan goddess-worshipping religions, women performed sacred dances, which are now being recreated by modern Pagans. The significance of dance for women means that women teachers will incorporate it into religions where it is unheard of, as Ruth Denison is doing for Buddhism. Her students find her body-based meditations, movement and dance help them go deeper in their practice, find more peace and acceptance in themselves and compassion for others.

### The Feminist Critique of Femininity – and Gurus

Osho displayed a fairly consistent hostility towards the women's movement (while acknowledging the historical sufferings of women), and sometimes expressed it crudely: 'that ugly movement called Women's Lib . . . [which] is turning women into wolves'. '["Lib" women] cannot be happy because the whole idea is nonsense.' His main criticisms were that through denying their femininity women were simply imitating men and losing their own identity, and that feminism made women vengeful, which was futile: 'Then the female chauvinist is born. And this is not going to put things right. Then the women will start doing harm to men, and sooner or later they will take revenge. Where is this going to stop? It is a vicious circle.'[9]

A number of women sannyasins had been involved in the women's movement prior to sannyas. While not reacting as crudely as their master, they felt that feminism had gone too far in its challenge to traditional femininity and become: 'stuck in reactive anger', 'blaming men', over-emphasizing the intellectual at the expense of the experiential, and denying feminine qualities.[10] For this reason, in 1989 the Osho Group for Women's Liberation was created, as explained by its leader: 'With the women's movement, many women started moving into hatred of men, or competing with men and behaving like them, so that their femininity has been lost. They are not really fulfilled because they have denied their feminine psychology.' As with secular groups, this one analyses socialization: 'an attempt to penetrate into these aspects of our conditioning that keep us in slavery, and bring them to awareness.' The difference lies in its esoteric approach: 'it is an alchemical group, rather than a therapy group, using rituals and Osho's meditations to go deeper.' The group includes techniques for awakening the inner goddess, an interesting new development revealing cross-fertilization from the goddess spirituality movement (see below).

Jungian psychology, despite its approval of gender 'archetypes', also criticizes feminism on these grounds:

> Seeing that men have failed to respect their capabilities, unique value, and potentiality, many women understandably react by asserting themselves and rejecting men. Yet their underlying model for personal expression has frequently been masculine so that often they appear to be mere imitations of the male. The crucial issue is to realize the value of reconnecting with the feminine, to understand what is essential to being a woman and to value that'. (Leonard 1982, 68)

In turn, the women's movement was highly critical of what was seen as a regressive choice – surrendering to a male master – especially after several founder members of the British women's movement became sannyasins. Their objections were linked to the critique of gender. One of these ex-feminists was interviewed by the leading British feminist magazine *Spare Rib*, and tried to explain the appeal:

> [Bhagwan] says that it is the logical thinking, organised, rational, male mind which prevents one from experiencing oneself, and one's physical being and sensations and feelings. My mind, I realise, is conditioned totally, 99% by what you could call a sort of patriarchal mind, a desire to be logical, realistic, materialistic. . . . Now I see trying to work out women's problems through the 'male' mind to be destructive and useless. In fact to work out any problem through the mind is useless because it doesn't really touch your own bodies or sensations. (Fell 1977)

This passage was denounced by the feminist writer Jill Tweedie as illustrating:

> the barmy acceptance by some women and even some militant feminists that the qualities men have described as 'female' through the centuries are essentially correct and only need dusting off and polishing up to take their rightful place in a deprived society. Men lay claim to rational thought and their claims are believed by women. Men say women are emotional and their judgment is believed by women. So all that women have to do is claim equal rights for feminine emotion (or, in the case of Bhagwan followers, exalt emotion's superiority) and all in the women's world will be well . . . What all this amounts to is a brainwashing campaign by men of women and women of themselves upon a truly staggering scale. (Tweedie 1977, 149)

This exchange typifies the dilemma facing, and to some extent splitting, the women's movement, and all women wanting to break out of the negative mould of femininity: whether to celebrate and make a virtue out of 'traditional' feminine virtues, or whether to compete and take on the values of the 'male' world. Jill Tweedie opts for the latter course, whereas Osho, on the whole, seems to opt more for the former.

Thirteen years later I interviewed the subject of the *Spare Rib* interview, who elaborated on her conversion process:

What took me into feminism was a search . . . Feminism helped me to understand how I'd been conditioned as a woman, but I didn't say, 'Wicked people conditioning me, it's their fault.' What I saw is that as women we allow ourselves to be conditioned, and what has to be changed is the mechanism through which we allow ourselves to be conditioned . . . When I met someone who saw conditioning on a much wider scale than just conditioning of women, there was no intellectual change for me. It was following the same path, because it's my allowing myself to be conditioned which is the problem.

The requirement to wear a *mala* particularly shocked and outraged feminists, being seen as a symbol of retrogressive bondage. One woman's reply to the question of how taking on a male master connected to her feminist principles clearly illustrates this culture clash, and the sannyasin solution:

> It didn't strike me with much difficulty, but it did to a lot of my friends – a man's picture around my neck! But I'd been moving away for some time from feminism. I found that it was restricting me and my development spiritually. And also when I looked at the truth of my life, I found that the people who really mattered to me were my son and my lover. Feminism didn't give me a framework to explain this.

I asked my female respondents how they had felt about surrendering to a male master. Nobody, not even the most committed ex-feminists, had found this a problem, although, as already discussed, some people had found surrender difficult in itself. Some women had never considered this issue; others had, but found that love overcame their objections. Other women perceived Osho as feminine or androgynous, which helped to equalize the relationship (see below).

Another factor that helped is that although lip-service was almost unanimously paid to the feminine ideal, and the majority of my respondents articulated it, some expressed a more robust and dynamic sense of femininity. In particular what emerged was the idea of a particular kind of female strength – different from male strength, softer, but equally powerful in its way. One woman described the main benefit from the meditations as finding her 'soft strength'. Another gave 'reliability and steadfastness' as the primary female qualities, which enabled her to give unwavering support to Osho. Another woman's comment assumed superior female strength in describing a male sannyasin as 'as strong as any woman in that commune, and as active'. Another said:

> I always felt that what Bhagwan was saying about women allowed women to become strong, have a greater strength than they'd had before – in a female way . . . It's the ability women have to change people, to move people, to connect with people in a way that doesn't involve pushing from the outside. Men tend to be more aggressive, women can do it with a softness that works very well.

Not everyone gave unconditional endorsement to Osho's ideal of femininity. Some sannyasins criticized the anti-intellectualism, the over-emphasis on subjectivity and intuition, and the exaggeration of female superiority. As one woman explained:

> I feel that I rejected a lot about myself in the world – my more impersonal, objective side. For me sannyas brought out a lot of the more personal, intimate side, and I missed the other side a bit. I think now we're back in the world we have to find our place in the world again by reclaiming this more worldly energy, which helps you set your own boundaries.

Men, being understandably less identified with the gender ideology, had a more developed critique. One joked: 'I used to say that in the ashram there's only one cock, everyone else is a vagina – because you have to be receptive.' More to the point it could be stated that there was only one mind, everyone else was a heart, hence there was no allowance for analysis, criticism or rational debate. Another man described how they had suffered from being 'conditioned how good it is to be female, receptive, surrendered. This was great for the ranch, because nobody popped their stupid head up and said, "Sheela, you're a bitch" – which is what she needed.' There is no doubt that the requirement of surrender encouraged a submissive passivity that allowed abuse of power, and was thus a significant factor in the demise of Rajneeshpuram.

Nevertheless, what emerged clearly from my interviews was that, however non-politically correct their experience, most women had found Osho's *via feminina* liberating: 'The feminine part of me was what I found difficult to be in the West. [Sannyas] did allow me to be that feminine side.' They were living through a period, still ongoing, in which historical certainties about sexuality and gender roles have been thrown into confusion. The Osho movement did not give them certainties, which most of them did not want, but it gave them a flexible ideology and a context in which to explore gender and spirituality:

> One thing that happened as a sannyasin was that the side of myself that was combative, felt I had to assert myself as a woman against men, making me rather aggressive and masculine, I was more and more able to shed. I could see what was truly beautiful about being a woman – not to be subservient, but powerful in receptivity. To be able to be loving was a freedom for me, not a bond. Love was taken out of my life if I was going to be a feminist .

## Are Women Better Disciples?

Much of what sannyasins said about their beliefs and subjective experience regarding femininity was connected to their experience of discipleship. Osho's affirmation of femininity was mostly in terms of the correlation with the qualities of a good disciple. Almost everyone believed that although men were theoretically as capable of discipleship, women tended to make better disciples. Several women felt women found it easier to surrender, whereas men had problems with it, or were less steadfast and more volatile.

Men themselves had mixed responses to this challenge, but were understandably more likely than women to minimize the significance of gender or propose alternative models of discipleship. But on the whole they endorsed women's superior discipleship. One explained: 'I began to see that my male ego is what stopped me from surrendering. The women had an easier time of it because they didn't have such a strong male ego.' This belief might be found problematic in terms of feminism, including feminist theologians' critique of the Christian

doctrine of sin as pride, as being damaging for women, advocating its replacement with a female sin of self-forgetfulness
and self-negation.[11]

Poonam, who worked as a centre leader for many years, had
a functional explanation:

> I think women make good disciples. They're willing to sur-
> render, they're willing to work more from the place of do-
> ing it for their master, whereas men tend to work more
> from their egos. It was difficult for them to let go of their
> role, their ego attachment. Obviously we all had ego attach-
> ments and power trips going on, but I think mostly for the
> women there was a willingness to let go of that and to re-
> cognize that the work or the commune or sannyas came
> first. It was much easier. To work with men you had to be
> a bit careful with their egos. With women it was easier to be
> straight, and you didn't have to eggshell walk around them.

One woman with some experience of goddess spirituality
gave a unique interpretation:

> There were certain moments when I felt he could really
> relate to us on an energy, being level, which perhaps a man
> would find much more difficult. I've often had this experi-
> ence where we create a wave of energy which sparks each
> other off and had an oceanic experience, a wildness and
> beauty that's very tangible, and that I feel men dancing
> together wouldn't be able to create.

However, although many women supported the statement
that women make better disciples, nearly a third made strong
qualifications or disagreed. One felt that 'the way he operated
drew forth the devotee quality' in women, but that he also
'drew that feminine quality out of men'. Another woman was
adamant that 'energetically there's no difference between a man
and a woman. There's a difference of vibration, but essentially
it's the being – not whether you're male or female.' Several
women felt that feminine qualities were important, but male
qualities had an equal though different significance, for example in terms of a distinction between the trusting receptivity
required in discipleship, and the assertive sharpness needed in
secular society. In other words, gender was essentially irrelevant, used as a 'device' to help people wake up and grow:

What he was trying to do in those early years was break down this incredibly thick crust of intellectualism, of head orientation that we all had, men and women. The women were slightly easier to approach because they weren't so heady, so I think he was encouraging these female attributes because that way was going to be easier for him to work with Westerners. My understanding was that he was never saying women can be better disciples, but that up to a point these qualities of softness and heartfulness can help you allow the master to work on you.

But there comes a point in the relationship between a master and the disciple that just sticking with it, stubbornness, more male qualities are useful – in another period of the relationship. Once that first opening of the heart has happened, then there's a period of very sticky going, and more male qualities are perhaps useful.

Finally, two more women felt that although this ultra-feminine model was predominant, there were other valid styles of discipleship. One had worked very closely with Osho as his dental nurse, and found that: 'the more feminine I was, the closer physically I came to him. I don't think he could have had someone around him who wasn't feminine.' But she then made the qualification that his personal assistant was not a feminine woman, so perhaps this was not essential. Another woman was adamant that 'the complete *bhaktis*, the devotional people' were not the only type; on the contrary, 'there were disciples very high up and close that weren't necessarily what you'd call warm, loving, tender women'. She went on to make the contrast with other religious traditions:

> One side of being a disciple is becoming a receptacle, letting your master pour in and emptying yourself out. But there are other ways I can imagine, how it would be in Buddhism or Zen, which is to really develop your awareness. One side is very much the love side, and the other side is meditation: to constantly take responsibility for yourself, constantly bring awareness to what you're doing.

Buddhists bear out this distinction. There are devotional elements within some Buddhist traditions but less prominently, and some Westerners who convert to Buddhism, like Joanna

Macy, miss the worship and adoration. Those for whom this side of religion is pre-eminent are more likely to choose a more ritualistic tradition such as Tibetan Buddhism (which has a disproportionately high membership of ex-Catholics). There is certainly less genderizing of spiritual tendencies. One Buddhist who had been a nun in Korea for many years found the idea of *bhakti* as a feminine path very limited:

> I'm quite devotional by temperament. I recite the chanting and I love it. I'm a woman as far as I can ascertain, and I've never been attracted by *bhakti*. But I know men who are incredibly *bhakti*. I've never wanted to get rid of my ego and surrender to someone else, though I'm aware I have my limitations and delusions.

**Mediumship and Ecstatic Religion**

Traditional, devotional and charismatic religions place a high value on emotion and ecstasy.[12] However, these qualities are often condemned by more rationally inclined practitioners and intellectuals as unmanly, dangerously close to the 'female' affliction of hysteria. For example, Weber makes the somewhat non-value-free observation: 'The influence of women only tended to intensify those aspects of the religion that were emotional or hysterical' (1963, 106). But against this sexist prejudice is Lewis's finding that it is untenable to interpret the prominence of women in possession cults as 'the reflection of an inherent, and biologically grounded female disposition to hysteria', since the movements are not restricted to women (1971, 100).

Within Christianity, the Pentecostalists or 'born again' Christians are the most ecstatic movement, and their success has led to the spread of charismatic movements within mainstream Protestant and Catholic churches. Members are born again in the Holy Spirit, and express their experience with great fervour, through glossolalia, laying on of hands, dancing, shaking, singing, laughing, crying. Those 'slain by the spirit' may fall to the ground and start rolling in the aisles (thus earning the name Holy Rollers). The latest manifestation of this style of religiosity is the Toronto Blessing, which began in the Toronto Airport Vineyard church in 1994 and has now swept

across the world. Participants express all the symptoms of
ecstasy common in other charismatic sects, specializing in animal noises such as roaring like lions and barking like dogs.
Critics quote St Paul's admonitions about maintaining decency
and order in the church service, and it seems that the degree
of a person's faith and openness to spirit may sometimes be
measured by the exuberance of its expression, but participants
justify their fervour in terms of its capacity for edification.
There are attempts to contain the 'wild fire' of enthusiasm,
combined with dualistic ambivalence towards these manifestations: interpreted as reactions of the corrupt flesh to the intense presence of God.[13]

At the heart of the master–disciple relationship in Hinduism is the ritual of *darshan*, an intimate evening meeting in
which questions may be asked but whose primary purpose is
*shaktipat* (energy transmission). All Hindu-based NRMs retain
some version of *darshan*, including TM, Elan Vital (formerly
Divine Light Mission), the Sai Baba Movement, and Siddha
Yoga, Mother Meera and Ammachi. In 1979 Osho developed
his meetings into 'energy *darshans*', a highly intensified process containing live music, singing and dancing, and flashing
strobe lights. The purpose was to generate ecstasy and altered
states of consciousness, which succeeded: 'I felt like glass shat-
tering in slow motion. I don't know how long it was – one, two
minutes? – then I fell back and someone held me. I was totally,
utterly blasted, and for three days afterwards everything around
me looked psychedelic.'

The unique feature of energy *darshans*, distinguishing them
from the traditional kind, was the use of female disciples as
'mediums'. Osho chose 10–12 women to come to *darshan* every
night with the aim of transmitting his energy to participants
and beyond to the whole commune, and eventually the rest of
the world. He described the purpose and process of mediumship in some detail, making sexual analogies similar to descriptions of marriage mysticism:

The function of the medium is to be utterly absent so that
I can penetrate your being totally, so that my energy can
start flowing through you. Your energy has to become at-
tuned with my energy. . . . You have to enjoy the sensuous
feel of the energy rising, with no fear, with great welcoming

and receptivity. . . . When the energy starts moving it will almost feel as if you are making love. And in fact it is so: you are making love to existence itself. So start moving, swaying, in the same way that you will move while you are making deep love, while you are in deep intimacy with somebody. Abandon yourself and go totally into it.[14]

Not much is known about the inner experience of being a medium, since they were instructed to keep it a secret. However, one of my respondents had been a medium, and spoke a little about the experience:

I think being chosen as a medium was incredibly important for my growth. The part of me that felt hard, unloving, closed, heavy, he was affirming something female in me – allowing me to be open, vulnerable, soft. I became much more emotional, and allowed it. It took many years to relax into that part of myself.

An interesting comparison can be made between Osho's mediums and the mediums used in Victorian Spiritualism. Skultans describes Spiritualism as a 'new religion' which typically 'involves a female medium and a male spirit or control' (1983, 15–16). She observed that: 'Victorian stereotypes of femininity . . . bear a remarkable resemblance to the conception of the ideal medium. The following adjectives can equally well describe the ideal woman as the ideal medium: unsophisticated, innocent, passive, young, tender, feeling, untuitive and so on' (ibid., 23). Victorian mediums were also attributed with an absence of high intelligence or at least education. Nevertheless, mediumship could be a very attractive way out of the oppressive drudgery of many Victorian women's existences, offering a star quality career including world travel and entertainment by royalty.

These observations could equally well be applied to Osho's mediums. Although most sannyasins were well educated, mediums, like all sannyasins, were required to 'drop their minds' and function from their hearts in order to transmit the energy without obstruction. Mediumship conferred the highest status on sannyasin women, who were also much sought after as partners by sannyasin men. An additional quality of Osho's mediums, perhaps different from the Victorian Spiritualists, was their ability to let go, be wild, spontaneous, ecstatic – not just submissively passive vehicles. In this respect they are closer to Dionysian worshippers or possessed Somalis. But the vital difference is that this energy was not simply perceived as what Weber terms 'orgiastic' abandon but as sacred. In Hinduism this primal, essential female energy is known as Shakti, the all-encompassing Goddess, whose power may be held and channelled through even ordinary women (though particularly virgins and faithful married women).

Sannyasins believed that Osho is 'transmitting the Shakti that rises in his body to the mediums, causing their Shakti to rise; and they are amplifying it, transmitting it to the women around them, who in turn are sending it to us' (Gordon 1987, 56). Even this derivative power gave the mediums a semi-divine status. Gordon also describes how 'The darshan mediums are regarded with the kind of awe that Greeks once reserved for sibyls and oracles' (ibid., 74). Franklin, even in her sceptical post-sannyas phase, remembers the mediums as 'temple goddesses' (1992, 119).

This power or charisma could be almost magically transmitted as transformative grace. A rank-and-file worker could be picked out of the crowd by Osho at *darshan* to act as a medium:

> The next morning, in lecture, Bhagwan started talking about Nandan . . . He spoke about how beautiful she was, how totally surrendered, and how beautiful her soul was. Everybody in lecture . . . immediately started looking for her, because being singled out this way always gave a person terrific energy. And everyone who knew her or saw her would also get a surge. A part of that energy was the idea that if it could happen to her, it could happen to anyone.
>
> Every few days he talked about how beautiful she was, and how surrendered. The whole commune would get a rush out of this. And the more he talked about her in that way, the more lovely she became. If you were picked out in a personal way like that, you did glow and glow. And Nandan grew more relaxed, silent. (Strelley 1987, 184–5)

The mediums thus became models for all sannyasins, exemplars of a spiritual path of egoless surrender. They were considered to have particular relevance for people in ego-boosting work as an antidote, above all the therapists who acted as a kind of priesthood for Osho. Rather than acting as professional experts, Rajneesh therapists were required to disidentify from their personalities and skills in order to function as mediums for the master: 'The therapist becomes just a vehicle for God's energy. He has just to be available like a hollow bamboo so that God can pass through him' (Osho 1978c, 126). Some therapists had to be 'broken in' to this role, such as the very successful and strong-willed Veeresh. Bharti describes the process of his increasing frustration trying to lead ashram groups through his ego and feeling undermined by 'Bhagwan's non-present presence'. Eventually Osho speaks to him in *darshan*:

> 'I wanted to shake your confidence in yourself so that you could begin to see how much you still have to grow. The group was bigger than the leader. They were all sannyasins; they were all a part of me, they were vehicles for me.
>
> 'Next group, you also become my vehicle and suddenly there will be a bridge between you and the others. When you go on working with groups, your ego is strengthened. That ego has to drop. Next time let Veeresh not be there. Just be my instrument. Not a leader really. At the most, a catalytic agent.' (1981, 37–8)

Most groupleaders and participants endorsed this model, but one ex-sannyasin therapist was critical:

> We were trained to be like hollow bamboos that were channels for his energy. We were to leave ourselves outside the grouproom door, and go in and be vehicles for this energy. We would walk back out the door into our true selves, which were whatever was going on, but when we were in the grouproom we were taught that absolutely nothing else existed. . . . One of the names we gave to these beautiful spaces that arose naturally was 'Bhagwan', because he was the symbol and embodiment for us of those qualities. We hadn't yet recognized that they were us – we were babies.

### Androgyny: Transcending Gender Stereotypes

The ideal that female and male sannyasins are striving towards is a balance and integration between the qualities so misleadingly termed feminine and masculine; between anima and animus, yin and yang. This desideratum of wholeness may be called 'androgyny', a concept that exists in many religions, representing a metaphysical ideal of fusion and wholeness.[15] The term is sometimes used in this sense by sannyasins as well as throughout New Age religion.

Androgyny has been criticized as predominantly a male experience, particularly by feminist theologians.[16] Inevitably in sannyas, given the reversed gender polarity, there was more emphasis on the feminization of men than vice versa, as in traditional *bhakti*. The sannyasin dress code was androgynous but closer to the feminine; men and women wore long shapeless robes, sandals and long hair – though the men were at least distinguished by their beards. Men had to adapt not only to the unprecedented role of a disciple but also to the expectation that they were less well qualified for it than women and therefore likely to do it worse. The 'male ego' – described by Osho as ambitious, competitive, goal-oriented, aggressive – was perceived as harder to 'drop'. Men tended to be more spiritually ambitious, focused on the goal of enlightenment. They were more likely to see discipleship as an apprenticeship for gurudom, to struggle to surrender and overcome their childhood socialization: 'The concept of being female has a negative side to me, a suggestion of weakness – in a male, not in a female. It's one of those lovely old conditionings, which probably all British schoolboys have, and which lives on forever.' This is doubtless the reason why most men preferred to describe themselves as 'soft' than 'feminine', and some believe the process went too far. There is now a men's group, and its leader sees the main problem as being that 'Many of us have chosen to move into femininity at the expense of masculinity', which therefore needs to be reclaimed.

One man spoke of having 'resisted the universal tendency towards feminization. I never saw the need to become more feminine, although I was under a lot of pressure from the female bosses in the ashram to do so'. Running the construction sector, such qualities were not necessary or appropriate: 'A more male energy was needed to make things work – cut through resistances, bang holes in walls. We had a slogan: If it doesn't work, hit it with a bigger hammer.'

Some men responded enthusiastically to androgynization, and described the process graphically:

I felt myself becoming much more vulnerable, softer, more reflective, introvert, less sexual, aggressive, stiller, more open, more feeling, more heart-oriented, caring and considerate. In some ways I felt I was losing my 'muscle', but really what I was losing was the toughness that my ego had built and wanted to protect me from being hurt.

The psychological and spiritual levels of androgyny were of more interest to sannyasins, but at least in imagination two men had had strong experiences of physical femaleness. One described going through 'a beautiful feminine period where all I desired was breasts'. Another said:

My body feels female sometimes, more graceful, especially when I'm not so busy. I was dancing in Poona one time, and had this incredible past-life experience of being a woman ballet dancer. I love this female side of myself, I really enjoy it. Sometimes I have this incredible desire to know what it would be like to make love as a woman.

There is inevitably a certain sexual ambiguity in the relationship between male disciple and male master when the emphasis is so strongly on love and devotion, as evidenced by the account given by Tweedie's guru (see p.74).[17] Some men handled it by not identifying with the dominant model of discipleship as a love affair, experiencing Osho as a heroic figure, resource, or role model, which enabled them to express their love and admiration without awkwardness:

I did love him, but more I suppose in the soldier's way. One loves one's commanding officer – the trust of the soldier for the commanding officer who can see much further than he can. He was my hero, and I saw him as a heroic figure. I had this vision of him leading his forces against the countless legions of the mediocre. He was my fearless leader.

For those who accepted Osho's model there were two options: a) they could become 'feminized' to the extent of feeling themselves as female in relation to Osho (as is traditional in *bhakti* yoga; see above); b) they could perceive Osho as a woman, falling in love with him in a spiritualized version of the male–female relationship. None of my respondents had chosen the second option, though some perceived Osho's femininity, but one described the first process: 'Gradually, as my mind started agreeing with him, my deeper, more physical and emotional layer of defensiveness started to loosen up. And that's why I began to feel more like a woman. When he would say "beloved", I understood that – as a *gopi*.'[18]

Women as well as men believed that male androgynization was primary, reflecting sannyasin ideology: 'I don't think women have to connect so much with their male energy, I think it's men who have to connect with their female energy.' Sannyasin women were also interested in exploring their 'masculine' side, whether conceived as animus, inner man, yang energy, or simply as ungendered attributes. They had more scope than the men to do this through relationships and work (see Chapters 5 and 7). However, it was equally important as an inner experience. For example, one woman who had been 'immersed in relationship' all her life felt:

> I'm just beginning the search to become one's inner man as well as the woman one knows already. The things I would look for in a man, I'm now looking for in myself. The things I admire in a man are courage, strength, decision-making – the things I've always looked to a man to take care of for me.

One of the most articulate descriptions of the differences between femininity and masculinity and the need for each individual to encompass both polarities came from a woman therapist who ran a group called 'Inner Man/Inner Woman':

> I started to explore the reality that I have a female body but also I have an internal male energy ... I started working with visualizing my inner male and inviting him to show himself. I started to identify if he was getting a chance to express himself in my life. I started noticing when I worked with other people if their male energy was functioning or not functioning, how the male was inhibiting the female energy, or the female the male.

Androgyny in the Osho movement was essentially a psychospiritual experience. The first step was to integrate one's own 'inner' man or woman. The next step was to 'transcend' gender altogether – experience one's true 'being' as 'beyond' both femininity and masculinity. This was Osho's aim: 'My work consists in freeing you from man/woman duality. ... I am

neither for men nor for women, I am only for transcendence
. . . being a sannyasin means you are neither man nor woman.
Finished – that game is finished!' (1987b, 82–4).

A few sannyasins claimed to have experienced this state temporarily: 'One day I was walking through the ashram and had
no sense of being a woman or a man, I was just a being, an
energy.' Another described it as 'the watcher, which has nothing to do with men or women.'

Many sannyasins described Osho as a model of androgyny,
both in the sense of combining male and female characteristics and as transcending gender altogether. This was partly to
do with external appearance – 'he wears dresses' – but also to
do with his personality and essence: 'he doesn't put out a very
male energy, he's very soft', 'a slightly mystical figure'. His
essence or soul was seen as transcending the duality of gender:
'As time went on, I couldn't say if he was a man or woman;
now he's just a very precious being'; 'I just saw him as a being
radiating love.' For most sannyasins, Osho had fully integrated
his animus, in Jungian terms:

> I found him very feminine at times, and yet a man. . . . There
> was a gentleness. When he shouted in discourse, that was
> male to me, but there were so many times when the love felt
> so round, he felt so receptive when you looked in his eyes,
> the way he moved his hands was so delightfully soft – that to
> me was very feminine.

There were only two dissenters from this view, both feminists. They experienced him as describing male experiences,
from a male viewpoint, but excused this because he had been
'brought up in a male-dominated society', or because 'he was
talking to something deeper than male or female conditioning'. For most women, one of the benefits of perceiving Osho
as beyond gender was to sidestep feminist objections to surrendering to a male master: 'I never saw him as a man to whom
I would as a woman surrender – that wasn't the relationship.
It was very clear that he was beyond being a man or a woman.
He was all love and receptivity, not my idea of a man in any
conventional way.'

For men, androgyny resolved the sexual ambiguity of the
relationship, or turned it to advantage, as in this description
using classical Hindu imagery:

He was definitely masculine, but interspersed was a tremendous softness, which I'd always associated with the female. On the one hand he could be roaring at you, you'd feel the wrath of god pouring down – in the early days he could really shout. And then in the next moment he could be so gentle that you felt you were being caressed by the lightest, softest thing in the world. At times I saw him as a cosmic dancer, not having any sex but drawing you closer and closer to him through this incredible mixture of male and female qualities.

The androgyny of the enlightened being is a common belief in Hinduism, as symbolized by Shiva Ardhanarishvara (the hermaphrodite god), whom Osho celebrated: 'That is tremendously beautiful. That seems to be the best image ever invented of God: half-man, half-woman' (1978d, 199). Prabhupada was described by an ISKCON member as 'above the dualities of male and female'. Again, despite the emphasis on the male process, women gurus may experience androgyny. Jnanananda, Mother Guru of Madras, explains the phenomenon: 'When the male and female elements are completely developed and complement each other in the same individual, the soul is fully realized. . . . For myself I no longer feel that I inhabit a body of particular sexual gender' (White 1980, 30). Andrew Harvey describes another contemporary example:

This time I saw the Maharshi as the Mother; not as Ma but as a man who was also Mother; Shiva, who was also Shakti, male and female at once. He lay on the couch with the openness and fragrance of a woman; age had distended his left breast slightly; the tilt of his beautiful, noble face gave it the tenderness of a mother welcoming her child . . . I understood why I loved especially this last image of his Play, for in it he was showing the last perfection, the complete marriage between Wisdom and Love, Male and Female. (1991, 172)

In some respects, Osho's model of discipleship was highly traditional in its derivation from *bhakti* yoga and Jungian psychology. However, its positive valuation of the feminine and the ensuing role reversals give it far greater contemporary significance, particularly for women. There was qualified agreement among women and men that women tended to make better disciples, and could therefore in an important respect be termed more spiritual. It still has to be asked whether this glorification of femininity was empowering and liberating to women, or whether it reinforced oppressive stereotypes. Despite the dangers and potential for abuse, however, it is clear that this model of female discipleship contained great flexibility and potential as a spiritual path.

Most women and some men embraced the model enthusiastically, as a means of reclaiming and exploring their femininity. It suited three types of person: a) 'feminine' women who felt validated; b) 'soft' men who appreciated a non-macho alternative to Western ideas of masculinity; b) women and men who rejected the harsher, over-intellectualizing tendencies of Western society and wanted rebalancing. The ideal of androgyny qualified the polarization and projection of femininity onto the disciple, masculinity onto the master, and allowed women and men flexibility in exploring their potential. Thus anima and animus could become integrated to transcend the limitations of gender. One of the best devices for this purpose was a sexual relationship.

# 5 Sexuality: Union or Opposition of Body and Spirit?

## Shifting Attitudes to Sexuality in the Modern World

Western society is going through a state of post-Romantic disillusion and deconstruction after 500 years of belief in the myth of romance and happily ever after. We are witnessing the breakdown of the nuclear family as we have known it, while harking back nostalgically to a golden age of shared values but also busy experimenting with new alternatives. The 'sexual revolution' has brought great changes. As our religious values and social communities have collapsed, sexual relationships sometimes seem the only source of emotional depth, intensity and intimacy. At the same time, the less welcome side-effects of 'free love' have become apparent, particularly for women, such as the increasing tendency to be viewed as sex objects; the pressure to have the perfect orgasm; the proliferation of pornography; and the increase of sexually transmitted diseases, especially AIDS.

The main progenitor of the sexual revolution was Wilhelm Reich, best known for his work on sexuality. *The Function of the Orgasm* (written in 1926 but not published till 1942) was a liberation tract to many, taking sex out of the religious/moral realm and into the domain of health, both of the individual and society as a whole:

> Psychic health depends upon orgastic potency... Mental illness is a result of a disturbance in the natural capacity for love. (1968, 28)

> The fact that man is the only species which does not fulfil the natural law of sexuality is the immediate cause of a series of devastating disasters. The external social negation of life results in mass death, in the form of wars, as well as in psychic and somatic disturbances of vital functioning. (31)

101

Reich speculated, in this and later books, that sexual repression led directly to fascism and its attendant evils. He also attacked religious morality, seeing 'moralistic hypocrisy' as 'the most dangerous enemy of natural morality' (39). Indeed, on this account he finally gave up training divinity students, because of the 'serious conflict between sexuality and the practice of their vocations' (160). His research culminated in the theory of 'orgone energy', which could be trapped in an orgone accumulator and used for general life-enhancement as well as improved orgasms.

Reich's work formed the basis of the new science of sexology, developed in particular by Kinsey in the 1950s, and Masters and Johnson in the 1960s. Kinsey, like Reich, found a negative correlation between sex and religion: 'Religion, which had had a negligible effect on men's sexual behavior, emerged as the most important factor influencing satisfaction for women. Women who described themselves as religious achieved fewer orgasms in any circumstances' (Archer and Lloyd 1985, 99). Masters and Johnson 'discovered' the existence and functioning of the female orgasm, and later the multiple orgasm, thus providing an empirical basis for the reclamation of female sexuality.

This psychological research undoubtedly helped create the climate for the 'sexual revolution' of the 1960s, fuelled by the development and availability of effective contraception and accessible, explicit sex manuals such as *The Joy of Sex*, and *Cosmopolitan* magazine. It was also supported politically by the radical left view that monogamy is a bourgeois construction and sexual possessiveness a crime.

The sexual revolution has had profound effects not only on our sexual and emotional lives but on social structures, and attitudes to marriage and the family. In America there is evidence that although only a small number of people were actively experimenting in the 1960s–1970s, half the population were affected, influencing a move away from marriage and the nuclear family as the dominant forms. During this period acceptance of premarital sex increased considerably and cohabitation increased by about 700 per cent.

In Britain a similar pattern may be discerned, involving radical changes in hopes and expectations of marriage, particularly over the last 10–15 years. Three related trends are a sharp fall in numbers of marriages accompanied by a rise in cohabitation; the rising age of first marriages for both sexes; and a dramatic increase in divorce. Moreover, a significant percentage of the population regard marriage as an outdated or dead institution, and a growing number are involved in extramarital sex and other alternatives to marriage. Even the Church of England's latest report on the family has recommended abandoning the phrase 'living in sin', though this is repudiated by the Archbishop of Canterbury. Another significant aspect of these changes is that they are spearheaded by women, who display more dissatisfaction with marriage and scepticism about its benefits, and initiate about 70 per cent of divorces. The main outcome of these changes is that serial monogamy has become the predominant, and increasingly acceptable, form of relationship, particularly among the 16–35 age group, accompanied by a flexible interpretation of commitment.[1] These changes are in line with Toffler's prediction that the norm of modern society would become close, affectionate but relatively ephemeral relationships.

As a response to both the benefits and the problems, two main, contrasting tendencies have emerged in both secular and religious society, which may be termed traditionalist and hedonistic. The hedonists are sex-affirmative, continuing to practise the freedom gained over the last 30 years as a path of personal development. In a religious context, the belief is that sexuality is to be celebrated and may be transformed into spiritual energy, and that a relationship can become a spiritual partnership. The traditionalists have retreated to a position of wider sexual conservatism, perhaps partly a backlash to the preceding antinomianism but certainly also a reaction to the AIDS crisis. They are sex-restrictive, believing that through restraint or even renunciation of sexuality, greater physical, psychological and spiritual benefits are obtained. The extreme end of this position is sex-denial, and there are signs of 'celibate chic' catching on even in secular society.[2]

## Sex and Misogyny in the World's Religions

Most organized religions and many NRMs are ambivalent or condemnatory about sex. Furthermore, religious beliefs, attitudes and practices regarding sexuality correlate with their ideas about women and nature: both are perceived as inferior, subject to control and domination. These associations are particularly clear in celibate traditions, leading to a polarized model of (celibate) holiness as male and (sexual) sinfulness as female. Women are thereby perceived as fallen, fleshly, earthy, trapped in matter. As Evil Temptresses they are sinful innately, actively, and passively as objects of temptation. Women's bodies, particularly their sexual functions, are impure and polluted. Women are therefore prohibited from participating in sacred rituals, or even entering a place of worship, particularly during such taboo phases as menstruation or post-childbirth. Even where women are held to have potentially equal souls (and in some religions they are held to have no soul or no capacity for spiritual advancement), their bodies 'represent the lower self of the bestial appetites and material, corruptible existence'.[3] This is the case not just in 'primitive' tribes but within the world religions and some new religions in the 'civilized' West. There are a few minority traditions, reformist movements and NRMs that attempt to create a holistic, body-positive, pro-female spirituality, with some success. But religions that equate celibacy with purity invariably promote a dualistic, body-rejecting and misogynystic philosophy in which women's best hope for salvation (if any exists) is to become a nun.

The body-negative and misogynistic attitudes of Christianity, with its close identification of sex with sin, are only too well known. The Catholic church has been particularly virulent and systematic in its condemnation, and the history of this hostility has been chronicled in relentless detail by Uta Ranke-Heinemann, from its origins in an emulation of 'heathen' ideals – rejecting its more body-positive Judaic roots[4] – through Gnostic dualism, St Augustine 'the man responsible for welding Christianity and hostility to sexual pleasure into a systematic whole', to the Scholastic theologians and Aquinas who 'paved the way for the demonisation of marriage itself' (1990, 133), right through to the 'elaborate antisexual edifice' of contemporary moral theology. She laments that 'Then as now, the cardinal sins of mankind are committed in the bedroom – not, for example, on the battlefield' (ibid., 25).

There are some attempts at a more body-positive Christianity, particularly within feminist theology and the creation spirituality of Matthew Fox.[5] However, misogyny is still so deeply ingrained that Fischer (1989) in her chapter on how spiritual directors should deal with violence against women makes no acknowledgement of the role of the church in fostering the shame and guilt that compounds this problem. Interestingly, since approving the ordination of women, the Church of England has been pronouncing more positively on sexuality.

Eastern religions display similarly misogynistic attitudes. In Hinduism, female sexuality is perceived more ambivalently, as simultaneously impure yet auspicious. However, 'For the ascetic, woman represented sexuality, reproduction, and the family, the very obstacles to liberation.'[6] Buddhism has been not so much ambivalent as paradoxical in its sexual attitudes. 'Throughout history ... puritan Buddhists who have attempted to ruthlessly suppress their sexuality in order to attain release have coexisted with Tantric Buddhists who wholeheartedly cultivated that same primal force, believing it to be an expedient to enlightenment' (Stevens 1990, 11). On balance, the puritanical tendency has predominated in all Buddhist countries, and 'an appalling proportion of Buddhist literature in all traditions is devoted to vilifying women as depravity incarnate – insatiable, vile, degraded, and nothing but woe' (ibid., 48). Christianity portrays women as the 'Devil's Gateway', but the Buddha literalized the metaphor: 'It is better that your penis enter the mouth of a hideous cobra or a pit of blazing coals than enter a woman's vagina' (ibid., 32).

Buddhism contains a range of positions on sexuality, including the more sex-affirmative and egalitarian tradition of Tantra (see Chapter 3). Many contemporary Buddhists are attempting to redeem its misogynystic history, drawing on Tantra and other more positive teachings.[7] Christina Feldman encapsulates this vision in the context of her search to 'deepen my fundamental understanding of what it meant to integrate my spirituality and my femininity':

> The authentic mystic extends herself organically, bringing the light of her integrity into her social, sexual and political relationships. ... The authentic mystic knows deeply and surely that, living within her body, she is sexual and honours the expressions of love, joy and sensitivity that are made possible through the body. (1989, 52)

The very first step towards ending estrangement is reclaiming our bodies. . . . To be a disembodied spirit negates a human spirituality. (ibid., 62)

A historical examination of sectarian attitudes to sexuality reveals a tendency towards extremism – either asceticism, or antinomianism. Contemporary NRMs continue this trend, particularly the more world-rejecting communal groups with charismatic leaders. The more world-accepting NRMs such as Soka Gakkai, merged into mainstream society, have little to say about sexuality. Another option sometimes encountered – which does not stand out historically because it reflects social norms, but is contentious in the modern West – is arranged or controlled marriage. The 'Moonie mass marriage' provides the most dramatic example of arranged marriage. The Brahma Kumaris are probably the most extreme and uncompromising example of the Eastern-based NRMs advocating celibacy, at least in Britain. The Osho movement, particularly in the 1970s, exemplifies the 'free love' ethic of the counter-culture.

## Spiritually Arranged Marriages in NRMs

Arranged marriages were sacralized by all the world's religions during periods when they were the cultural norm, and still take place in some conservative Christian sects and Eastern-based NRMs. Some women prefer arranged marriage with its accompanying clarity of family and gender role, despite the price of sexual restraint. They may also claim that not being treated as a sex object is a benefit of such customs as covering hair and body, although the religion itself traditionally interprets them in terms of purity and pollution. Examples are the Jewish *niddah* laws of family purity and the *mikveh* (purification bath), and the rituals around menstruation, sex and childbirth in all religions.

In evangelical Christian NRMs such as the London Church of Christ, marriages are not usually formally arranged but often rely on the advice and consent of the pastor. There are often restraints on sexual expression, including prohibitions on pre-marital and extra-marital sex, and divorce is forbidden except in cases of adultery. Homosexuality is particularly condemned, and such movements tend to interpret AIDS in apocalyptic

terms as God's punishment on homosexuals and other sinners. In the Jesus Army couples are required to sleep in separate beds. This is also obligatory in orthodox Judaism, in order
that men should not be 'polluted' by female menstruation,
but it is unclear if this taboo underlies the Jesus Army policy.
However, they do perceive marriage as the 'lower way', inferior to celibacy, which is catching on among men to the extent
that they now publish *Celibate Cutting Edge*, the 'inspirational
bulletin of celibacy'. This is accompanied by misogyny, which
presents as a militant version of the men's movement in which
the men give up being 'feminized' and don combat gear as
warriors for Jesus. It is a worrying tendency in evangelical
Christianity, one of the latest examples being the Promise
Keepers, America's fastest-growing religious group, led by Isaac
Canales. Among the seven promises required, vital relationships with other men is followed by the practice of sexual
purity. Harder concludes of the restraints on women in the
Jesus Army:

> Women are viewed as sensuous beings and as temptresses.
> Their bodies may cause men to have fleshly desires, so women
> must dress and conduct themselves in a manner which will
> not arouse males, and which will not show vanity or pride.
> They avoid tight-fitting, revealing clothes, shun cosmetics
> or other adornment. Women are given the responsibility of
> avoiding sexually charged situations and must take care not
> to stumble (sexually arouse) the brothers. (1974, 348)

Some Eastern-based NRMs may encourage or impose arranged marriage, especially those arising from traditional cultures. Reverend Moon's first followers were mainly women,
who thereby escaped arranged marriage and were able to
experience leadership. However, Moon's attitude to women
changed dramatically following his marriage to Hak Jan Han,
which symbolized the ideal family, leading to the ideal nation
in the ideal world. Mrs Moon herself became a role model to
women disciples as an ideal wife and mother.

In the 'Moonie mass marriage', up to 2000 or more couples
are married in one ceremony or 'Blessing'; most of the partners are strangers prior to marrying. The system operates like
a glorified marriage bureau, in which candidates send in
application forms with photos, then assemble in a hall. Moon

wanders around matching people up, reputedly under divine inspiration, occasionally assisted by lists of recommendations from local leaders. It is possible to refuse, but few do. There is no published research on the success rates of these marriage, but they are doubtless helped by the build-up of sexual charge arising from the restrictions. The marriages are preceded by at least six years' celibacy, followed by three years' celibacy in which the partners strive to become the Ideal Man and Woman before consummation is allowed. Finally, in a three-day ceremony following a seven-day fast, the marriage is consummated in a ritual that aims to reverse the Fall precipitated by Adam and Eve's premature sexual relationship. Mrs Moon in a recent address stated that sex within marriage was holy, expressing God's love, but the purpose is neither gratification nor procreation but sacrifice, particularly of women for their family.[8] Women may thereby attain equal or greater spiritual status than men as 'creatures of the heart', but at the price of total submission to husband and leader.

ISKCON also favours arranged marriage, though couples may come to a private understanding beforehand, and women may actively select their husband. However, they then need permission to marry from the temple president. Marital sex is permitted but only for the purpose of procreation, hedged around with restrictions. Partners may even decide not to share a bedroom, 'lest they "fall down" or "bloop" (which one devotee explained as "the sound the soul makes when it enters the material world")' (Palmer 1994, 22). Marriage improves the social and spiritual status of women but not men, who are held to be superior to women on all levels, particularly when celibate. As one female devotee expressed it: 'a man's body is a finer instrument for developing Krishna Consciousness and if he remains celibate he becomes very powerful' (Palmer 1994, 16). Devotees subscribe to the Hindu belief in the need to conserve semen for spiritual practice, as do the Brahma Kumaris. This is also fundamental to Tantric and Taoist sexual practice, but the energy conserved is used for spiritual purposes rather than simply conserved through repression.

Men tend to justify marriage as sacrifice for the good of the movement. This may lead to resentment against women as the cause of their fall in status, and even within the movement there are complaints of sex-related misogyny. The relationship between celibacy and misogyny is particularly clear in ISKCON. It had always been conservative, but only became overtly misogynistic in the mid-1970s after men had been initiated as celibate sannyasins. They then tried to stop the initiation of women, as obstacles to their own spiritual advancement. A woman may be perceived as 'a temptress first and a devotee second', and excluded from sharing power with the men so as not to 'sexually agitate them'. The men themselves appear to be absolved from responsibility by the Vedic imagery of woman as fire, man as butter: 'When butter comes near fire, it melts.'[9]

## Celibacy and Sex-Denial in NRMs

As these examples show, in NRMs that are ambivalent about sexuality, celibacy may be the ultimate ideal even if marriage is permitted and encouraged. Celibacy is unusual on a wide scale in non-monastic movements but is required for full-time members of the Brahma Kumaris (BKs). Like the Osho movement, the BKs are a Hindu-based movement founded by a man, Dada Lekhraj known as Brahma Baba, but run largely by women, who were promoted and praised by the leader. But in contrast to sannyasin attitudes to sexuality as gift and spiritual path, the BKs see it as a vice and obstacle to enlightenment.

Brahma Baba saw sex as springing from ignorance, leading to weakness, vice, and eventually 'total ruin', fatally wounding the soul for many births:[10] 'Hence you should treat it as the great enemy, the greatest source of violence that an individual can commit on another. It is indeed the greatest vice which needs to be totally renounced.' Even married love is not excepted: 'it is not an expression of genuine love between man and woman, but tantamounts to killing two souls.' Brahma Baba's main method for counteracting this 'vice' is to cultivate a dualistic attitude: 'to realise that you are souls and your body is mere dress.' This gave rise to a key BK mantra: 'I am a soul, my body is a garment.' The resulting chastity should be maintained even between husband and wife, so that 'they lose awareness of the physical relationship that subsists between them and, therefore, the feeling of sex does not enter their minds. On the other hand, they think of themselves as souls and are mindful of their spiritual relationship with God.'

The BKs view overpopulation as India's greatest problem,

caused by 'sex-lust', to which the 'only solution' is chastity. Osho made the same diagnosis regarding overpopulation, but his solution was not celibacy – hardly feasible on a mass scale – but birth control. Rather than lashing out at humanity in general for its immorality, he attacked religion, particularly Catholicism, for being against birth control.

In the West, although all the full-time BKs are celibate, the language tends to be toned down, and more emphasis laid on the benefits of celibacy than the sinfulness of sex. However, this underlying attitude remains, and Skultans found that 'Sexual activity of any kind is equated with lasciviousness and lustfulness and described as a vicious habit'.[11] Her hypothesis is that the purpose of celibacy is as much about secular as spiritual power, in a country where sex is inextricable from the bondage of marriage and children. To renounce marriage is the 'door to hell', and women have to venerate their husband, however unworthy. So the BKs see sex as the root of inequality, ignoring the role of child-rearing and housework in creating domestic slavery. Virgins have a quasi-Goddess status which they lose when they marry but may regain through celibacy. Celibacy may therefore be a price worth paying for liberation and power in India, enabling women to abandon their subordinate domestic role and achieve camaraderie, even equality with men. This may be the case in India, but the hypothesis raises the question of whether celibacy is the most appropriate means to empowerment for Western women.

My BK sample was too small to generalize from, but the data suggests that the movement tends to attract people who are uninterested in sex and for whom celibacy therefore has a positive appeal. The only single woman I spoke to had never been interested in sex, hence welcomed the practice of celibacy. As long as chastity is maintained, marriage and family life are allowed, even encouraged (perhaps to avoid the accusation of breaking up families). The married women I interviewed had been married for many years, and one admitted that this might have been a factor in easing the move into celibacy:

> Possibly our relationship had come to brother and sister anyway. He's a very modest person, and he loved it. I never told him about celibacy, I just moved out of the bedroom

one day. He must have wondered, but he never said any-thing. . . . I think we have a much better relationship now, it's great.

She was not specific about how the marriage had improved, but extolled the delights of purity: 'Oh, it's wonderful! It gives you such a sense of liberation. It's the best part of it.' One core member described the process of celibacy:

I felt the beauty of celibacy, and how much I feel that it gives a lot of spiritual strength. It's not a question of sup-pressing your urge and all that, because that's very unhealthy, but it's a question of using the energy in a different way. When we direct that energy into sexual energy, we lose a lot of energy, and that tends to make us very dependent on others, and on desires and physical gratification. But if you want to follow a spiritual life, then you want to direct your energy in a spiritual way, into a relationship with God, and the service of humanity.

I only spoke to one male BK, a core member, and the only respondent who admitted to any difficulty in the practice of celibacy. He had previously enjoyed sex, and found the auster-ity 'a struggle, which I only achieved gradually'. He quoted St Augustine: 'Give me chastity, but not yet'. He also admitted that he still occasionally became attracted to women, but felt this was more the fault of the women for 'putting out that kind of energy'. He was helped by coming to his own understand-ing that sensual pleasure gets in the way of meditation, be-cause body and soul are opposed. 'The body seeks pleasure, but we are here to seek spiritual truth. So you have to identify with the soul, not the body.' By continually sublimating sexu-ality through meditation he had learned to convert it into spiritual energy.

Buddhism, like Catholicism, has a developed monastic tradi-tion. In the West, discipline tends to be looser, but Theravada and some Zen groups impose celibacy on the monks, some-times accompanied by misogynistic attitudes. The Friends of the Western Buddhist Order (FWBO) recommends celibacy for the monks and as an occasional discipline for lay followers, although the rationale is as a discipline for the purpose of understanding the nature of desire rather than being against sex *per se* (Subhuti 1985). Another order member said that the FWBO policy on celibacy was flexible and compassionate, but admitted that it was regarded as a 'higher, ideal state'.

It is less usual to find women advocating celibacy in Buddhism, although the Zen teacher Kennett Roshi believes it is a precondition to attain enlightenment: 'If you're married, the singleness of mind, the devotion, the oneness with that eternal can't take place, because you're dividing it off for a member of the opposite sex . . . If you're going to follow the eternal, *he's* the one you're gonna be fond of. He-she-it' (Boucher 1993, 143). Most women who choose to become Buddhist nuns are older and have fully experienced relationships previously, such as Pema Chodron: 'I had explored my sexuality to the degree that I didn't feel there were any dark corners or unresolved issues' (Friedman 1987, 99). In the FWBO celibacy is practised long-term more by older women, which is also the case in other Buddhist communities. An 86-year-old nun I spoke to at the Tibetan monastery of Samye Ling in Scotland had been ordained in her sixties, and felt that this was a more sensible age to begin, as did a 52-year-old woman at the Theravada community of Amaravrati. At least Buddhism, unlike Christianity, provides a full range of techniques to deal with the problems and attain better results. But the middle way of witnessing sexual energy without repression or indulgence is subtle and arduous, and best for older, serious adepts, as recommended by a Chinese Buddhist monk:

> Most young men who keep themselves strictly chaste find themselves visited by sexual fantasies and torturing longings which are worse for them than occasional visits to the flower-houses, while marriage is far better still . . . Perfect chastity is dangerous, unless you really have mastered such longings . . . You must aim at so mastering your desires that they have no power to torment you. This, unless you are a budding Bodhisattva, will take you so long that it is far, far better for you to get married in the meantime. (Stevens 1990, 130)

A former nun from a Korean Zen monastery highlighted lack of affection as a much harder problem for women than lack of sex (whereas for men it was reversed), and stressed the importance of clarity regarding the aim of celibacy: that it should be undertaken only as an aid to practice and not to repress the body and one's full humanity. This point was made by other women, such as a former BK member who felt that their denial of natural human sexuality and emotions made them inhuman. Similarly, a current member of ISKCON felt that the rules imposed to control sexuality were an immature way of handling the issue of celibacy.

## Hedonism and Body-Positive Spirituality in NRMs

By the mid-1970s the widespread (perceived) practice of 'free love' had dramatically changed social attitudes, but in the popular imagination spirituality was still equated with the monastic virtues, particularly chastity. However, signs of a merger between secular humanism and spirituality were appearing in the counter-culture, where sexuality was attaining virtually sacramental significance as a process of discovering reality,[12] heralded by the high priest of the counter-culture, Timothy Leary: 'Sex is sacred.' There were a few group experiments, such as the utopian Kerista community in California, which practised a form of controlled hedonism called 'polyfidelity'. But this new ideology found its fulfilment in the Tantric teachings propounded by Osho.

### Celebrating Sexuality in the Osho Movement

The predominant media image of the Osho movement during Osho's lifetime was of a 'sex cult' led by a 'sex guru'. This view ignores and trivializes the spiritual aim of his (admittedly provocative) teachings: to create a scientific yet sacramental sexuality based on a synthesis between Tantra and Reichian psychotherapy. The main lines of his teachings on sex were established in a series of lectures in Bombay in 1968, later published as *From Sex to Superconsciousness*:

> All our efforts to date have borne wrong results because we have not befriended sex but have declared war on it; we have used suppression and lack of understanding as ways of dealing with sex problems. . . . And the results of repression are never fruitful, never pleasing, never healthy. (1979a, 89)

Osho taught that sexuality is a gift: our most powerful natural energy, a mystery to be enjoyed, celebrated, explored and used as a tool for enlightenment. This is a theory that has received some corroboration from empirical research.[13] He later developed a four-stage model of sexuality, corresponding to natural phases of growth. Children are autoerotic or narcissistic. They then move naturally into a homosexual stage, by which he meant simply exploring their own bodies.[14] If this is allowed, heterosexuality arises naturally, leading to a meeting between the polar opposite male and female energies. In its highest expression, the ecstasy thus created gives a natural experience of meditation, leading to a search for meditative techniques independent of a partner: 'Then the fourth phase, the ultimate phase comes, which is brahmacharya, which is real celibacy . . . Sex has disappeared; you don't need the outer woman, you don't need the outer man. . . . Now to be orgasmic is your natural state' (1984, 188–9).

Some psychologists believe this teaching distorted Tantra, encouraging orgiastic sexuality at the expense of intimacy and spirituality, but the books are full of detailed instruction and theory as well as inspiration. In particular, he prescribed and promoted multiple orgasms for women as a means of expressing and celebrating their sexuality to its fullest capacity. Once 'the energy was flowing' without hindrance or repression, it could be redirected inwards through the 'valley orgasm', a Tantric technique for prolonging the experience and transmuting sexuality into more subtle and spiritualized energy. This technique is the basis of the New Age practice of sacred sex (see pp.121–2). Most sannyasins found his approach inspiring and beneficial:

> The Tantric way fitted completely with everything I had so far found for myself. It was a natural progression and a liberation. It was a sexual liberation, a liberation from parents, from family, society's contracts. It was a final liberation from Catholicism and from any other religion.

Although not all my respondents used or even understood the word 'Tantra', many described experiences of sexual energy as leading both to deeper love experiences, and to deeper meditative states. One woman who had practised Tantra said: 'It's about meditation, about being still and silent. . . . It's not about eroticism.' Asked about the difference between Tantra and eroticism, she replied: 'Well, I'm not an expert, but more silence, more stillness, more real connection with the other person, totally on a heart level. . . . you just look into each other's eyes, really connect with each other, talk to each other – in a way, non-sexual.' Another ex-sannyasin who now practises and teaches Tantra has found sex a very important part of her spiritual search:

It was a manifestation of energy, and for me a very important part of how I experience energy . . . The spiritual search as I understood it then, and certainly as I understand it now, is about connecting with a very intense aliveness, vibrating at all levels. Whether it's about feeling one's heart opening or one's sexual energies being very alive, it's all part of life. If one was closed in that area, how could you be open in any other? . . . I learned to sense the body's energy field, where it's open and closed, so I have a very tangible sense of when a body's open or closed, where blocks are.

Paradoxically, Osho's teaching both promoted sexual ecstasy and encouraged transcendence. In a reply to a question from someone worried because he was becoming bored with sex, Osho replied that 'When sex is absolutely accepted it is bound to become boring. It is such a repetition. . . . The thrill, if you really want to keep it forever fresh, can be maintained only through repression' (1978, 63). In the past, religions had ensured that sex would never be boring, but post-Freudian man was bound to get bored. Tantra was the means to hasten this process, a curative measure to transform this energy:

People think that I teach sex. I am one of the persons who is teaching God. If I talk about sex there is a reason for it – the reason is that I would like you to know it before it is too late. Know it, know it totally, go into it headlong and be finished with it. Go into it meditatively, alert – that is the approach of tantra. . . . If you know something well you are free of it. Knowledge, understanding, liberates. (ibid., 66–7)

Sannyasins displayed a range of attitudes to this dichotomy. Some were content to explore their sexuality without worrying about the ultimate goal; others moved spontaneously in and out of celibacy; a very few were permanently celibate. Some were determined to resolve the paradox:

It's obvious to me that the two big difficulties and therefore attachments in this lifetime for everyone are sex and money. I really believe that these things are to be transcended and you cannot transcend anything until you've experienced it totally. Thanks to Osho it is possible that I may transcend sex in this lifetime, because I have learned to go into my relationships, my intimacy, my sexuality totally. I'm not saying I've experienced everything there is to experience, but it's my aim, my intention and my effort to do this thing totally with relationship – and I do.

Although the 'free love ethic' was normative, sexual behaviour was as varied as elsewhere in Western society, and serial monogamy was the predominant pattern, especially among long-term sannyasins.[15] Nowadays, monogamy is encouraged and practised even more, as a response to the AIDS epidemic – accompanied by an elaborate array of precautions, including condoms, rubber gloves, and compulsory three-monthly HIV tests. Osho encouraged an extreme position with his apocalyptic announcements that AIDS was the plague predicted by Nostradamus, which would kill two-thirds of the world's population, apart from sannyasins who would be saved by practising safe sex. Among the recommended alternatives to normal sex is 'Flex' ('fluidless sex'), achieved through an 'Oshoflex meditation' for non-sexual intimacy with a partner to achieve 'the energy orgasm for the New Man'.[16]

Osho's statements on marriage are mainly critical – 'the death of love', 'a painful suffering with false smiling faces' – although he would sometimes commend its potential as 'a deep spiritual communion'. In Poona there was no encouragement for sexual partners to marry, although the 'religion' of Rajneeshism later included a marriage ceremony.[17] Sannyasins' views and practices varied considerably, but whether or not they supported marriage their highest aspiration was usually to find a 'soul-mate', and many remembered past-life connections with their partner:

1) I have a sense . . . of him being a soul I've travelled with before, and [he] has that sense very deeply too. And here we are, still best friends, after all these years and two kids.

2) It was not just a relationship of the body, the mind and the feelings – this was a spiritual relationship in the sense that I felt connected to her at a place inside myself that I'd only reached in meditation, where I felt my being resonate with her being.

Nevertheless, experimentation was widespread, although one woman said, 'I think I was a lot more promiscuous before I was a sannyasin'. Not everyone felt at ease with this ethos, which was felt to encourage superficiality, lack of commitment and jealousy (by men as well as women). One of the main purposes of the therapy groups was to deal with these problems (see below), but they were mainly viewed positively as aspects of the spiritual growth provided by relationships. However, only five of my respondents showed a preference for partner change, and the most positive endorsement of this ideology came from two young women, one of whom had lived in the ashram since she was 16 and had a long-term but 'open' relationship: 'If I'm not around him and someone comes along and we both have energy for each other, then I will go off and be with that person. And if it doesn't, then that's fine too. I don't go round saying, "I'm free, here I am!" It's quite relaxed, I don't have a whole string of men.'

Relationships were viewed primarily as a means of personal growth, secondarily as a way of learning gender role flexibility – which could be problematic. Sannyasin men were encouraged to become new men, *avant la lettre*, and 'softness' was considered the highest masculine quality. Some women appreciated this change: 'I think it's lovely to find some soft, lovely men. I think it's one of the nicest things about sannyasin men, that on the whole they allow their feminine side to come out, they feel OK about it.' Other women were ambivalent or negative: 'I wanted a real man!' Palmer (1994) defines the Osho movement as a 'sex polarity group', viewing the sexes as separate and distinct, but sannyasin attempts at role reversal could blur the distinctions, causing confusion and frustration:

The female energy in me likes to surrender to a male energy, because that is what a female energy naturally wants to do. Sannyasin men tend to get softer and softer, and as I get softer, something in me – probably my ego – wants something to surrender to, and that can cause a lot of frustration.

I think ultimately a lot of relationships I've had have ended because of that surrender power game – because I veer between wanting to dominate and surrender to a man, and those two sides of me haven't yet harmonized.

The men had mixed responses to the relationship issues. Two felt that discovering their feminine side had improved their relationships with women:

1) I think women found it attractive. It wasn't as if I lost my balls, my passion – it was a kind of false masculinity that I began to lose. And as the changes occurred, I became softer, it became much realer. I could talk to a woman and be intimate with her, rather than try to dominate or seduce or manipulate or control her.

2) I think I always had plenty of female in me – also plenty of male. I was seen as not exactly macho, but somehow plenty of women were attracted to me, in their scores and hundreds. In a way, that makes people feel you're very much a man, but in fact women are attracted to female energy in men. A very strong male energy brings out the male in women, which they have to fight. Either they have to totally surrender and be walked on or they have to fight. If a woman wants to stay womanly – soft, gentle, receptive, flowing – then it's much easier to do that in a relationship with a man who is also the same.

On the whole, the men valued relationships with women but, perhaps predictably, were more likely than the women to put meditation first and see sex as a distraction, as evidenced in the following interesting contrast between a male and female response to sexual fantasies during a meditation group. The man found:

During the *zazen* group I did, sex became a major distraction. It became almost like a pornographic movie because of that. Basically these experiences of meditation and sex confirmed for me that what Osho was saying was true and sound. You can't suppress sex and meditate at the same time. I've no idea how the Buddhist and Christian monks get round that one, I certainly couldn't.

He therefore felt that rather than suppress sex it needed to be expressed, understood, and 'burned out' so that one could meditate in peace. However, a woman had a similar experience in a meditation group, but with a different outcome:

> I did a wonderful *vipassana* group on my third visit, where for two days I felt pure sexual energy. Then it clearly spread through my whole body until I was just feeling very present and open. That was the most tangible experience. I guess it's just part of the way I experience things generally. I do experience energy opening at different levels at different times, and that it's just energy that moves around. It's part of my everyday reality.

### Paganism and Sacred Sex

Paganism has had a bad press, partly on account of one of the main progenitors of its sexual practices: Aleister Crowley. He developed sex magick in his Rabelaisian Abbey of Thelema in Sicily, based on extensive experimentation with sex, magic and drugs to create altered states of consciousness, the results of which he published in a booklet *De Arte Magica*. It seems likely that Crowley was influenced by Tantra; some of the texts were available in translation, and there are Tantric elements in his Gnostic Mass.[18] His philosophy of sexuality also arose out of his channelled Law of Thelema: 'Do what thou wilt shall be the whole of the Law . . . Love is the law, love under will.' His community eventually collapsed amid lurid accusations, but has influenced various occult groups including the Temple Ov Psychick Youth, founded in the 1980s by the pop musician Genesis P Orridge, which practises sex magick but without passing through the previous degrees of initiation.

The main source of Pagan beliefs and practices is in the rediscovered (or recreated) mythology of the goddess, which affirms the female body and provides rituals for celebrating 'women's mysteries', particularly menstruation and childbirth.[19] As Starhawk, the best known witch and writer, expresses it: 'Sexuality is sacred because it is a sharing of energy, in passionate surrender to the power of the Goddess, immanent in our desire. In orgasm, we share in the force that moves the stars' (1979, 208).

The English Wiccan high priestess Vivianne Crowley believes

that the 'negative attitude to women displayed in Christianity has derived largely from negative attitudes to sex' (1990, 116), particularly following the glorification of celibacy. The resulting vilification of woman as temptress is bound up with another fear-arousing image: woman as witch. This is the term that goddess spirituality and Wicca are trying to revive in its positive meanings of wise woman and priestess.

Paganism may be seen as hedonistic but with provisos: Crowley's Law of Thelema is adapted to read: 'An it harm none, do what you will'. Vivianne Crowley describes Pagan sexual morality as simple: 'there are no barriers to sexual activity with other unattached adults; but we are expected to have regard to the consequences of our actions and to ensure that we do not cause unwanted pregnancy, spread sexual disease, or mislead others as to our level of commitment to the relationship'. Attitudes to homosexuality vary between different groups. In high magic groups where sex polarity is considered important, it is discouraged. Wicca is mainly liberal, while some feminist witchcraft groups actively support lesbianism. Extra-marital sex is forbidden if it causes hurt, while rape and child–adult sex are 'anathema' (ibid., 163–4). The Pagan response to AIDS is more compassionate and less apocalyptic than in the Osho movement, and is summarized by Starhawk:

> It is harder today, but perhaps even more necessary, to affirm the sacredness of the erotic. . . . AIDS . . . has become an excuse for an attack on the erotic, especially on those forms that do not meet society's approval. . . . If society valued the erotic as sacred, AIDS research would be a top priority, as would research on safe forms of birth control. (1979, 9)

Pagans are mainly uninterested in marriage as a legal institution, seeing it as a device to protect property and dominate women. However, a loving monogamous relationship is seen as a personal contract to be honoured. As Starhawk expresses it: 'Marriage is a deep commitment, a magical, spiritual, and psychic bond. But it is only one possibility out of many for loving, sexual expression' (ibid., 27). There is an ongoing debate between monogamy and 'free love' in paganism, and Starhawk herself has caused some protest in the Reclaiming movement by changing to a pro-monogamy position now that she is herself in a monogamous relationship. Various Pagan groups have created colourful wedding rituals, sometimes called 'handfasting', which are often celebrated at a seasonal festival, such as the spring festival of Beltain. Alternative marriages are increasing in Britain at about 50 per cent a year, including among non-Pagans, in reaction to the perceived outdatedness and sexism of the Judaeo-Christian rituals and the unspirituality of the civil ceremony.[20] So this may be an indication of changing social trends.

The myth of the Sacred Marriage between king and priestess to ensure good harvests and control of the land is fundamental in Paganism, and its re-enactment is a recognition of the power of sex. It is the basis of the Great Rite: ritual sex between the high priest and priestess in pagan rituals, including the third degree of initiation in Alexandrian Wicca. However, the evidence suggests that it is more often symbolic than actual, unless the participants are already partners. Some witches compare it to Tantra as a sacred ceremony to raise and release power, and channel it for the purposes of healing, consecration, creativity and inspiration. Witches do tend to worship 'sky-clad' (naked), but 'as a way of establishing closeness and dropping social masks, because power is most easily raised that way, and because the human body is itself sacred' (Starhawk 1979, 97).

The New Age answer to the failure of free sex is sacred sex, a syncretistic selection from Tantra, Taoism, humanistic and transpersonal psychology, and clinical sexology. It began in America in the 1960s but did not take off till the 1980s, when various teachers and psychotherapists began leading courses. There are now many books on the subject and many teachers in America and Europe, of whom the best known is Margo Anand, author of the best-selling *The Art of Sexual Ecstasy*. She is an ex-sannyasin who runs groups and trainings in 'High Sex' worldwide, and has set up SkyDancing Institutes in America and Britain. Her teaching emphasizes 'intimacy as a subtle set of skills, an art that has to be developed before sexual union is considered' (1989, 94), a Western requirement often ignored by Eastern Tantric masters.

Other well-known teachers are Caroline Aldred, who teaches sacred sex via nine levels of orgasm, as learned from Shunyata (Robert Ferris), the 'Laughing Guru' based in Bali. David Howe, head of the Institute of Higher Sexology in South London, teaches a 4000-year-old Seminal Ovarian Chi Gung. Zek and Mischa Halu are also based in London, and rose to media prominence as consultants for the video of the *Kama Sutra*. They have been dubbed 'the Masters and Johnson of the New Age' by the tabloid press, but their work is based on many years of study with Taoist masters. Like Margo Anand, they see sacred sexuality as a means of discouraging promiscuity, revitalizing marriage and enhancing intimacy, hence a vital therapy for the age of AIDS.

## Relationships and Charismatic Authority

Whatever style of sexuality is taught in NRMs, participants tend to validate their 'choice' as liberating and empowering. However, it can also be interpreted as a means of social control by the religion: to discourage the intimate private relationship of the couple, in favour of group cohesiveness and primary loyalty to the leader.[21] In a survey of 60 American communal groups, Aidala (1985) found that sexual norms received wide consensual support, whether they prescribed celibacy or hedonism. Furthermore, in groups where marriage was strictly controlled there was 100 per cent agreement on the need to submit to the leader's choice. In non-religious communes the norms were more fluid and experimental; shared standards were rare and harder to put into practice. She does not interpret these findings, but it could well be that the presence of a charismatic leader, more likely to be found in a religious community, was a determining factor in the differences.

In any group there is likely to be conflict between wider group interests and dyadic attachments, particularly romantic ones. Oneida, the nineteenth-century American spiritual commune founded by John Noyes, presents the most dramatic recent historical example of this problem. His system of pantagamy (complex marriage) appeared as free love but was controlled by a committee of male elders. The women had little or no choice of partners, and if they formed 'exclusive love' attachments were often forcibly separated. They were also required to sign a pledge resolving: 'We do not belong to ourselves in any respect, but that we first belong to *God* and second to Mr Noyes as God's true representative. . . . that we will if necessary become martyrs to science, and cheerfully renounce all desire to become mothers if for any reason Mr Noyes deems us unfit material for propagation. Above all, we offer ourselves "living sacrifices" to God and true Communism' (Kern 1981, 248).

Kanter postulated regarding Oneida:

> Two-person intimacy poses a potential threat to group cohesiveness unless it is somehow controlled or regulated by the group. Groups with any degree of identity or stability face the issue of intimacy and exclusive attachments and set limits on how much and what kinds are permissible or desirable. Exclusive two-person bonds within a larger group, particularly sexual attachments, represent competition for members' emotional energy and loyalty. (1972, 86)

It is clear that one effect of discouraging monogamous relationships is to destabilize even those that are achieved. Hence the only emotional security is in the one permanent relationship whose stability is assured – and to which all others are subordinated – that between the disciple and the master. Even in ISKCON and the Unification Church where marriage is encouraged, the couple's loyalty is – again – primarily to God, secondarily to the leader who represents him, and only thirdly to the spouse. Sheela's address at a sannyasin marriage ceremony in Rajneeshpuram inadvertently illustrates this priority: 'Remember I'm not asking you to make a commitment to each other, but to keep Bhagwan's love in your hearts for as long as you are together.'[22]

The most extreme example of the manipulation of relationships was the Children of God (now the Family). David Berg's Law of Love reached a peak of sexual freedom during the late 1970s (concurrent with the peak of the Poona ashram). Although as a biblically based movement, fornication, adultery, incest and sodomy were limited or forbidden, there is evidence that the first three were widely indulged in, although homosexuality was officially condemned. The 'Mo Letters', which were his main form of communication with his disciples, encouraged these antinomian practices, termed 'sharing':

> There is no such thing anymore as a Biblical law against adultery, as long as it is done in Love, because the 'Law of Love' supercedes *all* other laws.

God will have no other gods before Him, not even the marriage god . . . God is the God of marriage, too, and the main thing is to be married to Him and His work, and when a marriage is not according to His Will, He doesn't hesitate to break it up and form other unions to further His work!

Although Berg may not have intended to encourage total promiscuity, and different communities varied in their practices, monogamous relationships suffered and often broke up, partly as a result of the stress on both partners of Flirty Fishing (see Chapter 3). His daughter described a 'progression' from sharing inside the Family, then with outsiders, then homosexuality, child sex, child–adult sex, group sex, and finally incest. A 1980 Letter endorses virtually total antinomianism: 'As far as God's concerned there are no more sexual prohibitions hardly of any kind'. However, from 1983 behaviour changed, following the 'Ban the Bomb' Letter limiting sharing to the communities. Nowadays, particularly since Berg's death and various court cases regarding child abuse (see Chapter 6), the Family's sexual behaviour is more in line with conservative Christianity.[23]

Some women sannyasins experienced conflict between their commitments to their partner and their master. Two of my respondents resolved it by choosing their partner, one leaving Poona because she felt abandoning her partner 'would tear something apart that felt very special and valuable, and somehow that was what life had brought me'. Another woman's resolution of the conflict may illustrate a significant difference between typically female and male concepts of spirituality:

> I have to admit that until we split up, the relationship with a man was more important – I was totally committed and involved in him. I told him recently, and he was horrified, because to him the master is more important. . . . Most of the time I would have chosen [my partner]. But after this happened and I realized he wasn't mine any more, and I might never see him again, then I had no choice. Then it had to be Osho, and Osho became much more important – an experience I'd turn to whenever I was lost.

Most sannyasins believed that their commitment to spiritual growth, including their relationship with Osho, should come before their personal relationships. This is a fundamental principle of monastic life, and it could therefore be argued that it is primarily a spiritual position rather than a requirement of charismatic authority. Conflict may be an inevitable result of attempting to integrate the very different needs and approaches of family and monastic lifestyles. Tipton (1982) discovered that relationships in Buddhist monasteries ended as often with the partners separating as marrying.

It was generally recognized that the people who rose highest in the Osho movement were those who were totally committed, to the point of putting their meditation and work before their personal relationships. As the co-ordinator of Medina (the British community) expressed it:

> There was nothing but the work, and it was to me completely absorbing. It was my baby, I was living out what I wanted to do most – for Bhagwan, for people, for the commune. My relationships suffered terribly. The guys I was with had a very hard time of it, and got very grumpy about it often, because I wasn't available to them. My work came first.

It should be emphasized that this choice was voluntary, since even after leaving the movement her work still comes first: 'I did 10 years of marriage, and thought marriage was it, but since then I haven't focused on a relationship as being the centre of my life.' Most people were not so single-mindedly devoted, and thus had more difficulty in surrendering. Several people mentioned the strain on the relationship of having so little time together and being too tired after the long hours of work at Rajneeshpuram. The tendency was to accept this regime as a 'Gurdjieffian device', but Franklin, a disillusioned ex-sannyasin, has a different explanation:

> The only way lovers had time to be together was if they worked together, but couples rarely did. More and more, casual sex or celibacy was becoming a pattern for people. The severing of deep personal relationships has always been a classic way of fostering dependence on a group and its leaders. (1992, 261)

There is some evidence of relationships being deliberately manipulated in the Osho movement, though mostly by sannyasin leaders. Most of Osho's direct interventions appear to have been experimental, even playful – therefore open to challenge, even refusal. One sannyasin with a very close relationship to Osho, described a typical experience:

> One time at *darshan* he said to [a woman], 'You need a relationship, choose who it's going to be.' There were only two vaguely available men, and she chose me. So he said, 'He's yours, I give him to you.' I heard this, and I was furious: 'What right has this guy?' She came bouncing out of *darshan* and said, 'Well, you're mine!' I was really pissed off! The next day I was in the garden, so I said to Osho, 'I've got a bone to pick with you – you can't give someone away like that.' He looked at me, 'Can't I?' 'You can't turn love on and off like a tap!' 'You can't?' 'No!' At that moment I realized he had nothing to play with, he'd reached out for the first tool that was available, and as that was me he'd used me to see if it worked, but it didn't work.

Wallis notes how many of the sexually permissive youth communes of the 1960s 'characteristically failed to endure as a result of jealousy and a sense of sexual exploitation' (1979, 89). Osho believed that sex and money were the main causes of the dissolution of communities, and devoted much time to counselling couples on their problems. As a result, monogamy rather than experimentation was encouraged among the leadership and inner circle to provide a stable core group. The Rajneesh therapy groups functioned as a method of social control to avoid this: 'to encourage sexual communism of sharing inside the commune; to discourage ... "dyadic withdrawal" from the group by censoring possessive feelings and exclusive relationships; and to provide a forum in which members who were having difficulty adjusting to these new patterns and ethics could express their jealousy or other emotional dilemmas and receive counselling and support from the group' (Palmer & Bird 1992, 77).

Osho devoted attention to relationships because of their importance to his disciples, but saw them as secondary to meditation: 'I am not interested in your personal relationships; that is absolutely your own nightmare. You have chosen to suffer – suffer.' His last words to Shunyo were: 'Every love affair is a disaster' (Shunyo 1992). This attitude is reflected in his advice to one of my interviewees: 'I asked Osho a question:

"How can you know the difference between the thorns of a healthy and unhealthy relationship?" He said all relationships were unhealthy.' His teaching contained a further paradox: for those on the 'path of love', relationships were encouraged to 'open the heart', yet were also in a sense anti-spiritual:

> All relationships are just beautiful on the surface; deep down they are a sort of bondage. I am not saying don't relate to people . . . but no relationship is going to give you happiness – because it never comes from the outside. (1977a, 95)

> [Relationship] is a kind of concentration of the heart. But all concentration becomes a concentration camp! Basically it is fascist . . . Both are prisoners and both are the jailers. (1984, 32)

Osho made a fundamental distinction between romantic and spiritual love, similar to the Graeco-Christian distinction between eros and agape. Noyes also attacked romance as undermining the broader base of social love that pantagamy aspired to at Oneida. In Buddhism too, both celibate and Tantric, romance is perceived as dysfunctional, a fantasy imprisoning us in *samsara*. The FWBO deals with such 'immature and addictive' relationships traditionally by avoidance, prescribing single-sex communities (Subhuti 1985). Osho, by contrast, preferred the Tantric path of indulgence with awareness. Osho's expression of the contrast is:

> Love has nothing to do with relationship. It is more a state of being. You have to become a loving person. It is not a question of being in relationship. I am not saying not to be in relationship; be in as many relationships as possible because each relationship has its own uniqueness and each relationship has its own beauty and each relationship contributes its own joy and of course its own suffering, its own pain. It has its own dark nights and its own beautiful days. But that's how one grows: through darkness, through light, through sweetness, through bitterness. (1984, 37)

## Beyond the Sexual Revolution

The most positive benefit of the enormous range of NRMs on offer is the corresponding range of choices available to women regarding sexuality, as with other aspects of life. These fulfil different needs for different women, though each choice has its corresponding dangers or loss. Some women are attracted to the certainty and stability of arranged marriage, despite the sacrifice of freedom and status. Celibacy is a practical solution to the demands of a monastic regime but tends to work only for a few exceptional people; for those not ready or prepared it may cause immense frustration and psychological problems, and women in particular may suffer from the denial of the affective needs. Both these solutions are also associated with misogyny. Free love and variants such as sacred sex offer great freedom and potential ecstasy for those psychologically strong enough to handle the issues of jealousy and possessiveness. However, some women felt exploited as sex objects, as in secular society. It may be that NRMs whose sexual practices hold most relevance to mainstream society are those coming closest to the new norm of serial monogamy, such as the more world-accepting middle way of Pagan sexuality, which in its sacralization of sexuality offers a way of enhancing monogamy.

Most of the support for holistic spirituality, in all religions, is from women, and it may be that body-positive immanence is inherently more female, celibate transcendence more male, as believed by many sannyasins, Pagans, and feminist theologians. Restrictions and denial of female sexuality by male theologians, priests and charismatic leaders in the name of morality and spirituality clearly arise from misogyny, particularly when accompanied by explicit doctrines of female sinfulness. What is clear is the need for women – as well as men – to be in control of their own sexuality and emotional life.

# 6 Motherhood and Community: Beyond the Nuclear Family

One of the main accusations against NRMs, especially from the ACM, is that they break up families.[1] Given the small numbers of people involved in NRMs and the range of beliefs and practices regarding the family, this is an exaggerated reproach. As on other social issues, however, these experimental groups provide an interesting commentary and critique on the state of family and community. As with sexual practices, the conservative NRMs attempt to revive traditional, patriarchal family structures, whereas the counter-cultural movements experiment with alternative forms, particularly the commune.

The nuclear family is a relatively recent form of social organization that is already dissolving, partly through attacks from many sources, including radical psychologists, political utopians and feminists.[2] In the 1960s it was widely denounced as the root of most personal and social problems by such prophets as R.D. Laing, a hero of the counter-culture: 'families, schools, churches are the slaughterhouses of our children' (1971, 102). The Bergers analysed the main cause of the family's dissolution as the modernist belief in hyper-individualism, and the corresponding valuation of personal development over socialization: 'The very important consequence is that the individual becomes free to look for other support groups – be it in the therapeutic group, or the sisterhood collective, or the political cell, or what-have-you' (1983, 122).

Despite subsequent attempts to revive 'Victorian values', the structure of the nuclear family is breaking down rapidly. In Britain, 30 per cent of births take place outside marriage, many to women who are or soon become single mothers. Over the last 25 years the percentage of single parents (mainly mothers) has risen steadily and rapidly to 18 per cent. Through serial monogamy and divorce, the stepfamily is also becoming increasingly common as a household type. In addition, the birthrate continues to fall as a result of later births, smaller families, and the choice of some women to postpone or give up mother-hood altogether in favour of career and personal development. This pattern is similar in the rest of Europe and America.

## Intentional Communities

'Community' has become a buzzword of the 1990s, its absence perceived as the basis of most social problems. Yet despite the emphasis on individualism noted by the Bergers and others, and the Thatcherite belief in the non-existence of society, many people, particularly within the counter-culture, have been looking for alternative forms of family and community in which to live together and bring up children. Stability is needed for child-rearing, and whether or not the nuclear family is the ideal form, in its absence a community is needed to provide financial, practical and emotional support. Utopian communes are a perennial solution to the inadequacies of family and society, and religious persecution, possibly predating the development of agriculture, but certainly since the time of early Christianity, through medieval millenarianism, Protestant Dissenters, Ranters and Shakers, Enlightenment Owenites and American Transcendentalists. Communalism may have been the predominant prehistoric social form, but in the historical context it is a vehicle of protest and deviance, political, social and religious. Deviant communal groups flourish in periods of rapid social and economic change accompanied by a questioning of society's values. When they emerge as a prominent phenomenon, they may be described as a counter-culture.[3]

Communes, both spiritual and secular, were the preferred social organizational form of the 1960s counter-culture, based on an ideology of 'sex, drugs and rock'n'roll', personal growth, and spiritual revival. There were thousands of experiments in communal living throughout the 1960s and 1970s, particularly in America where they became increasingly commonplace. Indeed, the 1980 US census was designed with a special category for communal households.[4] Although the commune movement declined in the 1980s, many of the original communities have survived into the 1990s, which have also seen a widescale revival of what are now termed 'intentional communities'.[5] They are enormously diverse in structure and ideology, including ecovillages, co-housing groups, student co-ops, urban housing co-operatives, farming collectives, monasteries, ashrams and millenarian religious sects. Some have become internationally renowned, such as Findhorn in Scotland, Esalen in California, and the Farm in Tennessee. The closest one can come to a common definition is their basis in values that may be broadly termed holistic. The majority have grown out of a spiritual philosophy, but even those that are political tend to have the religious character and social form of a band of true believers, presenting a heretical challenge to the established order. Many communal groups developed directly out of NRMs, themselves radically deviant groups experimenting with new forms of spirituality, relationship and social organization.

Whatever the motivation for joining, a communally based NRM clearly represents an alternative to the family of origin, and therefore a rival and threat. Kanter found in her study of nineteenth-century communes: 'Utopia is the place where a person's fundamental emotional needs can be expressed and met through the communal group. The community seeks to become a family in itself, replacing or subsuming all other family loyalties' (1972, 72).

Opinion is divided as to whether contemporary NRM communes arise out of positive or negative family experiences, although there is some evidence that members have had disrupted or dysfunctional childhoods.[6] Whereas the ACM tends to view membership as a rejection of the family and a factor in its dissolution, it is also clear that joining an NRM is partly a search for an ideal family, with the charismatic leader as an ideal father figure (see Chapter 3). Robbins and Anthony argue that positive experiences of family lead to a search to replicate the experience, particularly following the sharp discontinuity of impersonal educational and workplace relationships. In contrast, NRMs provide 'multiple possibilities for alternative kinship promising unequivocal acceptance, warmth and structure' (1982, 68). Jacobs agrees with their view of NRM as alternative family, but contests their interpretation of NRMs as a means of transition between the private and public sectors of society. Pointing to the massive evidence on strained and broken families, and child abuse, she argues that the overidealization of the family in the 1950s produced correspondingly strong disillusionment in the 1960s. 'Accordingly, a segment of disenchanted youth was drawn to these movements in search of the ideal family' (1989, 4). Palmer agrees, seeing the 'spiritual families' established by NRMs as an attempt to create the old extended family (1987). What is clear is that community is an important element in the appeal of NRMs as substitute families, from the Unification Ideal Family to the Pagan coven, but that they do require a certain level of maturity to work. As Subhuti asserts of the FWBO communities, 'A community is no place for the inadequate since it demands, again, responsibility from its members' (1985, 169). When communities do work, they provide a coherent social context, ideological framework, and inspirational value system, often promoted and held together by a charismatic leader.

## Motherhood versus Personal Development

It is particularly within marriage and motherhood that feminists see woman's 'self' as most at risk of being negated. Patriarchy demands that women should sacrifice their own needs and demands to their family, valuing selflessness over self-realization, caring for others over creation of self. The publication in 1963 of Betty Friedan's *The Feminine Mystique* was the milestone exposing the paradox that love and oppression are tragically interwoven for women. Liberation therefore meant freedom from the family, from the duties and burdens of childbearing, in order to experiment with alternative sexual and family norms and paths to personal development. Feminism also developed links with the HPM through the mutual emphasis on self-realization.[7]

Most religions sanctify motherhood as a woman's destiny and true vocation. The more patriarchal the tradition, the more motherhood is glorified, as in Roman Catholicism, the more fundamentalist movements within all three Western religions, and NRMs such as the Unification Church (itself Christian-based) where Mrs Moon as a 'devoted wife and mother' is a role model for Unificationist women. Women who are themselves conservative, internalizing and upholding these beliefs, may be drawn to such religions. The benefits are clearly defined gender roles and stable families, but the downside is a rigid control of sexuality, of work and worship by husband and elders, loss of status and opportunities for direct spiritual advancement, and a high incidence of wife and child abuse.

Conservative Christianity is now the main preserver and legitimator of traditional family values in the West, and again herein lies the main appeal for certain kinds of women, looking for discipline and stability in contrast to the 'decadent experiments' of secular life (Rose 1987). The women may find it hard to give up their autonomy to a husband, particularly given 'the lack of strong sensitive men to head the godly institutions of church and family in a loving and responsible manner'. Yet this requirement is enshrined in the social organization, as in all patriarchal society, here upheld by the ministries' Director of Counselling: 'The Bible clearly states that the wife is to submit to her husband's leadership. . . . Two-headed households are as confusing as they are clumsy' (ibid., 247–8). Rose found that the women did finally make this sacrifice, deciding 'they would rather follow than be left behind to struggle with their own individual identities.' She concludes: 'While they may be relatively content in their relationships with their men, their bench mark is embedded in the old system of patriarchy which continues to perpetuate the costly contradictions that trap both men and women' (ibid., 257). Another irony of the purportedly 'pro-family' stance taken by evangelicals is their tendency to oppose legislation for the rights of women and children, including 'shelters for battered women, mandatory child abuse reporting, and family planning clinics' (Rose 1990).

Lynn Davidmann did some interesting research on the increasing numbers of women who join orthodox Judaism from liberal or secular backgrounds. They usually convert not out of a search for God or spiritual experience but out of a desire for a conventional family life. In exchange, they are willing to give up successful careers, control over their sexuality and the gender-role flexibility of secular life. Even exclusion from public and religious life is not objected to. Having achieved public success, 'they are actually glad to have a private sacred sphere in which they do not have to be "out there" asserting themselves' (1990, 391). As noted earlier in this chapter, it is often women who themselves have suffered childhood deprivation who most idealize the Jewish myth of the warm, close-knit family. What is interesting and perhaps unique about these Jewish groups is that the rabbis themselves are conscious of the reasons women are attracted to their synagogues, and promote them as marriage bureaus: 'This has become a selling point of the synagogue. One woman told me that when she told the Beginners' rabbi about her engagement his response was, "Great! That's good for our statistics"' (ibid., 397).

The legitimation of nuclear family life is also central to the appeal of Islam to women, who are attracted in increasing numbers. In Britain there are around 20 000 Muslim converts, mainly women; in America 80 per cent of the 80 000 white converts are women. The appeal lies partly in the moral certainties and clearly defined gender roles for those confused and frightened by the uncertainties and challenges of freedom, but many are attracted to the high value Islam places on motherhood.

The one interesting exception to this pattern of patriarchal dominance over women and children is the women's spirituality movement, where there has been a resacralization of motherhood. This is based partly on the power and pre-eminence of the myth of the Great Mother, which gave rise to the archetype of woman as earth mother, and the womb as cauldron of transformation. Some Pagan women claim that performing goddess rituals, and sometimes simply reading the myths, helped them become fertile. A feminist witch and healer I interviewed was told she had 'defrosted the ovaries' of one of her patients, who had a child a year later. Wicca may also legitimate a woman's choice to be conventionally feminine, finding her main identity in motherhood. It is seen as a path for developing caring, nurturing feelings, although not necessarily only for offspring; they are also considered important for society in general and the land. As one priestess explained, 'Motherhood is valued, considered a proper job, but whether one is or is not a mother is not going to define one's status.'

The dangers of reverting to biological determinism through overemphasizing and romanticizing female bodily existence have been incisively analysed by Ursula King:

I consider the excessive importance placed by some feminists on the experience of birth as dangerously romantic, especially as most women in the western world give birth far more rarely than women in the past or women in the third world. . . . In addition one might observe that an excessive insistence on the experience of motherhood can be considered as a form of 'retraditionalization' emphasizing, admittedly in a new fashion, what women have so exclusively experienced for far too long, often to their own regret and at the loss of a wider human experience of self-development and greater fulfilment. (1989, 80)

## Motherhood in the Osho Movement

The Osho movement was one of the most militantly anti-family NRMs, which both reflected and approved the break-up of the nuclear family. Osho provided a critique of family and society in tune with counter-cultural values. He believed that only 1 per cent of families were beneficial – in line with America's influential Recovery movement, which claims that 90–99 per cent of families are dysfunctional. They should therefore be abolished in favour of a spiritual family:

> The most outdated thing is the family. It has done its work, it is no more needed. In fact, now it is the most hindering phenomenon for human progress. . . . The family is the root cause of all our neurosis. . . .
>
> The real family is not your father, your mother, your brothers, your sisters, your wife, your husband, your children; they are just accidental. Your real family is the family of a Buddha. If you are fortunate to feel joyful in the company of a Buddha, then dissolve into that company – you have found your family. (1984, 505–8)

Despite this fierce attack, Osho would sometimes describe motherhood as potentially the peak of female creativity and responsibility: 'becoming the mother of a Buddha'. However, his main emphasis was firmly on self-realization for women:

> A woman is not only capable of giving birth to children, she is also capable of giving birth to herself as a seeker of truth. But that side of woman has not been explored at all.[8] (1987b, 18)

Sannyasins had fairly representative family backgrounds and childhoods, some from broken, unhappy homes, but some from quite stable, happy ones.[9] Their rebellion against the family appears to stem from the counter-cultural belief in the need to create the 'real' self independently of family conditioning and a spiritual belief in the benefits of living with a group of fellow-seekers. Many had had experience of different types of commune, political, feminist, or psychotherapeutic (including Laing's community) prior to becoming sannyasins.

Attitudes towards motherhood and children were ambivalent. Osho discouraged women from having children on the basis that a) most people were incapable of positive parenting, and b) children were a distraction from the spiritual growth that was the main purpose of being there. Abortion and sterilization were sometimes used to discourage childbirth, which Osho is believed to have endorsed although he never spoke publicly on this subject. Estimates of the numbers of sterilizations vary, but it is probable that there were not more than 200–300. These were mostly undertaken voluntarily, apart from some kitchen workers who were allegedly coerced by their supervisor, Deeksha, an Italian woman rumoured to be Mussolini's granddaughter. For most sannyasins sterilization was either a symbol of their devotion through renouncing biology in favour of spirituality, or simply a practical alternative to contraception. It was an easily available option in India, and it is ironic that though encouraged by the West for poor and/or non-white women, in this instance it was used by middle-class Western women who would not have been allowed to have the operation in the West.

Most sannyasins were of the first generation to have easy access to birth control, and were in favour of contraception or abortion as a fallback, legitimated by a belief in women having control over their bodies and biological processes. Sannyasins also believe in reincarnation; it follows that an aborted foetus simply chooses another womb. The experience of a woman who had experienced two self-induced miscarriages is typical:

When a woman conceives, the child chooses the parent – that's how I was looking at it. Something had entered me, and what was the most intelligent and loving way to help it to leave? I didn't want to have an abortion because that was too violent, though if it had to be done I would have done it. I tried a sort of experiment. I thought if it's something that's come from outside me it will feel a detachment from me if I sit and talk to it. So I used to close my eyes and feel this something inside me and say to it, 'Just leave. I don't want to hurt you, I don't want to go to a hospital and have you extracted, I don't want to be violent towards you. I'm not the person you need to come to – just leave, and find someone else.' I did that for a week, 10 days. I had an abortion booked, but two days before I had a miscarriage.

Official attitudes against childbirth became more stringent after Poona I, and it appears that no children were born in Rajneeshpuram or Medina. Pressure was sometimes exerted, and there are instances at this time of women being made to choose between having the baby and staying in the commune. Some women later regretted getting sterilized, especially if they dropped sannyas, but now some are having the operation reversed. There is a growing trend for sannyasin women to have babies, whether or not they get married. It is interesting that the anti-motherhood phase coincided with a time when the birth rate in the West dropped dramatically as women celebrated their newly won freedom, whereas the present tendency coincides with the now fashionable return to motherhood.

Nevertheless some sannyasins had children, though mainly born prior to joining. Those who had children in the ashram would often practise some form of sacred sex in order to conceive in a state of higher consciousness. The belief was that the woman would thus be empowered to invite a 'higher soul' into her womb. Some of the ashram children were known as 'Buddha children' and were believed to be reincarnated Zen masters or *bodhisattvas*. This status was perhaps a mixed blessing: it conferred high prestige but also required appropriate behaviour. Such children would sometimes later rebel against this 'family icon' by indulging in normal teenage behaviour. However they were not subjected to spiritual disciplines, unlike the boy *tulkus* of Tibetan Buddhism, who left their mothers as babies to enter a monastery of celibate men and undergo a rigorous regime of education, meditation and etiquette. June Campbell (1996) describes their sufferings and the unfortunate consequences in adult life, including fear and hatred of women. The main problem for parents, especially mothers, was that the commune was set up primarily as a monastery, for childless adults choosing to pursue spiritual development as the main priority. Traditionally seekers have been required to sacrifice everything, including family life, for this goal.[10] Women with children were committed to 'giving birth to themselves as seekers of truth', but also, naturally, to their children. As has been seen, sexual relationships in a monastic setting can be highly problematic, but children and family life can be even more so, setting up conflicts with the spiritual objectives: 'There wasn't a great deal of room for children, motherhood wasn't encouraged. I didn't expect them to provide anything, but I felt you had to prove your okayness as a mother. Obviously you wanted to get involved with the work or the meditations or groups, but you also wanted to make sure the child was getting what she needed.' Having made the choice to be in effect a working mother, women had less time for their children and some later regretted the missed joys of motherhood. But the consensus was that even if the children had been somewhat neglected, they had still been better off in a commune than a single-parent family.

Some women resolved the conflict by leaving their children behind when they went out to India, but this was rarely accomplished without pain. Belfrage (1981) describes the struggle undergone by one woman whose children had chosen to stay with their father. When I interviewed this same women she had become reconciled to the situation, and said the children, now in their late teens, appeared to be undamaged by their 'broken family'. Bharti (1981) also describes the recurrent pain of leaving her children in America, which she analysed in her post-sannyas book: 'I made my abandonment of my children into a moral principle, clothing it in spirituality. What could I offer them that was more important than my own Buddhahood? If I wasn't free, how could I hope that they would be?' (Franklin 1992, 56). Despite this *post-hoc* ambivalence, she admitted that 'Despite missing my kids, there was never a moment when I wanted to be anywhere else' (ibid., 135).

However, some women found motherhood and personal development more compatible. One woman had found motherhood 'one of the greatest gifts that's ever happened in my life', and managed to combine it easily with meditation and communal living. Another had experienced the conflict between motherhood and 'growth' with her first children, when she felt 'much more concerned with going on my own trip, doing my things, than being a mother, and I sometimes felt being a mother was in the way – I couldn't be a mother and devote myself to my own spiritual growth.' However, this had now changed with her younger child. Asked whether motherhood was a distraction to discipleship, she replied:

> It is and it isn't. It is in that you cannot give yourself the time, the space, the attention to grow spiritually, and at the same time give that time and attention to a child. But the other side of it is that giving that total motherhood to a child is a clear path to spiritual growth. For me it's a very clear path to discovering all kinds of very deep things about myself. I wasn't ready for it first time round, but second time round I was absolutely ready for it, and I felt I was growing as a person by giving my own needs up, putting my own needs aside for a while and being totally with this child.

Interestingly, the men I interviewed who had children were all divorced and did not have custody, nor any regular contact. My sample was too small to generalize from, but it is still significant that, as in the wider society, it was the women who were left holding the baby, often at the expense of their spiritual practice. One of my female respondents had separated from her husband in Poona and returned to Britain with her children, while he remained in the ashram pursuing his spiritual growth: 'There was also no question for him that it was exactly right. He realized that he needed to be without a family, without those ties, without kids, without a wife – to be there for nobody but himself.'

Any monastic community that allows families produces the same dilemma, including Buddhist monasteries: 'The monastic role takes precedence over marital and parental roles, and it can take time and energy away from them' (Tipton 1982, 148). Some people believe the main reason for imposing celibacy on monks is practical, to avoid the emotional and financial distractions of family life, as expressed by one of my respondents who had been a nun in a Korean Zen monastery. The FWBO has experimented with various community structures and found that single-sex ones work best, reducing the psychological dependence, conflict and entanglements of family life. The individual 'can then live with others who are also trying to become free, and together they can inspire each other to yet greater freedom' (Subhuti 1985, 166).

In America, on the other hand, there is a growing tendency

for Buddhist monasteries to be non-segregated, combining single and married practitioners, sometimes including children. Boucher interviewed mothers in many monasteries and found a variety of experience: 'Some mothers are bitter because their needs are not addressed by the male-biased groups with whom they've practiced. Some women who plunged deeply into practice when their children were small now feel guilty for having neglected their family responsibilities; others chose to sacrifice formal practice and sought to realize mindfulness within the perfection of their domestic duties and their work to earn a living. A few women speak of motherhood as a path in itself' (1985, 326).

Some Buddhist groups are finding ways to accommodate mothers and children, appreciating the particular benefits they can bring to a community. Some members see mothers as the strongest and most grounded members, with 'the clearest overall picture of what it's like to be a woman and a mother and Buddhist and worker and sometimes priest' (ibid., 253). But in other communities there is much prejudice, and women 'have been forced to choose between their duties with their children and their spiritual quests, and have sometimes been treated as lesser beings' (ibid., 328). As in the Osho movement, some women feel guilty of neglect, even though their children do not feel neglected. Again, other women were able to successfully integrate their lives through incorporating their domestic duties as 'mindful practice': 'I was just determined that wherever I was would be practice. At my work, that would be practice, at home it would be practice, and here [in the monastery] it would be practice' (ibid., 333).

## Childcare and Education

It may be that communes are inevitably hostile towards couples and families, since these relationships drain emotional energy away from the group, competing with community feelings. In most successful nineteenth-century communes, family life was minimalized. Children were often separated from parents and cared for communally, reducing the emotional and functional importance of the family. At Oneida, children were reared by women other than their mothers in a Children's House, thus encouraging women to renounce 'selfish philoprogenitiveness' and direct their maternal love to the whole community.[11]

The best known large-scale attempt at communal child-rearing in this century is the Israeli kibbutz, which has aroused much interest and admiration but has been criticized by the Bergers for producing a personality and value system that is 'emphatically collectivistic and conformist' (1983, 158). However, they admit to writing a 'defense of the bourgeois family' (ibid., 192) and also denounce the child-rearing practices of American communes in somewhat emotive terms:

> The data collected on these experiments are overwhelmingly negative: children subjected to bizarre and frequently damaging experimentation, instability in all the relationships significant to the child, neglect and neurosis, and children suffering from all sorts of physical and emotional deprivations. (ibid., 158)

Child abuse and indoctrination are the two most frequent and contentious charges made regarding the treatment of children in NRMs, particularly by the ACM. A recent report investigating organized and ritual child abuse by Jean La Fontaine, commissioned by the British government, confirmed that evangelical and fundamentalist religious groups were at the root of most allegations, but that there was no evidence of ritual or satanic abuse. She warned that 'concern with satanic abuse draws attention away from the very serious state of the minority of damaged children' (1994, 31) with the result that the real causes of their disturbed behaviour may not be properly investigated. Her conclusions offer an explanation for these delusions:

> A belief in evil cults is convincing because it draws on powerful cultural axioms. People are reluctant to accept that parents, even those classed as social failures, will harm their own children, and even invite others to do so, but involvement with the devil explains it. . . . Demonizing the marginal poor and linking them to unknown Satanists turns intractable cases of abuse into manifestations of evil. (ibid.)

Objective research has found that children in NRMs are usually brought up with at least as much love and care as are children in mainstream society – and more than in children's homes or some boarding schools. The loss of intimacy and privacy may be compensated by gains of freedom, richness and variety of adult relationships, as well as the benefits to children and parents of shared childcare. Generalizations are often made – as so often in childcare issues – without taking the children's own views into account or the differences between movements. In general, there is more evidence of child abuse in the mainstream churches and fundamentalist Christian sects than in NRMs, particularly of severe corporal punishment in fundamentalist sects and sexual abuse by paedophile Catholic priests.[12]

The most offensive instances of abuse have been found in a Christian NRM, the Children of God (COG). The daughter of the leader, David Berg, accused him of incest and sexual abuse and of encouraging such behaviour in his followers (Davis 1984). His main concern seems to have been for children to grow up free of problems by loving their bodies and discovering sex naturally. He encouraged such activities as sexual self-examination, nude mixed bathing, and sex and marriage among young teenagers. In addition, some Mo Letters do endorse child–adult sex and even incest, using the Bible as justification (Melton 1994). However, the COG claim they did not follow Berg's advice on incest, which is abhorrent to them. The British leader claims to have only known of three perpetrators of child–adult sex, who have all been excommunicated (Hardman 1992). There have been various court cases concerning child abuse in the COG recently, including one in Australia in 1992 in which 140 children were taken into care in a dawn raid, but quickly returned owing to lack of evidence. A 1996 case in Britain also found no evidence to warrant giving custody of a child to her grandmother in order to remove her from the movement; there was no statement that the mother was bad or inadequate, the sole grounds being her membership of the COG. The price of winning the case was for the COG to denounce their leader's earlier pronouncements on childhood sexuality. Since Berg's death last year, the childhood guidelines have been rewritten, and he is said to have made statements from beyond the grave condemning his excesses and apologising for any harm caused.

There is no evidence of child abuse in the Osho movement. All the parents I interviewed as well as the children who had grown up in a sannyasin commune felt that the children had mainly benefited thereby, that they were loved and mostly well taken care of. They were mainly positive about motherhood in India, despite the difficulties of health and nutrition:

> I felt a child in India was a hell of a lot safer than a child growing up in the West. They love kids there, they're holy. I think kids have a charmed life in the East. When we walked into a restaurant, she would be taken to the kitchen, played with, fed chappatis. You could never take your kid at that awful squawky age when they're one to a restaurant in England. But there I could take her everywhere I went, there was space for kids, they were a part of life. And I think that's very healthy.

Nowadays there is much concern in the West about the growing number of single-parent families, but the consensus is that children suffer more from the poverty trap and its ensuing problems than the loss of a parent *per se*. In the Poona ashram these disadvantages were largely overcome through cheap local childcare, the ashram's own rather rudimentary school, and the willingness of other sannyasins to help. The weight of responsibility was also eased psychologically by the widespread belief that Osho himself had taken on personal responsibility for the children, and had a psychic connection with them even if he had never met them. One quoted him as saying 'Don't worry about your kids, I'm looking after them'. Thus mothers were released from the burdens of childcare for meditation. This is an advantage also appreciated by Buddhist mothers (Boucher 1993).

Research is divided on the effects of an absent father in society and in NRMs, but Osho, in common with some spiritual feminists, gave fatherhood diminished significance:

> Kids should belong to the commune, and the commune should take care of the kids. The mother should be known, who the mother is, but the father should not be known – there is no need. That was the original state of humanity: matriarchal. Then society became patriarchal: father became important. And with the father came a thousand and one illnesses. (1978, 305)[13]

For sannyasin mothers, the problem of the absent father was largely offset by the major perceived benefit of communal life: the children's experience of an extended family, especially the availability of other adults as carers, close adult friends and as alternative role models. Although some mothers felt that more stability and more commitment from the fathers would have been beneficial, most people echoed Osho's teaching on the damage done to children by looking for a partner moulded solely on their opposite-sex parent as role model, and valued the communal model:

> Probably the best thing we could do was be there, because [my daughter] did have father figures, good men friends who reached out to her, loved her, took an interest in her, and she still has those connections. And she now has good, balanced relationships with men, no problems with boyfriends.

In Rajneeshpuram and Medina, proper schools were opened in line with government regulations, and the children were also integrated into the community through working part-time as part of their education. The Medina children lived in a 'kids' house', but were allowed to see their parents whenever they wanted and to sleep with them. The long working hours during this period meant parents were unable to spend much time with their children, so the relationships tended to suffer. Some mothers later regretted this deprivation, but in general the system was felt to work well: 'It was wonderful to have the kids taken off my hands. The relief of not having to keep together the house, the business, and the kids! And it was wonderful having so much help with the kids.'

There is now an international sannyasin school with 70 students, Osho Ko Hsuan in Devon, England. Attendance is voluntary, but full-time sannyasins normally prefer to send their children there if they can afford the fees. The school initially provided a liberal, non-academic education based on Osho's somewhat eccentric theory of 'five-dimensional education', containing a balance between informative subjects, creativity, the art of living and the art of dying.[14] At the request of the children – with some resistance from the more libertarian staff! – the national curriculum has been introduced, leading to the GCSE examination, the results of which are in line with the national average. Government inspectors have given positive reports on the educational and social aspects of the school, highlighting the good atmosphere and relationships.

The vision of the school is strongly child-centred, based on Osho's ideal of sannyasins as harbingers of the 'New Man'. Adult sannyasins were considered too socially conditioned to reach this state themselves, but could become parents of the New Child, who would flourish free of the conditioning that had obstructed the spiritual development of their parents.[15] There is little authority structure, with an emphasis on co-operation rather than discipline. In practice the rules are created and maintained by staff, but often in response to students' requests. Teachers and students have equal status, and a relationship based on trust and friendship. Policy on social organization, as on education, is flexible according to changing needs, so that order and stability are now valued over the earlier more experimental approach, helped by cooking and cleaning rotas. Weekly meetings are attended by staff and students, who have equal voices and air any complaints uninhibitedly. Altogether, it amounts to an impressive demonstration of pupil participation in management, a process now being introduced in state schools.

As they grow up, sannyasin children have diverged in different directions. Some have dropped sannyas, merging into society. Some are full-time sannyasins, spending most of their time in Poona or travelling round the world. Whether they leave or remain sannyasins, more nowadays are going to university, training or working in a career, usually creative or service-oriented like their parents. They tend to stick together in a group, but this is typical of any children who have grown up in a close community segregated from the rest of society, such as ex-pupils of Summerhill or, indeed, any boarding school.

## Socialization and Indoctrination

A common charge against NRMs is indoctrination of the children. It is ironic that most accusations come from the ACM, which is largely composed of conservative Christians, whose schools inculcate the heaviest indoctrination. The Christian School Movement claims: 'The battle for the Christian school is thus the battle for the faith' (Rose 1990, 100). Their schools provide a deliberate programme of indoctrination involving subtle socialization as well as explicit teachings, with the aim of producing Christians and reinforcing traditional authoritarian and patriarchal values. Hardman (1992) researched the similar Accelerated Christian Education (ACE) in Britain. Their schools are institutions proclaiming 'one doctrine, one truth and one way', providing a 'highly censored and disciplined education' in which the children are isolated from their peers and beaten for disrespect and defiance. Their philosophy of education may be summarized in their own words: 'Disobedience is a sin. Rebellion is anathema. God punishes sinners.' A simple theory of gender roles is also instilled: 'A boy needs to learn submission to God, a girl submission to her husband.'

Rudin (1984) accuses 'cults' of actively recruiting children. The Osho movement did not recruit children, but most parents give sannyas to their children, sometimes while they are still babies. Other children take sannyas voluntarily at a later age, as with the few non-sannyasin children at Ko Hsuan, though this may be through peer pressure. None of the parents feel they are imposing a religion on their children, but rather that it is the best gift they can give them, which the children are free to reject later. One mother explained:

> My experience of sannyas is not as a religion. It's an invitation to live life as honestly, as creatively, as spontaneously, as caringly, as totally in the moment as possible. To me it's the opposite of giving [my son] a fixed religion. It's inviting him to see what his reality is, and how he experiences life, rather than giving him a list of set rules.

This is in line with Osho's teaching: 'When I give sannyas to a child, it is not that you have to impose an ideology on him. You have just to persuade him towards meditativeness. . . . One day he will be grateful for it – that you helped him' (1984, 185).

The next question is whether once in the movement, members (and in this case children) are subjected to indoctrination processes. Point 9 on the Ko Hsuan Manifesto reads: 'There is no religious, political or moral indoctrination.' Observers agree on the lack of systematic socialization, even in the more authoritarian communes of Rajneeshpuram and Medina.[16] Sannyasin ideology perceives family and society as the most abusive agents of indoctrination, as expressed by one spokesperson:

The real damage that the family perpetrates on the occupants of this planet is the indoctrination of each new generation. Successive waves of new young people are thus involuntarily inculcated with belief systems and values that conveniently support the status quo and the vested interests of the ruling elites, particularly the beliefs that maintain the church, the state, and the family itself – from which all other vested interests gain their nourishment. (Amrito 1989, 40)

At Ko Hsuan there are no signs of political or social indoctrination. Little interest is shown in world events by staff or students (who rarely read newspapers), apart from a general concern with environmentalism. Otherwise, the school reflects the libertarian values of the membership. There is some awareness of sexism among the staff, who are keen to combat unfounded beliefs and encourage boys and girls to study the same subjects and share roles. Accordingly, girls play football and boys chop carrots.

In terms of religious indoctrination, both staff and students insist that 'This is not a religious school.' There is no morning religious assembly and no formal religious education. Osho's meditations take place daily but optionally, and few teachers or students participate. Some feel it would benefit the ethos of the school if they were compulsory, but there are no attempts to coerce children into religious observance: 'We don't shove it down their throats.' This policy is considerably more liberal than the schools of organized religions and most other NRMs, where there is a far greater degree of compulsion. Even state schools are legally compelled to provide more in the way of religious education – which might be termed indoctrination, however soft in intent.

Sannyasin children accept Osho as their master, but in a relaxed, low-key way. Their attitude is less devotional than the adults, and they seem to see him less as an authority figure, more as a loving father or occasionally wise teacher. One girl who had grown up in Poona and Rajneeshpuram described Osho as someone who had 'opened my eyes a lot' but not as someone who could lead her to enlightenment, which she felt she could only do on her own. She also disliked sannyasins using Osho's words as an authority, since 'he's always contradicting himself, so you can't take him seriously. You have to

laugh, but some people take him totally seriously.' This attitude may be contrasted with Sahaja Yoga, where the emphasis
is on total devotion to the guru. Since members are perceived
as psychically linked to Mataji via their *chakras* (energy centres), children are particularly vulnerable to charges of being
mentally abnormal or possessed by evil spirits if they do not
comply.

Inevitably, sannyasin children are socialized, as happens not
only in an NRM but in any school and society. The point is
that the process is less overt, programmed and intensive than
in a typical British public school, let alone an evangelical school.
It is a case not of indoctrination but shared values. These
values bring Ko Hsuan closer to the English tradition of free
schools than to most other religious schools. Free schools
comprise a spectrum from secular schools like Summerhill,
through the more systematic Montessori schools, to the Steiner
schools that are within an NRM (Anthroposophy) but attended
by many non-members. Steiner schools are a popular choice
among New Agers, particularly one in Totnes, Devon (a centre
of the New Age in Britain), and another set up in conjunction
with the Findhorn community.

As in free schools, sannyasin children appear eminently
'normal', but with a preponderance of bright yet difficult pupils.
The children clearly enjoy their school, and receive an excellent personal and social education. The school can be said to
go a long way towards fulfilling Osho's vision of the commune
as a superior substitute for the nuclear family, particularly in
a context where most pupils come from split families. As such,
it may offer a model to the wider society. The key difference
between Ko Hsuan and a typical free school lies in its spiritual
vision. One teacher commented that in many ways it was
similar to Summerhill, but 'There's nothing like a master
behind Summerhill, though Neill himself [the founder and
headmaster] was a great guy.'

There is clearly an important distinction between fundamentalist religious schools that practice systematic indoctrination and schools influenced by more liberal ideologies such as
the Human Potential Movement and Eastern meditation. This
is important at a time when all schools are grappling with the
paradoxes of education in a pluralist, multi-faith society. On
the one hand our democratic ideal of tolerance, particularly

in a multi-faith society, requires freedom of worship rather than imposing the dominant religion on other faiths; on the other hand ethical and spiritual concerns are crucially on the agenda, requiring some form of educational response and input. Whether the New Child becomes the New Man/Woman has yet to be seen, but in the meantime Osho Ko Hsuan offers an original and challenging model of alternative education.

In terms of social organization and lifestyle, the commune worked well for sannyasin mothers and children. The perceived benefits were an ideology that was paradoxically pro-child though anti-family; the convenience of communal childcare; and a varied, stimulating social environment – an emotional substitute for the extended family. This last benefit helped compensate for the widespread absence of fathers in the children's lives. On the whole, the experiment was a challenging but successful alternative for children and their mothers, particularly for single mothers. Self-realization was perceived as a prerequisite for good parenting: a path that offered women a radical fulfilling alternative to the traditional paths for social, emotional and spiritual development. As Ursula King says:

> An exclusive insistence on the special experience of womanhood does seem to give biological dimensions a priority over all other considerations of human experience. Why not equally emphasise other spheres of women's experience, especially those of work and creativity? Why not consider all dimensions of the self-creating, self-defining and self-transcending activities of women? (1989, 79)

As with other social and spiritual issues, NRMs offer women a range of options from the traditional nuclear family to childless freedom. The choices and experiences of women regarding religion have close parallels with their secular equivalents. Women who accept motherhood as their vocation and are looking for a stable, secure family life therefore tend to be drawn to conservative old and new movements. The price of these benefits, as with non-working mothers, is a loss of liberty, self-determination and other possibilities for growth. Women who prefer to focus on their personal development tend to choose religions such as Buddhism, the Osho movement, and Paganism. The price paid by women with children in these movements, as with career women, is the stress of combining motherhood with an often arduous regime of work and spiritual practice. But where a good system of support for mothers and children is provided, the commune may be seen as a positive and practical alternative to the nuclear family.

# 7 Gender Roles, Work and Power

Women who are full-time members of NRMs have to cope with similar problems to working women in secular life such as combining work and motherhood; challenging unequal opportunities and glass ceilings; discovering how to be a female manager, whether imitating, surpassing or departing from the male model. The workplace is, however, changing in favour of women, partly as a result of women's presence in larger numbers and higher positions, partly through the influence of HPM values on management training and business philosophy. The result is an increasing emphasis on ethics, human values and personal development, including teamwork rather than hierarchy; co-operation rather than competition; relationship as against status; sharing, mentoring, helping and supporting colleagues and junior staff for mutual benefit rather than personal gain. These changes are encouraging a more caring, collaborative style of management within flatter structures. The process is sometimes termed the 'feminization of work' and promoted in some training approaches such as action learning (Weinstein 1995). It leads to the logical argument that women are more effective managers of these new-style working environments.

As with businesses, some of which have produced innovative, creative and humane solutions, while others are changing slowly and reluctantly or becoming even more entrenched in sexism, NRMs show similar ranges of response to the issues. Most NRMs are Christian-based or Eastern imports, hence tend to reflect the traditional values of these societies, including sexism. However, a few support equal opportunities and even positive discrimination, recognizing that women have unique talents and are equally capable of displaying leadership qualities.

## Gender Roles in NRMs

In most of the world's religions women have played a subordinate role, excluded from participating in public rituals and often barred from even entering places of worship. One might expect more liberated practice in NRMs, particularly in the light of feminist advances. Yet despite the range of radical experimentation around sexuality and family structures, research demonstrates that women tend to perform traditional – that is, subservient – work and religious functions.

It is perhaps predictable that the ACM should present negative evidence on female status in NRMs: 'the low valuation of women in cults is often expressed most directly in a common cult practice that demands males be eagerly served as avatars by the cult's females. Most females are only tolerated as economic resources as they serve to advance the patriarchal lineage of the cult leader'.[1] Unfortunately, sociological research tends to agree with these findings, particularly in conservative Christian movements.

Harder's research on 'Sex Roles in the Jesus Movement' demonstrated how 'this movement of young women into the traditional, rigid, submissive roles of the Jesus Movement contrasts with another current social movement, the women's liberation movement'. She exposed the hypocritical contradiction that 'All jobs done by the brothers and sisters have equal status according to the fundamentalist theology of the group, even though they are rigidly separated on the basis of sex and in reality are accorded quite different statuses.' She concluded that 'the behavioral expectation of submissiveness is perhaps the dominant expectation for all role positions filled by females in this religious commune'. The only ray of light in this grim picture was that there were a few changes towards greater equality during the two years of her research. Her sceptical interpretation was that: 'We view these changes as indications of the pastors' attempts to gain more female members . . . the basic role structure of the group remains the same' (1974, 345–9).

Rose also chose to study a New Christian Right commune 'because they have chosen to adopt and participate in a meaning system that emphasises submission of women to men in a time when the mainstream culture defines such blatant male domination as oppressive and archaic'. The women in this community called themselves 'prayer warriors' and 'exercise power through prayer'. In a religious system that legitimates male dominance, 'the majority of them are . . . active partners in decision-making and their husbands are active child caretakers'.

Yet despite these signs of progress, Rose's conclusion is that 'It appears that this group is representative of many other new religious groups that put much energy into thinking about and defining gender issues but which, in the end, tend to reassert traditional rather than new gender roles' (1987, 246–57). The fundamentalist hierarchy may be summarized as a chain of command from God to man to woman to nature.

Hindu-based NRMs have also tended to continue the Asian tradition of male dominance. Even in Sahaja Yoga, which is led by a woman, devotees are urged to follow traditional roles. In ISKCON men and women are philosophically equal, but 'the empirical evidence points to a certain reluctance to put [the principles] into practice' (Knott 1987, 125). Prabhupada himself was ambivalent, sometimes emphasizing that the soul is beyond gender which is therefore irrelevant, sometimes endorsing traditional Hindu views of gender, including the conservative mores of Manu (see p.202). In the 1970s, male devotees took advantage of this sexist tendency to reinforce female subservience. Women were made to stand at the back of the temple, a custom that shocks educated Indians as restrictive. They are still segregated from the men but at least now stand side by side. Their access to Prabhupada was restricted: the women had to cut vegetables while the men accompanied Prabhupada on his morning walk.

Since Prabhupada's death there has been a strong reaction by women and some men, and gender policies are being openly debated within the movement. A recent issue of their magazine was devoted to women's viewpoints. While acknowledging the Vedic belief that 'women must be protected, they should be naturally chaste and submissive, and they are naturally shy', there was much questioning of the policy that women are welcome to cook and clean but excluded from spiritual and secular leadership positions.[2] This challenge was led mainly by vocal women speaking out, writing, participating in management structures and lobbying for reform. It was, however, supported by some men who realized that their marriages were falling apart on account of their mistreatment of women. The balance has at least shifted dramatically from 20 years ago, when 80 per cent of women devotees agreed that women should be submissive to men; nowadays only 30 per cent believe this. Women in the Western temples are now beginning to participate a little more in the priestly role, at least in the upkeep of shrines. There are also now a few women on the governing body, but the most influential function in the movement is teaching, and older women members are too subjugated by past humiliation to want to teach. The younger women do want to but are hampered by lack of encouragement or role models. The highest post of all is guru; women are theoretically now entitled to hold this office, but so far no women have been appointed.

The only Hindu-based NRM that directly challenges Indian misogyny is the Brahma Kumaris movement, which 'is without doubt a movement where women control men. Women occupy positions of power and status, whereas men, both in their secular and religious roles are subordinate to women' (Skultans 1993, 47). In some respects it offers a complete role reversal: 'Men look after the practical aspects of living thus freeing women for higher spiritual duties.' In other words, they 'appear to be playing the role of wives'. This leads to the interesting and rare phenomenon that 'male pupil and female mentor is a typical combination' (ibid., 50–1). The BKs are demonstrating their theory that sexual abstinence produces more energy for service, and their style of engaged spirituality may be compared with more world-accepting orders of nuns engaged in teaching and social work. Although Skultans does not implicitly term it a feminist movement, her study makes it clear that there is an implicit feminist ideology. This is admitted by some of the women leaders but not stressed. Babb found that 'gender and sexual issues are muted in the movement's current persona, which has been deliberately focused on the culturally less provocative theme of world peace' (1986, 153).

Buddhism presents the interesting paradox that despite its freedom from doctrinal inequality, patriarchy arose, until it became: 'an overwhelmingly male-created institution dominated by a patriarchal power structure. As a consequence of this male dominance, the feminine is frequently associated with the secular, powerless, profane, and imperfect' (Paul 1979, xix). This was exemplified by the eight extra rules for ordained women, which are still imposed in the Theravada tradition. Buddhist misogyny has been vigorously challenged both in writing and practice, particularly in America. Boucher (1985) and Friedman

(1987) based their books on extensive research into the growing number of women teachers in America, who are introducing many changes through their questioning and pragmatic attitudes towards the tradition (see Chapter 8).

The FWBO in Britain shares in this questioning, though perhaps less radically than their American counterparts. The official line is that 'men and women enjoy equal "status" and have access to the same opportunities and facilities for serious Dharma practice', via a 'middle way between the traditional subordination of women within the sangha ... and a demand for equality in a purely secular sense.'[3] This could be interpreted as a compromise, and the problems have been more frankly addressed in an internal newsletter. One long-term member expressed disquiet to me at the under-representation of women in the higher echelons, while an ex-member felt that Sangharakshita was unsympathetic towards women and reluctant to ordain them.

Comparative research on gender roles in NRMs has found an across-the-board subordination of women, even where the ideology was non-discriminatory. In the Eastern groups she studied, Aidala found that ideologically 'No differences were seen in the abilities of men and women to attain self perfection or "higher consciousness" which was held to be the only relevance in life.' However, translated into daily life, 'Concern for such mundane matters as the tendency of male members of the commune to avoid household chores was scorned as evidence of wrong or limited consciousness.' In other words, 'The quest for personal transcendence in such groups most often resulted in the reproduction of traditional patterns of gender relations, however refurbished with spiritual explanations' (1985, 295). But whatever the ideological differences, 'in none of the religious communes did ideological formulation or practice pose a direct challenge to the traditional allocation of greater social and economic power to men' (ibid., 297). Even in secular groups the findings were the same: 'socio–metric analysis of informal power structures and comparison of the sexual division of labor within communes shows relatively little difference in the subordinate role of women in religious and nonreligious groups' (ibid., 310, note 14).

Jacobs's (1984) study was also comparative, including Christian and Eastern-based groups. All the groups researched were male-dominated with a male leader, and the members were mainly young women. Again, the women were usually confined to subordinate roles, mainly domestic service. They were initially happy because of their affective ties to the leader, but this often led to exploitation, which ultimately resulted in deconversion. Jacobs found that all the women's responsibilities 'were related to the domestic service aspect of affiliation rather than to specific spiritual duties' (ibid., 159). Furthermore, in the secular realm they had no access to decision-making and lost control over their personal lives as men controlled all areas including marriage, children, work. 'The overall effect is a system in which men are dominant, women are submissive, and the exercise of male power leads to almost total subordination of female devotees' (ibid., 158).

More recent research finds changes, probably reflecting the impact of feminism throughout Western society. Robbins notes that although most of the research on women and gender roles in NRMs has revealed 'a regression to absolutist, sexist and patriarchal patterns ... there is also evidence of women being *empowered* by NRMs', particularly in the women's spirituality movement.[4] However, Goddess-worshipping and other Pagan groups tend to be part-time religions whose members have outside jobs and meet specifically for spiritual work. They may live in small communal households, but these rarely provide full-time work, so the issues of inequality and discrimination in work do not arise.

So far the only research finding evidence of female empowerment in NRMs with male leaders is by Palmer (1994), whose interview data and sex ratio surveys challenge prevailing notions that 'cultswomen' are the passive victims of the ineluctable forces of charisma, 'brainwashing' or 'patriarchal authority', leading her to the conclusion that 'the innovations in sex roles and sexual mores presently developing in NRMs, far from representing a neo-conservative reaction against "mainstream" experimentation and feminism, might more accurately be characterized as offering even more extreme, intensified and diverse versions of the ongoing experimentation already occuring outside these utopias.' Wiccan covens are normally led by a priest and priestess with equal status, and a strong emphasis on female empowerment (see Chapter 9).

## The Feminization of Work in the Osho Movement

The Osho movement is not included in any of the comparative studies of gender roles in NRMs discussed above, which
is surprising, given the unusualness of the movement in this
respect. The difference is that, apart from the Brahma Kumaris,
it is the only movement that has a female majority in leadership and administrative roles. Yet inevitably most sannyasins
in Poona I, male and female, were rank-and-file workers,
sometimes in creative occupations such as the various arts
and crafts, but often unskilled, low-status work such as cleaning. As discussed, women doing domestic work in NRMs is
generally interpreted by feminists as exploitative, but the issue
is complex, as even Jacobs notes: 'women are both attracted to
and repelled by traditions that prescribe femininity and do-
mesticity'. She interprets this phenomenon as 'indicative of a
larger cultural phenomenon in which contemporary women
choose to adopt and live by rigid patriarchal norms in exchange for the promise of familial security and male approval
and love' (1991, 347). Simple manual labour could be a positive choice, however, sometimes in reaction to parental pressure to succeed: 'I could relax, and didn't have to prove I was
as good as a man. It was OK just to do female things like
cleaning, cooking, housework. I enjoyed it and could admit I
enjoyed it. I didn't have to be a scientist, doctor, lawyer or
something.'

Goldman found that this opportunity to work for a purpose
other than ambition had a particular relevance for sannyasin
women, whom she had researched as a possible 'extreme example of the many American women who, whatever their age
or social position, equivocate and back away from the fruits of
occupational success' (1988, 18). Her findings showed a positive result: 'The high-achieving women of Rajneeshpuram found
a sense of completion and release in their work. They were
honored for their skill in serving Rajneesh and his commune,
while in the outside world they had previously received ambivalent social responses to their achievement' (20).

Tipton noticed a similar problem and resolution in Zen
students, which he analysed as part of the counter-cultural
dilemma:

Zen Center makes high demands for active accomplishment
and inner discipline on sixties youth earlier socialized to both.
... In the professional and managerial world of upper-
middle-class adulthood, these sixties youths faced the duality of individual success or failure.... They shied away from
this ultimatum, as much from fear of success as failure ...
they have found in Zen Center the possibility of transcending the predicament of these conflicting life plans. (1982,
166)

These are secular explanations, which assume a negative
rejection of the career path out of fear of failure or success,
ignoring the positive counter-cultural rejection of scientific
materialism and the Protestant Ethic: 'In the new paradigm,
work is a vehicle for transformation'.[5] For seekers, the spiritual
rationale for simple work is uppermost. Sannyasins believed,
'The work was your meditation, and if you were total in your
work then meditation would happen.' The technical basis for
this belief is that simple, repetitive work slows down the mind
'so there wasn't time to daydream; one's mind had to be in
the present moment.' The combination of awareness and
energy (a frequent admonition was 'Put your total energy into
your work') could lead to profound spiritual experience:

Perhaps just making shoes ... but making them with such
intensity and totality that you are completely lost in the act,
and you are far more blessed than any president can be.
The moment you are lost in work, you become almost like
a flute on the lips of existence itself.... You become a vehicle.
(Osho 1987, 247)

Working with meditative awareness, commitment and total
energy would lead more easily to creativity, another important
goal. Osho taught that any kind of work should be creative,
even cleaning:

Cleaning a floor can be a tremendously creative act. Remember, creativity has nothing to do with any particular
work. Creativity has something to do with the quality of your
consciousness.... Creativity means enjoying any work as
meditation; doing any work with deep love. If you love me
and you clean this auditorium, it is creative. If you don't
love me then of course it is a chore.... Are you thinking

that if you paint, you will feel creative? But painting is just as ordinary as cleaning the floor. You will be throwing colors on a canvas. Here you go on washing the floor, cleaning the floor. What is the difference? (1984, 273–4)

This purpose was enshrined in ashram practice. Strelley describes being taught how to clean a room: the elaborate ritual but also the spiritual purpose, as explained by her co-ordinator: '"You have to remember: You're not just cleaning the outside, you're cleaning the *inside* of yourself".... She illustrated [the technique] with quick, graceful movements, for all the world like an impromptu ballet' (1987, 89; her italics).

A further spiritual dimension was work as devotion: 'There's part of me that loves devotion, and creating a beautiful space for people [through cleaning]. I loved the fact that sannyas created the opportunity for devotion, because it is very alien in the West.' This belief could be interpreted as dangerous for women, but unlike most NRMs there was no gender segregation of work roles. As many men as women were cooking and cleaning, and men also appreciated the opportunity to develop nurturing, devotional qualities. The culmination of devotion was work directly concerning the guru's person:

> Since I had been with Osho my life had changed in a way that I could never have imagined. I was so happy and fulfilled that to do Osho's laundry was my way of expressing gratitude. And the funny thing is, the more lovingly and carefully I did His clothes, the more fulfilled I felt and so it was like a circle of energy that kept returning to me. (Shunyo 1992, 20)

This sanctification of menial work for cultivating humility is common in all religious traditions, including Christian monasticism. Herrera describes her mother's shocked exclamation at seeing her ironing Maharishi Mahesh Yogi's robes: 'Do you even have to do his laundry?' to which she replies, 'Yes, darling, and I consider it an honor' (1992, 145). In an interview published in the feminist magazine *Spare Rib*, the interviewers questioned the morality of Osho being 'looked after hand and foot', and the interviewee offers a rationale: 'people who are around him feel that what they want from him and what he can give them is so important that they want him to put energy into that. For him to put energy into cooking his food and cleaning his room is a waste, as we would see it' (Fell 1977, 9). However, this practice is not confined to devotional religion. In the Theravadin Buddhist community of Amaravrati, feminists found it hard to cook and wash up, but then 'discovered the beauty of yielding' (Goswell 1989).

A couple of my respondents had difficulty initially with being given such menial work, but became reconciled eventually. One 'felt it as a putdown' but grew to love it. Another discovered how to 'make it into an art you could be proud of', encouraged by Osho's teaching on cleaning as creativity. However, another woman failed to find creative fulfilment in cleaning:

> I've always experienced ordinary simple work as something that gives me tremendous deep experience – as long as I'm not tired out and anxious. I experienced it as worship when there were creative possibilities, but if I had to just clean toilets and bedrooms which I thought were very grim and bare anyway, and I couldn't make them look nice, all I could do was make them clean, I got very bored and found it very barren. And that happened more and more towards the end.

Whereas cleaning was considered primarily an opportunity to express devotion, kitchen work was believed to be about 'working through resistance', which could be problematic:

> The kitchen was the hardest department to work in. I was totally in love with massage, and people loved the way I was working. I'd moved into the ashram with these great expectations about being the massage therapist, but basically found myself chopping carrots and sweeping floors, and I went through my resistance, and was always getting into trouble, being told to surrender. Finally it ended up with me having a huge fight.

Reflecting on the experience later, she deduced:

> Surrender was very easy when it had a spiritual dimension like sitting in front of Bhagwan in meditation, when it was love and heart. But if you asked me to surrender to 12 hours

of chopping carrots or being dictated to by some obnoxious fool, I wasn't very good at surrendering at all.

Another woman described the kitchen as 'a horrible hell-hole', which through her determination she transformed into 'an enlightenment box'. This attitude reflects Osho's doctrine of 'devices', which he traced back to Sufi and Zen masters via Gurdjieff. Whether in the form of a sudden shock (the 'Zen stick') or a prolonged test, the purpose was to dissolve the ego's 'blocks' and resistances to provoke an enlightenment experience. Bharti has a chapter on 'Work as a Zen koan', and explains: 'Bhagwan doesn't give us koans to meditate on; he gives us koans to live. He does that continually with the work around the ashram' (1981, 60). This belief was reflected in the language of disciples: 'The whole thing was to drop the ego: opinions, illusions about who I am, what is right and wrong. So I was constantly being tested, and in a way getting a "Zen stick" from the master in the work I was doing, in everything that was going on for me.' Despite the claimed link with the Zen tradition, this is where Osho's concept of the purpose of work begins to diverge. Tipton makes no mention of this purpose at Zen Center, which appears to be a more straight-forward 'diligent, careful, quiet effort, unattached to outcome yet attentive to process', the purpose being 'to fulfill one's own life, serve others, and express their interdependent unity' (1982, 155).

In Poona I there was widespread agreement that this un-usual but not unprecedented approach to work as spiritual growth was benevolently motivated and effective. This subjec-tive conviction must be set against the outside perception of these processes as instruments of social control, although even at this time there were some abuses. On the one hand, un-skilled jobs were perceived as a test of surrender and commit-ment, and therefore to be welcomed as a 'gift'; on the other hand, they could also be used as a punitive measure. Strelley claimed that this negative attitude intensified later as the hier-archy became more defined, so that such work became per-ceived 'as a punishment, rather than a unique learning position' (1987, 264). One of my respondents believed that she had been given hard, menial work as a punishment for being a rebel. Another described extreme mistreatment by her boss, but had remained there because she had felt it was all 'leading somewhere'; she also believed she had 'grown' by eventually finding the courage to stand up to the abuse.

In Rajneeshpuram, as already described, the utopian vision of 'doing Bhagwan's work' began to turn sour until the City for the New Man began to resemble a glorified labour camp. Sannyasins worked a seven-day week, in which the hours kept increasing until in the later stages a 16-hour day became the norm and 18 hours not uncommon. Responses to this tough regime varied, but eventually even the most dedicated disciples began to find the exhaustion insupportable. Yet even following the bitterness of the débâcle, and with the wisdom of hindsight, many continued to support the experiment. It is hard to assess a social experiment that provoked such polarized responses. Franklin, who suffered for years at Rajneeshpuram, could not make up her mind whether the experiment was a Gurdjieffian 'spiritual technique of awareness under pressure' or 'a sadistic experiment to see how far people could be pushed before they collapsed' (1992, 221).

## Women in Power: an Experiment in Positive Discrimination

The most interesting and significant aspect of this attempt to create a new work ethic is that it was largely managed by women. From Osho's teaching two opposite models of femininity can be extrapolated. The ideal of woman as devotee has already been discussed in detail. The second model – which could be perceived as conflicting, but was understood by sannyasins as complementary – was an equal opportunities vision of woman freed of the shackles of centuries-old conditioning, reclaiming her power:

> My own vision is that the coming age will be the age of the woman. Man has tried for five thousand years and has failed. Now a chance has to be given to the woman. Now she should be given the reins of all the powers. She should be given an opportunity to bring her feminine energies to function, to work.[6]

This ideology was reflected in the social organization. Osho was always clearly in the position of ultimate authority, but as the movement grew he came to rely more and more on his deputies, who were mainly women. Almost every department in Poona and Rajneeshpuram was headed by a woman, including the technical and construction services, the administration, press office, publications, as well as more traditionally female-run areas such as the kitchen and cleaning department. Estimates agree that about 80 per cent of the top jobs at Rajneeshpuram were held by women.[7] As Franklin noted at Rajneeshpuram: 'The only sexist roles were administrative ones: the majority of coordinators were women' (1992, 191).

Interpretations of the reasons for this positive discrimination vary. Osho's explanation was inspirational: 'I want [the commune] to be run by the heart, because to me, to be feminine is to become vulnerable, to become receptive. To be feminine is to allow; to be feminine is to wait. . . . Yes, the ashram is run by women because I want it run by the heart.'[8] This policy also had a pragmatic goal. He often quoted Buddha as stating that his commune would have lasted 5000 years until he allowed women, as a result of which it would only last 500. Osho believed that, on the contrary, '*My* commune can live 5000 years or more, because I have started it with women!'[9] Fitzgerald argued that Osho 'put women in charge of practical matters', in order to 'ensure that his authority would remain unchallenged. As he himself told his disciples, "The open secret is that you can be free only if you have put too many women around you. Then they are so concerned with each other, they leave you absolutely alone . . . Their jealousies, their envies are enough to keep them occupied."' (1981, 321) Although presented as a joke, his comment may reflect a certain sexist prejudice as well as revealing the workings of charismatic authority. However, it was widely believed by sannyasins that it was logical to put women in charge of a feminized workplace. Decision-making processes were based on intuition rather than reason or empiricism. Caring was considered a higher value than efficiency in work processes. Devotion and meditation were higher goals than productivity, and gains in these areas more significant than financial profit. Competition was to be renounced in favour of co-operation, placing public good over personal advancement. Power-seekers were frowned upon and regarded as less spiritual. It was believed that administrators were worldly, while therapists had big egos; the cleaner was the paradigm of right livelihood – humble, devoted, creative and contented.

Latkin's (1987) PAQ test found that both male and female sannyasins described their ideal leader or manager as high on female qualities, which is the opposite to the norm. The sannyasin model of management worked well in Poona and the early days of Rajneeshpuram as a two-tier co-operative system, with men running the technical side and women in charge of the administrative and personnel aspects. This produced a good balance between efficiency and a nurturing, motherly workplace ethos. The system began to break down in Rajneeshpuram at top management level. One man who had worked closely with Osho, thought that

> The biggest handicap was that Osho would determine what people would hold key positions, and in my and a lot of people's views these were sometimes totally unsuitable. The only thing I could think was that it was a Gurdjieffian device, but I thought it was a mistake. Like Gurdjieff he would issue impossible orders, but whereas Gurdjieff supervised his experiments directly, Osho ruled by proxy. I felt the urgent priority was to get things done, and the time for those sorts of games was past.

In Poona the system had worked partly owing to small size and simple technology, but in America the problems were exacerbated by an unwieldy, top-heavy bureaucracy, organized by women with no technical expertise responsible for sophisticated technologies. A further problem was increasing competition among the female co-ordinators, who were often new sannyasins without the training and experience of working in organizations. They were often appointed less for their professional or spiritual qualifications than for their loyalty to the woman who was now in charge of the entire operation: Sheela.

*Female Leadership in the Osho Movement*
There is evidence that women have sometimes been historically significant as the power behind a prophet's throne.[10] This was certainly the case with Osho, whose main emotional support in the first phase of his teaching was his devoted cousin, Kranti. The most important single follower from 1969 to 1981

was Laxmi, the daughter of a prominent Jain businessman and member of the Indian National Congress Party, and herself secretary of the All-India Congress Women's Conference. Osho's biographer Joshi describes how 'First as Bhagwan's secretary and later as managing trustee of the Rajneesh Foundation in Poona, Laxmi has been largely instrumental in the expansion and growth of Bhagwan's work'. He describes the importance of her devotion and total belief in him in his transformation from Acharya to Bhagwan, and later in the maintenance of his charisma within the movement.[11] Laxmi perfectly illustrated Osho's dual idea of woman as devotee and power. In Osho's presence she was the epitome of nun-like meekness, following him into *darshan* with head covered and eyes downcast. Osho once said of her: 'Laxmi never does anything on her own. She is a perfect vehicle. That's why she has been chosen for that work' (1979b, 313).

The most prominent co-ordinators in Poona I were all markedly Amazonian in style, although, like Laxmi, they were all transformed into soft, receptive disciples in Osho's presence. One example was Deeksha, who ran the kitchen and was regarded as a Zen master for her toughness. Osho said of her: 'Deeksha is my device! I have given her total power . . . because she is so loving, so soft, so caring. She wounds people, but she heals also. By one hand she hammers, by the other she caresses' (1982a, 178). This dual function was confirmed by my respondents who worked under her: 'she was considered a very tough "dragon" master by lots of people, but was fine with me, very motherly but very firm'. Another of Deeksha's workers confirmed this impression, though more ambivalently, describing her as 'a very powerful, big fat lady. She was put there for a purpose, as Bhagwan described it. She was a perfect mother, because with one hand she's caressing you and with the other hand she's beating you.'

The woman with the greatest power in the history of the Osho movement was Sheela, who took over from Laxmi as Osho's personal secretary in 1981 and ran Rajneeshpuram until she left in September 1985. She was Indian by birth and American by marriage, and had known Osho since childhood. Like Laxmi, she seemed a very meek and simple person when she arrived at the ashram, but after her meteoric rise to power from humble beginnings in the kitchen to Laxmi's assistant, she was perceived as a tough and determined power-seeker. Davis describes a similar process in the Children of God: the rise to power of her father's companion, Maria: 'As we were pushed out little by little over a period of years, Maria grew to be more powerful and consequently more assertive. The "sweet, meek little kitten" began to feel the intoxicating lust of power and soon exhibited the cunning of a street-wise cat. Her desire for power, hidden at first, shortly emerged and burgeoned into "the Queen"' (1984, 62).

Attitudes and feelings towards Sheela, as a person and as leader, varied enormously. Franklin, who had been one of her few friends in Poona, described her as 'a brash, spunky kid' who 'could be warm and loving when she wanted to be, but it was impossible to have an intelligent conversation with her' (1992, 73). Franklin became disillusioned and dropped the friendship after Sheela's power drive started escalating, but others were attracted to her charismatic energy. Strelley, who worked for Sheela as her personal assistant for several years in Poona, gives the most detailed and intimate portrayal of Sheela. Disarming frankness was part of her appeal. When she offered to train Strelley she warned her: 'I'm the biggest bitch you've ever met – or will meet. I'm totally ruthless. My offer is that you can work with me, you can learn from me, and you become exclusively mine' (1987, 169). Despite this threat, which was sometimes carried out, Strelley adored her:

> It wasn't the fact of *what* I felt she was going to become that so intrigued me, it was *her* – the energy, the power, the *charisma* I sensed there. I wanted to imbibe it *so desperately*. She seemed so clear, so centered, so graceful – I sensed this in everything from her hand movements to her laughter. (1987, 192–3; her italics)

Strelley experienced Sheela as a 'high priestess', and claims that her ultimate effect was empowering: 'She was always a great "zen stick" for other people; whether they were being struck or stroked by her, they were getting something out of the encounter' (208). Her charisma grew almost supernaturally powerful:

> Meeting Sheela, I felt I had tapped into some unlimited power in myself – though I could not have said exactly what

the nature of that power was. I had a curious double vision of her. Something about her suggested death, the grim reaper; and yet she embodied the ultimate in life. It was almost as if she could only live life to the fullest on the edge of death. (ibid., 194)

Sheela rose rapidly to power and prominence in Poona, until she took over from Laxmi as Osho's 'secretary' in 1981, and organized the move to America. At Rajneeshpuram she reigned supreme, deferring to Osho in name but seemingly making many decisions on her own.

Many sannyasins admired Sheela for her energy and drive, seeing her as responsible for the initial success of Rajneeshpuram: 'She was not to be underestimated, a very skilled administrator who made a lot of good decisions as well as bad ones, and a good judge of people.' Others were critical but still supported her: 'In defence of Sheela, she had always been unpleasant and abrasive, but she did try to make it work for us. Every time they put a barrier in our way she made it twice as hard for them, so we had that much strength.' One woman who had worked closely with her made a revealing distinction: 'Now I feel she wasn't being aggressive in the way [Osho] wanted – the best she could do was be obnoxious.' Unfortunately, this quasi-fascism constituted her appeal for some people: 'I totally loved Sheela, she was so dynamic, out there, outrageous. . . . I had this very strange admiration for her, all the guns. I felt, "Fucking right, we need to protect ourselves."'

Fitzgerald also mentions 'rumors of an inner sanctum where the goddess Kali was worshiped and where there had been a human sacrifice'. This is the only mention in the literature of such goings-on, which sound highly unlikely. However, there is an aspect of Sheela that resonates with the Hindu goddess Kali, mythologized as an aspect of the divine mother, who represents death and destruction. The ambivalence and polarization of people's feelings and attitudes towards Sheela reflect the fundamental Hindu understanding of *shakti* (the female principle): 'It is protective, benevolent, bestower on the one hand, and malevolent, destructive on the other . . . Thus, there is an essential duality in the concept of the female in Hinduism. She is both the creator and the destroyer, she is both mild and terrible, and good and evil' (Gupta 1986, 168).

There is a further ambiguity in this powerful goddess energy. O'Flaherty asks: 'how can a goddess have authority, being female, but how can she not have authority, being a goddess?' to which she answers, 'Authority is the social force (male) needed to tame, control, and channel pure power (female); to say that he has authority and that she has power is to say that he directs and shapes the life force that comes from her' (1980, 118). She continues later: 'The Goddess is the incarnation of the power of the god (sakti) but she derives this power from the authority of the male gods in the first place' (ibid., 129). King also discusses this relationship but gives it a slightly different interpretation, perceiving the female power as primary: 'The Great Goddess, the Mahadevi, is related to male deities, as to all that exists, not through an external relationship as consort, but internally, as their very power or shakti, the very energy through which all Gods act' (1993, 28).

There is thus disagreement on the balance and relationship between god and goddess power, an unresolvable question. Similarly, it is impossible to calculate the balance of power and charisma between Osho and Sheela, hence to assess their relative responsibility for the 'failure' of Rajneeshpuram. What is clear is that Sheela was originally a strong and effective leader, whose ruthlessness became increasingly tyrannical. The extent of her crimes and misdemeanours was not proven, but it was evident that she created a totalitarian regime at Rajneeshpuram, with the active or passive support of Osho. Meredith (1987), as official spokesman, asserts that sannyasins must take the responsibility for allowing Sheela to gain power, whereas Osho in his spiritual state of 'choiceless awareness' simply confirmed that she had taken the job. This viewpoint absolves him from the charge of choosing an unsuitable deputy, but at the time it was universally believed that 'Bhagwan appointed Sheela'. Because of their trust in him, sannyasins fought any doubts they might have, believing, like Poonam: 'There must be something about her that he sees that I don't. This is all for his greater vision' (Gordon 1987, 160).

It seems probable that there was a large element of collusion in the relationship between Osho and Sheela. There is also a strong current of opinion that Sheela was scapegoated by Osho, 'setting himself up as the good guy and Sheela as the heavy'. It is well known that Sheela was in daily contact with him and that he supported and praised her publicly, though after her departure repeatedly attacked her for her 'fascism'.

It was Osho's refusal to take responsibility that was the sticking point for some, including Poonam, herself the leader of a large commune, who suffered personally at Rajneeshpuram:[12]

> I don't blame Sheela for what happened, I feel that it was Bhagwan's commune and he knew everything that was going on and subscribed to it. . . . When I was running Medina, then I felt responsible for everything that went on there. If I put someone in charge of running a department and they weren't capable of running it, then I wouldn't turn round and say, 'You have messed up this commune.' I would say, 'I made a mistake putting you there, it seems you're not ready for that one yet, and maybe you do this.' So with Sheela I saw her neurosis and paranoia the moment I knew her, so I don't see how he couldn't have done. But he was blinded, and then he blamed her, and I didn't like that – not taking responsibility. I can see he can make mistakes, and I don't care a bit about him making mistakes. But I felt he blamed her for his mistakes.

Poonam herself exemplified a different style of female leadership. She was the most important and powerful of the movement's centre leaders and one of the main therapists, through whom hundreds of people took sannyas. She ran Kalptaru, the London centre, from 1972 until she set up the 'city' of Medina in Suffolk in 1981, which she ran until 1984 when she was invited to Rajneeshpuram. She described the experience of running Medina:

> I think the main thing about me and Medina was that at that time I was totally committed to Bhagwan, and that was the paramount thing. The paramount thing for me wasn't actually power. I felt this was it, that this was the only way. And I would have done anything for him at that time. I was willing to tell lies, to do things that didn't feel right to me because I felt so convinced that he was the way for the world. And that commitment gave me the strength and the power, because in a sense I knew that I was supported by him, because he knew that I was committed to him. . . .

In terms of enjoying or not enjoying or feeling power, I did enjoy creating something, or hoping to create something, which was a way of life that felt absolutely agreeable to me. I enjoyed Medina because I had a lot to do with it, I was in control there too, I had the ultimate say most of the time. I would also have to go along with messages from the Ranch and directives, but pretty well, especially in the first two or three years, I had a pretty free rein and did it the way I thought things should be done. Also I think I'm really a good manager, a manager of businesses. I know how to co-ordinate businesses and co-ordinate teams of people, and work with people and bring out what's available in people and find skills in people, that sort of thing.

Poonam agreed that these characteristics could be termed 'leadership qualities'. Asked about whether she felt women had particular qualities to bring to positions of power, however, she reverted to the 'vehicle' concept of leadership: 'I think women make good disciples. They're willing to surrender, they're willing to work more from the place of doing it for their master, whereas men tend to work more from their egos, which in the real world is fine, but in the world of the commune was difficult.'

Responses to this absolute commitment and near-absolute exercise of power varied tremendously. What is clear from research and personal accounts is that however feared and disliked Poonam was by some, she was not regarded as an Oriental-style despot in the manner of Sheela.[13] Many people, both in interviews and privately, have expressed their tremendous love and admiration for Poonam. Even though she was 'excommunicated' after leaving the movement, sannyasins are still friends with her and participate in her therapy groups. Even the London centre leader said, 'There was a time when [Osho] apparently put out, though I didn't hear it from his mouth, that sannyasins shouldn't work with people like Teertha, Poonam, etc. I'm still going to do it anyway, because I love Poonam very much and I love her work, and therefore I will continue to work with her.' Another said, 'I think she did a great job for Medina, and got quite badly pushed around towards the end.'

However, another woman had a very traumatic stay at

Medina, having given up everything including her home to live there, and felt she had been very badly treated and let down. 'The "hook" for me was Poonam saying she felt I'd be much more nourished there – in fact, the last thing I felt was nourished! I think if I have any regrets about my sannyas life, it was probably going to Medina.' Several women were ambivalent, both towards Poonam and in terms of their own feelings about having power – whether or not they wanted it, whether they were prepared to 'play the games' thought necessary to enter the inner sanctum. A woman who worked very closely with Poonam in her 'inner circle' described the effects of power on the psyche:

> One thing it did was give me the experience of being invulnerable, so I lost touch with my vulnerability. But it was a very heady experience, like a drug ... and when I came off it I really crashed, because I did really think I was special. I did have an inner hierarchy, and I was very keen on moving towards the top of it. I got caught up in the power system.

Asked if she thought women had any particular qualities for these positions, she replied:

> Well, they poisoned people instead of shooting them, and they sneakily wiretapped instead of having bar-room brawls. ... I think power does the same things to women as to men, it's just a different form. Maybe women had to have that experience of power after so long of being powerless, relatively. Maybe in some collective sense it had to be balanced, and for an individual woman to become whole she would have to go through the experience of power, because it's a part of being alive and it's a hard one for a woman to get.

The experiment in female leadership within the Osho movement has so far been at best a mixed success, and has certainly produced some disastrous results. However, many sannyasin women claim to have learned valuable lessons through the exercise of power, and through experiencing both sides of the fence: 'I had difficulty with the powerful women in the ashram. ... When I came back [my lover] and I ran Kalptaru for a while, so I did have to get into my powerful self. That was lovely, very good to get into that.' Asked if she had felt any conflict with the receptive, devotional side she had described earlier, she replied, 'No, why not? It just felt different aspects, somehow. It felt all part of just becoming more me, bigger, moving out of the little, constricted me into a bigger one.' Many women felt empowered through being given responsible work, which boosted their confidence and self-esteem: 'I still had quite low self-esteem and didn't feel I was anywhere near good enough to be in charge of people, but I kept being given those jobs. And over the years I started to realize I was capable, strong, able to do a lot of things that I hadn't been able to give myself credit for.'

Another woman initially had very hostile feelings about the women in power, but then discovered a different style of leadership for herself: 'I hated them, loathed them, because they were bitchy, arrogant, nasty, full of themselves, ugly, unfeminine. I wanted to be myself, find my own strength, but definitely not be like that.' When she ended up running the London centre, she felt she had found a way of being in power without losing her femininity: 'I was into having fun, enjoying myself. I wasn't into being a boss, I was into expressing my creativity. The boss bit was completely irrelevant, the point was to be there and express myself as fully as I possibly could with my friends. I think it worked. I never had a heavy moment, or very occasionally.'

During the month after Sheela left Rajneeshpuram, one of the questions Osho answered was: 'You always said that women are better than men as far as ruling and governing people is concerned. You said that they are better than men because their starting point is from the heart. Considering recent facts, do You [*sic*] still have this opinion? Do You still trust women?' To this question he replied that 'Just one Sheela does not make any difference ... there are thousands of women who love me more than Sheela ever did ... Now we need a softer quality of people who can destroy all the hostility that Sheela has created' (1985, 162–4). He affirmed that he was still putting women in power because they were more capable than men, had more to contribute, but that they should do so in a feminine way – not according to feminism but 'according to their nature' (see Chapter 4).

Nevertheless, there is some evidence of disillusionment with the feminine after the experiences of Rajneeshpuram. On the one hand, the surrendered devotee polarity of the feminine ideal led to the extreme passivity and submission that allowed all the abuses and exploitation. On the other hand, giving women the opportunity to have power and responsibility did not work: women turned out to be no better at it than men, perhaps worse, especially without the checks and balances that 'male' rationality and pragmatism might have given to the worst excesses. However, women were not blamed; with time, even Sheela stopped being the target, which shifted to the American government. Currently there is a move towards a more natural equality and balance between male and female in the work situation – away from positive discrimination towards a more democratic meritocracy.

In terms of results, the experiment of female leadership was a mixed success. Its failures may reveal more about the nature of power and the kind of person attracted to it than about female leadership *per se*. Clearly, most women in these positions were not submissive devotees in their handling of power, though they may have been in their personal relationship with Osho. Some were more ruthless and aggressive than men, and became progressively more so the longer they held their positions. In fairness, due allowance should be made for their inexperience, after millennia of repression: 'I think when you've been submissive and you first start being assertive, it comes over very raw, bossy. I've mellowed out a lot now, but I think at the time it was my suppressed stuff coming out.'

What has been shown is an organization run largely by women in its first two phases, though within the context of charismatic authority – ultimate authority residing in a male charismatic leader. Despite this limitation, women had a great deal of power and scope. Their financial support, hard work and loyalty were vital to the growth and success of the Osho movement. It was widely felt by sannyasins that there was a genuine attempt to run the community through love and intuition, and that this worked as a successful antidote to the technocratic and left-brained bias of the modern Western approach to work.

Kim Knott (1987), discussing the low status of women in ISKCON, suggests that it is unfair to make comparisons with the ideal of gender roles in liberated American society. ISKCON is unliberated even by Indian standards; educated Indian women do not follow the policy of standing separately from men during temple functions. But the main crticism of this position is that to set different standards and criteria, making a special case of religion, is to marginalize these movements even further, as well as setting dangerous precedents that can be used to maintain women's inferiority. Furthermore, it leaves open the risk of such arguments being reapplied from religious to secular life, as has happened so often historically. Within the Osho movement, despite the excesses of Sheela and a few other coordinators, many women used the opportunities of power and responsibility to develop a gentler, more nurturing style of leadership, incorporating traditional 'feminine' qualities, rather than becoming an imitation male. It is a dilemma that faces all women today in positions of power, whether spiritual or secular, and there is clearly no easy answer.

# 8 Female Spiritual Leadership in NRMS

Female leadership in secular life is still relatively rare and contentious, despite the advances of feminism and other forces over the last 30 years. Religious leadership has been rarer still, unhelped by theological legitimation of female inferiority and sinfulness. Women have barely been acknowledged as possessing souls and capacity for spiritual growth, let alone allowed to achieve rank and status in religion. Religious titles betray this bias, either possessing no female equivalent or a debased meaning: priest, master, guru, pope. Only priest has the counterpart priestess, but overlaid with ambivalent connotations. Recognition of spiritual equality between men and women is the core issue in the struggle over female leadership and status. It is still under debate in the Church of England, despite the recent formal ratification of the ordination of women, and it is unrecognized in Catholicism.

Often the founders of religion have had progressive, compassionate theories of gender, but these have been subverted by succeeding priesthoods and theologians who produce orthodoxies in line with socially entrenched sexism. As already discussed, this conservatism is still current, indeed the predominant trend – to such an extent that, arguably, one of the primary functions of successful religions has been the subordination of women to male authority. Religion is also a root cause of the inequality of women in secular society and the workplace, in that until the advent of psychology it was the creator, maintainer and sanctifier of most of our ideas about psyche and society including gender. Although psychology now has greater scientific authority and respectability, its theories are deeply influenced by religion, through the religiously conditioned beliefs of its founding fathers and many of its current practitioners.

In the past women have sometimes been revered for outstanding gifts and virtues as mystics, hermits and saints, although sainthood has been mainly earned through the masochistic passivity of martyrdom, perceived as a peculiarly female accomplishment (see Chapter 4). Such women rarely attain temporal position or power and when they do, tend to attract hostility, as with St Teresa of Avila who was accused of heresy. Despite the restrictions, even within the most misogynistic religions and societies there have always been examples of women as writers, poets, scholars and occasionally as charismatic prophetesses, teachers and leaders. Sometimes they have been influential but often unrecorded and soon forgotten.[1] For example, early Islam was relatively egalitarian, and Mohammed's wife and daughter played prominent roles in the formation of the religion, but over time both religion and society restricted and subordinated women to men. Sufism (the mystical sect within Islam) encouraged women as mystics and teachers, though only Rabi'a al-Adawiyya is officially recorded. Some of the best-known Sufis such as Ibn Arabi and Bayazid had (less well-known) women teachers. A modern Sufi example is the successor to Meher Baba's organization Sufism Reoriented, Murshia Ivy O Duce.

Stark and Bainbridge postulate that 'one of the things that attracts particularly ambitious women to cults is the opportunity to become leaders or even founders of their own religious movements' (1985, 414). Most such women will have been frustrated, but a few have succeeded. The lack of opportunity within their own religion will sometimes drive women to convert to completely different traditions, as happened with a well-known Zen master:

> The only reason she turned away from Christianity, Roshi Kennett told me, was her incredibly deep calling to become a priest. And, as a woman, 'there was no way I could become a priest in Christianity.' It was the sexism of the Church of England that compelled her to cut loose from Christianity and finally become a monk in a foreign country, in a foreign religion, in a foreign language. (Friedman 1987, 173)

There are three main routes to leadership for women in religion. Firstly, movements founded by men are sometimes taken over by women on the founder's death or at a later stage, usually by a close relation or disciple. Secondly, some movements have been co-founded by a male–female team, usually husband and wife. Thirdly, rarely, groups may be founded by a woman.

## Women Leaders in Male-Founded Movements

As discussed, Hinduism has not generally been supportive of women's spiritual development, beyond the performance of minor domestic rituals. A woman's best hope for advancement is to serve her family dutifully in the hope of being reborn in a male body next lifetime. Yet despite these restrictions, women have been more prominent in Hinduism than in the Western religions. This is probably partly because Hinduism is such an ancient and broad tradition, encompassing paradox, complexity and a multiplicity of approaches; partly because its expression of divinity includes the Goddess as well as the God; partly because of the feminine aspects of *bhakti*, the most popular religion.

The most famous historical female mystics are Lalla and Mirabai, medieval poets who composed and publicly sung ecstatic, devotional lovesongs to God – songs that have remained part of the literary and religious heritage. Although they had followings, they did not found ashrams or traditions. Similarly with the Tantrics and *dakinis* rediscovered by Miranda Shaw (1994) and others; they wrote poems and sacred texts, and were sometimes dominant in their spiritual partnerships, but were not leaders with large followings. Tibetan Vajrayana Buddhism allows the possibility of divine beings taking female human forms, but only a handful of female *tulkus* are documented, of whom Dolma is the best known. Even these had lower status in the hierarchy than their male equivalents. These women did at least set precedents, allowing some continuity of female religious leadership that is also found in some NRMs, particularly the more Westernized ones.

The Osho movement, as discussed, is an example of an NRM founded by a man but run mainly by women, in which Sheela appears to have had equal or greater power than Osho for several years. She was sometimes unofficially called the queen of Rajneeshpuram and also – as acting head of the new 'religion' of Rajneeshism – the 'Pope'. Thus she united secular and spiritual power in her own person. However, the formal religion of Rajneeshism that was set up at Rajneeshpuram was not taken seriously by sannyasins or the American government; it was perceived as primarily a device to attain an American visa for Osho as a religious leader. Thus, although Sheela had formal priestly powers, such as the performance of birth, marriage and funeral rituals, the real spiritual power – the charisma – was still perceived as residing in Osho's person. Sheela's charisma was at best reflected, despite her temporal powers and forceful personality.

Osho delegated very few spiritual powers to any disciples. This was partly became he was profoundly anti-clerical, seeing priesthoods as the 'source of all kinds of ugly institutions' and the root of all misery and repression, instilling obedience through fear and guilt. Nevertheless, his therapists performed certain priestly functions. The catharsis and breakthroughs experienced by group participants were comparable to the experience of absolution produced by the confessional. As with religious rituals, these groups had a socialization function, educating sannyasins into discipleship.[2] As with most priest-hoods, the majority of the therapists were men, including the most respected and charismatic practitioners, one of whom was regarded as Osho's unofficial chief disciple. At least there was no disbarring of women from this role, and some were highly regarded.

The Osho movement presents a paradox: in the inner realm women were clearly perceived as superior, and this status was reflected in their temporal powers. Yet, as with ISKCON, Hin-duism in general and other Eastern religions, ultimate spir-itual authority derives from the ability to be a teacher or guru. Osho was frequently asked why there were so few women masters. His replies were fairly consistent, and made it clear that although female virtues were pre-eminent in discipleship, they were not qualifications to become a master: 'I know women have a much more feeling heart, are more loving, are more open, are more receptive. But these are the qualities of a dis-ciple, not of a master' (n.d. [1985b], 65).

Although he occasionally emphasized the motherly, caring function of the master, Osho mainly described it as a man's job. There were two reasons he gave why women could not become masters. Firstly – paradoxically – the mind that was so condemned in sannyas had to be reclaimed by the aspiring master. Since Osho saw men as intellectually superior, they had the edge here. Even the few women who had made the grade were not 'really' masters:

The man has a tremendous capacity for logic and reason. Once he has found reality, enlightenment, he can use the mind to spread the fragrance he has found. The woman cannot do it. That's why there have been not only no great masters, there have been no masters who were women. Even the famous religious women saints were disciples. [St Teresa, Mirabai, Leela] became enlightened, but they remained devotees. (ibid., 66)

Another reason why 'only the male mind can be a master' was: 'To be a Master means to be very aggressive. A woman cannot be aggressive. Woman, by her very nature, is receptive. A woman is a womb, so the woman can be the very best disciple possible' (1978a, 44). This belief reverses the principle of androgyny fundamental to the teaching, whereby both men and women are required to access and develop their opposite-sex characteristics in order to attain wholeness and transcendence. The master–disciple relationship is a very polarized, patriarchal model: the disciple carries all the feminine qualities, the master all the masculine qualities. Now that Osho has died, there is less emphasis on gender polarity. He appointed not a successor but a committee of 21 senior disciples (11 women, 10 men) called the 'Inner Circle'. This is currently chaired by a man, but one of its members is his former secretary Anando, an Australian woman. On his deathbed he appointed her as his 'medium', without explaining the meaning and function attached. Since the Inner Circle was set up with practical, secular functions but no spiritual powers, Anando is probably the closest Osho got to appointing a spiritual successor: a continuation of the vehicle concept of leadership.

The Brahma Kumaris present a similar pattern of a founder who favoured and promoted women, and has been run mainly by women since his death. In some respects the role reversal is more complete than in the Osho movement, since women are teachers as well as administrators, and there is a very comprehensive doctrine on gender equality, as expressed by the movement's female leader, Dadi Janki:

To a soul born in a male costume, as a man, the characteristics are probably going to be bossiness and ego; for a woman it will probably be timidity, dependence and fear. But when the awakening of the spirit takes place . . . then the man who is a yogi will have the strength of being a man but it will be tinged with gentleness, humility, so that ego and bossiness disappear. And for a woman, having the experience of detachment from the body and being in yoga brings a lot of strength, a lot of courage so that she is fearless now. (Bancroft 1989, 126–7)

The BKs are concerned with women's issues and spiritual leadership; they publish leaflets and run workshops on the subject. Dadi Janki has a very high profile as an international religious leader, meeting many top political leaders, involved with the UNO at a high level as well as other global organizations and causes. The British leaders, Sister Sudesh and Sister Jayanti, are also very active as teachers and in religious, social and environmental causes. The theological emphasis is on service, self-effacement and humility, but not to the detriment of action and expansion. Sister Sudesh claims: 'Feminine qualities such as love, tolerance, compassion, understanding and humility are also qualities of leadership' (1993, 40). These virtues might well be more widely acknowledged as producing a more humane, holistic style of leadership and she qualifies this list with the need for balance with 'courage, determination, clear thinking and self-respect'. However, as with sannyasins, BK women become core members by being fully 'surrendered'. Dadaji believed women made good devotees because they were used to renunciation and hardship, which fostered humility and service. Again as in sannyas, women's prominence derives from their mediumistic capacities, channelling *murlis* (sermons) from their dead founder. This material contains no new information or changes to the teaching, and the result is: 'their power is veiled . . . through the device of possession. Women, even when they possess power, cannot be seen to wield it. Hence, the importance of spirit possession where women are the instruments or mouthpieces of a male spirit' (Skultans 1993, 52).

Most Hindu-based movements founded by men tend to perpetuate a male lineage, if a sole successor is appointed. An exception is Siddha Yoga, which was founded in the early twentieth century by Nityananda, expanded and Westernized by his successor Muktananda. Before his death Muktananda appointed a female successor, Chidvilasananda, known as Gurumayi. As with most Hindu-based NRMs, Siddha Yoga theology has a misogynistic streak, with a particular emphasis on *maya*, the illusory state of consciousness that causes suffering – personified as a woman. Gurumayi herself sometimes uses such language, but has gained much respect as the leader of a movement that has grown in appeal in the West, despite allegations of misconduct.[3]

Gurumayi visited London in 1996 as part of a world tour, and filled a conference centre that holds 5000 people. She led the chanting with a powerful voice, and then gave a one-hour talk interspersed with devotional songs. Her performance was highly charismatic, but the devotion was almost all channelled towards Muktananda, her own guru as well as the former guru of many current devotees. It is traditional in Hinduism for gurus to acknowledge the pre-eminence of their own guru, although the more charismatic modern male gurus have a tendency to outshine their predecessor with claims of cosmic supremacy. Gurumayi is at least acknowledged as being a fully enlightened Siddha Master in her own right, with the capacity to awaken others through the transmission of *shaktipat*. After the talk she gave *darshan*, smiling graciously at her devotees and flicking them with a peacock feather as they filed in front of her. Once again, she is a mediumistic leader, a vehicle for divine grace via her dead former guru, but she is also active in setting up and directing meditation centres throughout the world, and many devotees travel to Shree Muktananda Ashram, the main centre in America, specifically to be taught by her and spend time in her enlightening presence.

As we have seen, Buddhism has a mixed history regarding gender, with a tendency towards misogyny. However, women mystics and teachers have existed in all Buddhist countries, particularly in Tantra and the Vajrayana and Zen traditions, though less so in Theravada, to some extent reflecting the status of nuns.[4] All the well-known Tibetan lamas are men, but one of my interviewees had met a woman teacher who 'was revered by the greatest male masters. She never spoke but she was extraordinary, and she was promoted as the feminine.' There is also a 22-year-old Tibetan woman lama who speaks good English and is said to be very impressive.

Following the immigration of many Zen and Tibetan teachers to the West, there have been great strides in the improvement of women's position. It is significant that the first American Zen student was a woman, and there are now increasing numbers of women teachers in America.[5] As with the organizational transformation of business, women are at the forefront of the creation of a distinctive new style of Buddhism, both Westernized and feminized, emphasizing human values. As Maurine Stuart succinctly puts it: 'Don't worry if you've forgotten a form, just do it from an open heart.' Whether overtly feminist or not, these changes are often regarded as subversive challenges to the male establishment, which is formal, hierarchical, entrenched in complex rituals and customs that may be incomprehensible and inappropriate to Westerners. Again as in business, the first priority has been for women to get established in leadership roles; once accepted, they can start questioning and changing. Women tend to take a pragmatic, flexible approach to Buddhist forms, innovating and modernizing, even at the price of friction with their own teachers. Hence their approach tends to be more compassionate, with less hitting and shouting involved. They are egalitarian, sitting at the same level as their students and not wearing distinctive robes. They simplify the practice, omitting the elaborate complexities of bowing and chanting, exchanging chopsticks for knives and forks. As Joko Beck explains: 'Neither tradition nor innovation is the point. The point is, what best serves a live, vital practice? All changes should arise from that consideration . . . I question accepting any fixed format for sesshin as sacrosanct. I'm willing to look at *everything*' (Friedman 1987, 123).

Some women exemplify a fairly traditional, 'masculine' model of power, such as Maurine Stuart who tells her students: 'We are warrior women.' Her comment on the rigour and toughness of Zen training is: 'this is also an essential part of being a woman – to be strong . . . this strength coming from a really solid inner discipline that our practice gives us.' This approach may be compared with the BKs as incorporating traditional masculine virtues, though more forcefully. It may also be contrasted with the so-called women 'prayer warriors' of the New Christian Right who must submit to their husband in all respects, and whose only power lies in petitioning God for their needs (Rose 1987).

Kennett Roshi calls both male and female practitioners monks, and herself is described as 'forthright in style', with a voice 'by turns commanding, funny, sardonic, rousing, hortatory', expressing strong views in strong language: 'in religion you have a lot of people who're insulting because you're a female . . . but that's *their* problem, it's not *mine*. Somehow or other women have to get to that stage, if they want true spiritual equality. They've gotta stop letting the men put them down.'[6]

The main tendency is towards a more feminine style of leadership, sometimes to the point of self-effacement. The 'reluctant *dharma* teacher' Joko Beck asserts, 'People like to project their power onto someone else . . . But I won't accept that.' On the whole, self-effacement does not appear to become self-abnegation in the weak sense, and there is acknowledgment of the issue. As Karuna Dharma says: 'women are seeing dependency as a crutch they need to get rid of.'

Probably the most successful and relevant model of female leadership coming out of Buddhism integrates so-called feminine and masculine qualities, as with Sharon Salzberg who 'combines gentleness and compassion with her intellectual power, clarity, and rigor of practice', an approach that is 'empowering to women'. She sees a widespread shift towards feminine values and believes that Buddhism 'will be truly successful only if there is a great deal of feminine energy and responsibility involved.' This is also the approach of 'engaged' Buddhists, who become involved in (non-violent) political protests, antinuclear demonstrations, environmental work. The term was first applied to the work of the Vietnamese monk Thich Nhat Hanh, but there are also some prominent women teachers involved such as Ruth Klein, American president of the Buddhist Peace Fellowship, and Joanna Macy, who specializes in despair and empowerment work and is one of the leading lights of the deep ecology movement.

## NRMs Co-Founded by Women

There are very few NRMs co-founded by men and women, although wives, mothers and daughters may be very influential behind the scene, usually unacknowledged. For example, Margaret Fell married the founder of the Quakers, George Fox, and became known as the Mother of the Society. Ramakrishna's wife ran the ashram while he was in blissful trance.

The best known recent spiritual partnership in the West was between Helena Blavatsky and Henry Olcott, who co-founded the Theosophical Society in America in the late nineteenth century and popularized the idea of India as the source of spirituality. Theosophy was partly a transformation of Spiritualism, itself dominated by women, and is the most important historical influence on the New Age. Blavatsky outshone Olcott both as a charismatic leader and formulator of Theosophical doctrine, and is much better known than him, but has been widely condemned as a charlatan – a fate perhaps more likely to fall on female than male leaders.[7] On her death, the Society was taken over by another partnership, between Annie Besant and Charles Leadbeater, again with Besant as the dominant partner. Shortly after the establishment of Theosophy's headquarters in Madras, Shri Aurobino opened an ashram in nearby Pondicherry teaching Integral Yoga. One of his early followers was Mira Richard, a Frenchwoman who became his co-guru, known as the Mother. After his death she became a charismatic leader in her own right, chief administrator and *inspiratrice*, who founded several major projects including Auroville, City of Human Peace.

As with the Aurobindo ashram, the Summit Lighthouse was originally founded by a man, the aptly named Mark Prophet. On his death in 1973 the leadership was taken over by his wife, Elizabeth Clare Prophet, known to her followers as Guru Ma, who renamed the movement the Church Universal and Triumphant (CUT). The teachings are allegedly channelled through hidden masters, though also largely derived from two women, Blavatsky and Alice Bailey. The CUT has been strongly criticized regarding its recruitment techniques and treatment of its members. It is theologically highly exotic and esoteric, but takes a hard conservative stance on political and family issues, against communism, abortion and rock music.

The Chrisemma Foundation was co-founded by Chris and Emma in 1990, and flourished for a few years in Totnes, a centre of the English New Age. It reversed the pattern of female supremacy, in that although both claimed to be enlightened masters, even God, it was Chris who 'discovered' God in Emma and set up the teaching partnership on attaining enlightenment through sexual relationship. He did all the talking while his 'silent guru' partner sat on the sofa staring into

space. Not much is known about them except that their followers are mainly ex-sannyasins, probably attracted by the diluted version of Osho's teaching on offer. Eventually the couple
moved to Bristol, where they split up, and the work was carried
on by Chris alone through the Chris Orchard Foundation.[8]

## Women Founders and Leaders of NRMs

There are a number of contemporary Indian women gurus
teaching in their own right, such as Amritanandamayi, known
as Ammachi or 'the hugging guru'. This is because her whole
teaching and practice consists of hugging, a ritualized expression of love and grace. Her *darshans*, which last till 2 or 3 a.m.,
are similar in format to Osho's energy *darshans* (though without mediums), beginning with singing, swaying and clapping
till she reaches an ecstatic state. Then a line of devotees and
visitors passes before her and she enfolds each one in her
arms, hugging and kissing them. On her annual week's visit to
London in 1996 the ritual was more restrained, but the audience of about 1000 urban professionals per day queued for up
to five hours for their hug. This phenomenon surely says something about the state of Western society. For some people the
experience was electrifying, 'like being plugged into a genera-
tor'; for others it was soft and melting.[9] Ammachi is a typical
*bhakti* guru. Her devotees look after her and organize her visits
overseas, where she has thousands of followers and admirers,
but the organization is minimal and her charismatic leadership is still in a 'pure' state. Her charisma is enhanced by
association with Krishna. Her mother is said to have had visions of him during pregnancy, she herself sang prayers and
songs to him without instruction from the age of two, and has
worshipped him throughout her life, having visions of him
until she began to take on his appearance and *bhav* (mood) –
a sign of divinity in India. These experiences are similar to
those of the revered nineteenth-century mystic Ramakrishna,
of whom Ammachi has claimed to be a reincarnation. Nowadays she also takes on the *bhav* of the goddesses Devi and Kali
in her performances of sacred dance, and in this she is similar
to another revered woman mystic, the late Anandamayi Ma.
Her *puja* culminates in a powerful invocation of the divine
feminine through the chanting of the 108 names of the goddess,

and prolonged repetition of the mantra, '*Om Parashakti Namoha*' ('Salutations to the supreme female power').

Mother Meera became well known in the West primarily through Andrew Harvey, a writer and seeker who has promoted many spiritual teachers including Sogyal Rinpoche. He describes in vivid detail the transformative effect of her presence, for example: 'Meera seemed to know intimately each head she took into her hands; and her eyes changed for each person who approached her. She did not take the worship offered for herself. There was no self in her; only a Presence like the red-gold sunlight and warm wind that filled the room.' Often she is described in nurturing, maternal terms, though she can also appear in an infinity of forms, 'a blaze of Light', or fierce and frightening. He has promoted her publicly and successfully as the avatar of the *shakti*, the primal female goddess/force, which is the highest conceivable manifestation of the feminine. In an interview he persuasively extolled her virtues and the merits of discipleship as against the delusions of 'false individuality': 'You have to fall in love with the holiness and beauty of the master – forever – and the desire to become like them engenders the discipline that slowly transforms you, with their grace. . . . I have seen her power and have no doubt that she will alter the whole history of this period.'[10]

Recently, in a dramatic, public *volte-face*, Harvey rejected Mother Meera along with all gurus who claim to represent the sacred feminine as 'Jehovah in drag', reproducing patriarchal hierarchies and lies and accruing personal power and wealth. He proposes: 'The revolution of the sacred feminine . . . can now, I believe, only happen if we get rid of the old guru model, if we empower ourselves, if we establish a direct relationship with the divine mother herself, who is willing to initiate us directly.' He admits that the trigger for his denunciation was her refusal to bless his homosexual 'marriage' and accuses her of homophobia, which she denies, as do her devotees and admirers. He also admits that he had had an obsessive, undiscriminating adoration for her, based on maternal projection. His film-star mother had given him a fascination for powerful female stars, and he saw Meera as 'the Garbo of the spiritual Hollywood. She is the one who is rarely seen, the mysterious one who never speaks.'

Thus the guru-maker became the guru-breaker, although

his rejection does not seem to have affected Mother Meera's popularity. She remains in her ashram in Germany, and has not yet visited Britain or America, but visitors and devotees pour in from all over the world. Again, the format of her *darshans* is traditionally Hindu, and participants report strong experiences of energy and bliss. The emphasis is on *bhakti*, but insight may be a by-product: 'During the last *darshan* I felt a lot of warmth along my spine . . . and then a sense of blissful emptiness. I had prayed to be shown what the obstacles are to my spiritual progress and to be given help to remove these, and this was answered.' This seeker was powerfully affected by Mother Meera, yet still felt that the chemistry was not quite compatible enough to become her devotee. What is interesting is that she was particularly attracted to the idea of a female guru, yet this factor was not enough to induce that choice.

One reason for Indian female gurus' failure to build large organizations and disseminate their teachings, past and present, is their lack of formal education; most are poorly educated or illiterate, like the majority of Indian women. In contrast, the male gurus are often highly educated. Both Osho and Prabhupada were professors of philosophy, whereas Ammachi and Meera are uneducated, as was Anandamayi Ma. These women are leaders in the traditional *bhakti* style, which I have already argued may be called feminine (Chapter 4). For their followers – rebels against reason – this non-intellectuality may be perceived as an advantage. Many of them are devotees, aspiring to emotional and spiritual experience rather than formal teaching and practice.

Another well-known woman guru is Nirmala Devi, known as Sri Mataji, founder of Sahaja Yoga. She was once a disciple of Osho, although she is publicly critical of him, as he sometimes was of her. Osho claimed that she was an *ersatz* guru who imitated his style. His version of events is that after they had visited Muktananda together and been unimpressed, the idea entered Nirmala's head: ' "If such a fool like Muktananda can become a saint, then why can't I become a saint?". . . . Once she could see that this fool can raise people's kundalini, then "Why can't I raise it?" And she is certainly far more intelligent than Muktananda, far more capable' (Osho 1981, 318). Kundalini yoga is the basis of Sahaja Yoga, so Mataji appears

to have based her praxis on Muktananda but her style of charismatic leadership on Osho.

Like Osho – and Gurumayi – she is anti-feminist, and her
teaching on gender is as traditional as ISKCON's. She advoc-
ates clearly defined, traditional gender roles: men should be
leaders in the movement, active, assertive, dominant, protecting and providing for their families. Women should imitate
the ideal of the Indian wife: submissive to their husbands,
passive, nurturing their families and not actively involved in
the organization. Women who behave like men, becoming
dominant, will lose their femininity. Mataji does not follow
her own prescriptions; although she is married with two
daughters, she has always played an active, dominant role.
As a young girl she worked with Mahatma Gandhi, and as a
guru her status has increased until – like Meera, but on her
own behalf – she has claimed the ultimate female Hindu
position of Adishakti. Like many of the male gurus, Mataji is
believed by her devotees to possess psychic powers; she appears to them in visions and dreams, sometimes as a saviour or
divine being. She has healing gifts and may work miracles.
Like the BK leaders, she is a high-profile international figure.
Now in her seventies, she travels round the world overseeing
her centres and organizing projects with seemingly boundless
energy.[11]

Christianity has not on the whole been supportive of female
leadership, but there have been periods when women have
flourished in a variety of religious roles. There is a growing
body of evidence for the extensive participation of women in
early Christianity: as followers of Jesus, witnesses of his resurrection, and as apostles, prophets, missionaries, priests and
even bishops in the early church.[12] The Roman church restricted and suppressed this activity, but in the Middle Ages
women again found some expression for their leadership abilities as founders and abbesses of religious orders. The proliferation of sects in the Reformation gave women new leadership
opportunities, although most sects were originated by men.
Mother Anne Lee is the best known, who founded the Shakers
and established them in America, which has ever since been
the country most open to women as religious leaders. Also in
America, Mary Baker Eddy founded Christian Science, while
Ellen G. White founded Seventh Day Adventism. Elizabeth Cady

Stanton is still remembered for her creation of *The Woman's Bible* (published 1895), which was attacked at the time but is now recognized as a landmark in feminist scholarship. As discussed, America also produced a number of well-known women spiritualist and occult leaders such as Helena Blavatsky (see above), and Alice Bailey who created the Arcane School.

Britain has been less encouraging of radical movements such as sectarianism and feminism. However, there was an upsurge of spiritual fervour during the early nineteenth-century Industrial Revolution, prior to the first wave of feminism, which included some prominent women among its leaders. Most famous and successful was the charismatic Joanna Southcott, said to have converted 100 000 with her millennial prophecies, healing and psychic powers. Victorian women tended to put their energies more into social action than religion, partly because the churches became so unsupportive of their efforts and have largely remained so to the present. As a result of this 'glass ceiling', British Christianity has failed to produce any notable women leaders, although feminist theologians have paved the way for future generations of women priests who may help revive their traditions.

In the occult movements that flourished around the end of the century, however, women once again played a prominent part. These comprised a revival of the Western Mystery Tradition that emerged concurrently with the Eastern-inspired esoteric revival, with a certain amount of cross-fertilization. Four of the leading magicians in the Hermetic Order of the Golden Dawn were Maud Gonne, Moina Mathers, Florence Farr and Annie Horniman.[13] The best known and most influential British magician of the early twentieth century was Dion Fortune, a psychologist and ex-Theosophist who emphasized women's superior occult powers. She believed that although in the outer world men were active and women passive, these roles were reversed in the inner world, whereby women became active as priesesses. Her work has inspired many of the women who are now leading and shaping magic and occultism, such as Dolores Ashcroft-Nowicki, Director of Servants of the Light. Wicca was founded by a man, Gerald Gardner, but with much help from Doreen Valiente and largely based on the writings of Margaret Murray. The next main development, Alexandrian Wicca, was created by a husband-and-wife team, Alex and Maxine Sanders.

Most of the well-known figures in Paganism are women: in Europe, Janet Farrar, Vivianne Crowley, Marian Green, Freya Aswynn, Monica Sjoo, Caitlín Matthews; in America Szuszanna Budapest, Margot Adler, Starhawk.

In both occultism and spiritualism women have been in the majority as both leaders and followers, and their ideas about the spiritual nature of women both complemented and contended with the emerging feminist ideology – an ambivalent relationship that still continues. In Victorian spiritualism in Britain and America women predominated as psychics and mediums, as they still do. Their reputation was generally low, partly due to lack of education and socio-economic status, partly to frequent allegations of fraud and occasional financial scandals, but perhaps also as a direct result of their predominance in their profession: 'Men's work is generally valued more highly than women's, and occupations that shift from being male to female preserves generally lose status' (Archer & Lloyd 1985, 239). Spiritualists and mediums still have a relatively low public profile, giving private consultations, speaking in spiritualist churches, sometimes doing promotional tours. It is also still a route to success and status for women, even without education: 'Though [Spiritualism] fails to address the problem of women's empowerment in any explicit way (i.e. ideologically), it nonetheless accepts women's legitimate role as religious authorities without question or hesitation, and encourages some empowerment of women through its modification of the conventional identity of women' (Haywood 1983, 165). A few mediums do rise to public prominence, such as the best-selling author Betty Shine.

In America the term 'channelling' is used for mediumship, and again women are predominant. Helena Blavatsky (see above) and Alice Bailey who created the Arcane School are the main forerunners. The modern phenomenon began in the 1960s, with Jane Roberts channelling the entity Seth, and continued with the more Christian-oriented *Course in Miracles*, implied to be teachings of Jesus. They were originally channelled by Helen Schucman, whose work is now being further popularized by Marianne Williamson. Other well-known channellers are Pat Rodegast with Emmanuel, and J.Z. Knight with the 35 000-year-old Lemurian warrior Ramtha. There are also husband-and-wife teams such as José and Lena Stevens, channelling the entity Michael. The Michael teaching is unusual in being also channelled by a number of other people, probably because it provides the most sophisticated philosophy and cosmology accompanied by the most comprehensive methodology for personal development.

Channelling, healing and divination are the three main New Age practices, and women predominate in all. The two best-known healers and best-selling authors are Louise Hay and Shakti Gawain. Divination is the main outlet for the development and practice of psychic powers, comprising a variety of systems, tools and techniques of which the best known are: astrology, tarot, runes, crystals, dream interpretation, dowsing, palmistry, graphology, numerology and the I Ching. The most popular method by far is astrology, and in Britain all the women's magazines, the tabloids and some of the quality newspapers have a 'sun sign' column, usually written by a woman. Yet the doyen of astrologers was a man, Patrick Walker, celebrated astrologer of the *Evening Standard,* who wrote a highly profitable column syndicated across the world. He was a charismatic figure who, like Gurdjieff, gave many of his students to understand they would be his successor, but upon his death his mantle passed to a woman, Shelley von Strunckel. The feminist astrologer Sheila Farrant has analysed the gender bias in Western astrological symbolism, developed under the Graeco-Roman patriarchy, such as the dominance of male imagery in the Zodiac, the subordination of the moon to the sun (they were originally equal), the trivialization of Venus, and the relative values ascribed to masculine and feminine:

> The qualities of drive, leadership, nobility, active energy, creativity and aggression (Fire), and intellectualism, invention, speed, communication and reform (Air) are classed as 'masculine' and given high status, while practicality, grounding, caution and endurance (Earth) and feeling, sensitivity and intuition (Water) are classed as 'feminine' and given low status. Earth is stolid and unimaginative in much astrological writing, Water too emotional for words! . . .
> The message of astrology for women is in fact very clear. *Masculine* forces and influences give us our drive, our inventiveness, our intellect, our science, our leadership qualities (if we can ever put them into practice!). *Masculine* deities

rule our death (Pluto), signify our birth (the Sun) and dictate our Fate (Saturn). (1989, 3)

Female and male imagery and symbolism are equal and complementary in Kabbala, alchemy and tarot, and Farrant sets out to reclaim astrology as a tool of self-knowledge and healing for women. The influence of Jungian psychology through the work of Liz Greene and others, though problematic in some respects (see pp. 77–9), has also had a rebalancing effect on gender meanings as well as leading astrology away from prediction towards personal development. The sheer predominance of women as professionals and clients combined with the pervasive influence of feminism has also enabled this shift of meaning.

## Is There a Feminine Style of Leadership?

Out of all these examples of female spiritual leadership, past and present, is it possible to discern any trends, defining characteristics, similarities or differences from male leaders? Clearly, despite the restrictions and lack of opportunities for women, they demonstrate a great range and variety of leadership style, as is the case in business and the professions. The issue is complicated in that there is no clear correspondence between successful female leadership and feminist ideology. Indeed, some of the strongest leaders are explicitly anti-feminist, such as Nirmala Devi and Gurumayi. Three types or styles of leadership emerge, which may be classified in gender terms: a) masculine or 'male-identified'; b) feminine; c) non-gendered or androgynous.

Historically, the masculine style of female leadership has sometimes taken the form of transvestism. Male transvestism has already been mentioned (Chapter 4), but this took place for ritualistic rather than social reasons. There are examples of female ritual transvestism in traditional religions, but Western women have used it more as a means of entry into spheres of action where they were debarred, such as the military, and religious life. In the Middle Ages there was a trend of female saints who disguised themselves and lived as monks.[14] The best-known is Joan of Arc, who was called 'Maid' but wore a colourful male uniform. For the contemporary leaders discussed here, transvestism has not been necessary. However, Blavatsky has been called 'male-identified' on account of her masculine role-behaviour. 'She insisted on wearing men's clothes, being called "Jack" by associates, and continually denied having given birth to her son' (Hutch 1984, 258–9). She also held a jaundiced view of traditional female aspirations: 'Woman finds her happiness in the acquisition of supernatural powers. Love is but a vile dream, a nightmare.' Dion Fortune, who also suffered from turbulent relationships, held similar views.

Masculine styles of leadership are not found among *bhakti* women gurus, understandably, since they would then be challenging the fundamental approach of this tradition. Yet there are examples of extremely fierce women leaders in India. One notorious contemporary example is Uma Bharati, one of three female sannyasins spearheading the Hindu revivalist movement. They engage in acts of violent destruction, invoking Kali's name and meditating on the spears and swords of Durga, the manifestation of Kali as demon-slayer. Another example is Phoolan Devi, a gangleader, folk heroine and feminist icon known as the Bandit Queen, who was recently released from prison and has been elected as a member of parliament.

Buddhism can be described as more 'masculine' in style, particularly the tough regime of Rinzai Zen with its oft-used metaphor of cutting off the student's head to attain enlightenment. Maurine Stuart and Kennett Roshi successfully exemplify this style and teach it to their students, though they might not describe themselves as masculine. It is a question of emphasis, cultivating qualities traditionally perceived as masculine, such as strength and courage.

Most women in religious life hitherto have acquired the title 'Mother', including those such as nuns who are debarred from biological motherhood. Women who identify with motherliness as a defining characteristic will tend towards a more feminine style of leadership. Christian women who have attained leadership positions tend to take on the title, such as Mother Anne Lee; abbesses and prioresses are addressed as Mother Superior. It is also a virtually universal title in Hinduism. Women teachers and sages are addressed as Mataji (Holy Mother), such as Nirmala Devi. Others take on the title in some other form, as with Mother Meera, Anandamayi Ma and Ammachi.

Sannyasin women were also given the prefix Ma to their

names. Despite the relative devaluation of motherhood in the movement, several women referred to 'motherliness' as an important feminine quality. The nurturing aspect of motherhood was seen as very important in the work, especially for the co-ordinators, who were known as 'moms' and 'supermoms' or collectively as the 'ma-archy'. The BKs are given the prefix Sister, but motherliness is one of the pre-eminent qualifications for female leadership. When I asked one why she claimed 'Women are excellent teachers' she replied, 'Well, they're mothers, aren't they? They have mothering qualities, patience. And this is the teaching that came through Brahma, that the mothers must go in front.' All my BK respondents emphasized that women's 'maternal' qualities such as nurturing and compassion were more conducive to spiritual growth than 'male' competitiveness, in line with the official doctrine.

Receptivity is the most-cited quality to epitomize both femininity and spirituality, particularly in movements based on discipleship or mediumship. Although some sannyasin leaders failed spectacularly in this respect, others, such as Osho's first secretary Laxmi, the therapists, and the mediums were perceived as 'vehicles' for the divine. As discussed, this is the approach most embodied by Indian *bhakti* gurus. In spiritualism and channelling, receptivity is the primary qualification, which probably explains the predominance of women. Other qualities that women leaders have frequently defined as positively feminine and beneficial for leadership are practicality, intuition, tenderness, body-affirmation, caring, healing, devotion, forgiveness, holism, social engagement and social mysticism.

Probably the most flexible and relevant model of female leadership for the future is of a more androgynous kind, which steers a middle path between imitating and cultivating the traditional masculine models, with the danger of taking on their flaws to an even greater degree, or adhering too closely to a feminine model, which lacks toughness in a confrontation or crisis.[15] Osho offered women opportunities to experiment with this approach, which some adapted more successfully than others. The BKs also make conscious efforts towards this kind of integration, although the result is much closer to the feminine, probably owing to the influence of *bhakti*. Gurumayi and Nirmala Devi both manage to combine active, assertive roles building their organizations with a more graceful, receptive style of teaching and giving *darshan* to their devotees. Within the world religions, Buddhism offers most scope for a truly androgynous style of leadership. In itself it contains a balance between wisdom and compassion which in Tibetan Buddhism (surprisingly to Westerners!) are represented as respectively feminine and masculine qualities. Particularly in America, but increasingly in Britain, Buddhist women are leading the way towards a post-modernist, post-feminist, androgynous style of leadership.

One NRM where women have been prominent in leadership roles from the beginning – since its creation or revival this century – is within Paganism and the goddess spirituality movement. The next chapter examines these movements in more detail.

# 9 Goddess Spirituality: The Feminist Alternative?

## The Divine Feminine in the Judaeo-Christian tradition

The most fundamental problem for women in the Judaeo-Christian tradition is the overpowering dominance of the male perspective, which has constructed and distorted the core symbolism and language of the tradition. The most obvious manifestation of this sexism – both underlying and overriding – is the lack of any concept of the divine feminine: there is a God but no Goddess. In Judaism, Jahweh reigns supreme. Christianity possesses a Trinity with two male figures and a neuter or asexual Holy Ghost. The Virgin Mary is the centre of a cult, Mariolatry, for some Catholics, but although she is honoured as the Mother of God in the Orthodox Church she is not God the Mother – she does not partake of Godhead. In some quarters (particularly the mainstream Protestant denominations), devotion to the Virgin Mary and other female saints is seen as the preserve of folk religion, a relic of primitive pagan superstitions. Furthermore, this lack of respect or even acknowledgement of the divine feminine legitimates the lack of female leadership within these religions.

Despite the sexism of the Judaeo-Christian tradition, some feminists continue to believe in the authenticity of the core revelations of both religions. They therefore choose to remain in these religions, tackling sexism from within while exploring and developing feminist alternatives to existing rituals, doctrines and exegesis. They seek out the few biblical references that may be construed or interpreted as goddess-oriented, feminine imagery for the divine, pro-women statements by Jesus or Paul. They write liturgical material calling on God as Mother, and books of positive, constructive, alternative theology. Carol Christ and Judith Plaskow refer to this choice as the reformist option: the belief that by cleansing the core teachings from millennia of misogynistic deviation, the essential truth of the tradition may be once more revealed in its pristine purity. They contrast reformism with revolution: acceptance of the hopelessness of uprooting such rigidly entrenched prejudice and leaving to create new spiritual possibilities and expressions for women. However, their next book took account of criticisms that this classification appeared to overly favour the revolutionaries as 'more radical, profound and courageous', failing to acknowledge the great diversity of approaches within both camps, whereby women who remain in their religion of birth may be more concerned with transforming than reforming tradition. They therefore decided that a continuum model might be more appropriate than a dichotomous one, although one could argue that the original terms do encapsulate a significant and fundamental divergence.[1]

In Judaism, reformist feminists are revisioning Lilith, Adam's first wife. Not many people know about Lilith, who does not feature in Genesis, although Asphodel Long (1992) argues that it is she who is the breath of life, the spirit of God, and thus the original Creatrix. Rabbinic legends describe her as Adam's first wife – an attempt to rationalize the two versions of the creation story in Genesis. In the first version, man and woman were created equal, whereas in the second – significantly, better known – version, Eve was created out of Adam's rib. The rabbinical explanation is that Lilith was too independent and argumentative, giving Adam a hard time. The last straw was her refusal to adopt the missionary position, and as a result of this unthinkable chutzpah, Adam complained to God. Lilith still refused to comply and so was banished, and eventually demonized as a danger to women in childbirth and killer of children.

Some Jewish feminists are reclaiming Lilith as a Goddess, exemplifying female power and sexuality. There is also a theory that in early Judaism, Jahweh had a consort, Asherah. Even more radically, there is a movement in America to recreate the kind of pagan, polytheistic Judaism that existed before it became the state religion in 621 BCE. Another proto-goddess is the Shekhinah: God's indwelling glory and presence in the world. The Hebrew word is feminine, and within the mystical tradition of Kabbala referred to the feminine side of God. For centuries this teaching was only available to men, but is now being discovered and reclaimed by women as the divine feminine. The Shekhinah also absorbed some of the attributes of another important manifestation of female divininity, Hochmah.

For many feminists in Judaism and Christianity, the figure of Wisdom (known as Hochmah in Hebrew, Sophia in Greek) is a rich source of inspiration. Wisdom may be seen as the exemplar of the divine feminine in the Old Testament, bearing a striking resemblance to earlier prototypes such as Cybele, Queen of Heaven and mother of the gods. In the Book of Wisdom she is personified with many attributes of divinity. Yet this text which apotheosizes her also describes her degeneration, and the book ends with her enslaved, her riches made over to the Sage who has conquered her. Wisdom reappears in Christianity, but as the fallen Sophia in need of male redemption. Her attributes are absorbed by the Torah and the Shekhinah in Judaism, and by Christ as Logos in Christianity. Here her identification with the Goddess is lost completely, although it was partly preserved in Gnostic groups until these were banned; then re-emerged briefly in a medieval heretical sect, the Cathars. In the Middle Ages, Sophia was also partly recovered through Mary in her role as Mother of God – though lacking divinity in her own right.[2]

Christian attempts to recover the Goddess have also focused on the Virgin Mary and Mary Magdalen – most famous exemplars of the Virgin–Whore dichotomy that Christianity did so much to create and promote. The Gnostics are believed by some feminist theologians to have been especially radical in their promotion of the divine feminine and the role of women in the church. There is even some evidence of an esoteric tradition passed from Jesus via Mary Magdalen.[3] As the first witness to the Resurrection and possibly the most important early disciple, Mary Magdalen was highly regarded by the Gnostics and other early Christians as the companion to the Saviour, the woman he loved most, and the Bride of Christ. However, she is best known in her traditional role of repentant sinner – victim and scapegoat – and is only recently being reclaimed as the quintessence of female sexuality, fused with mysticism. This re-evaluation has given rise to a spate of scholarly reconstructions as well as fiction, most notably Michèle Roberts's 1984 novel *The Wild Girl*, based on a feminist-romantic interpretation of the Gnostic gospels.

Mary the Virgin is harder to reclaim as a feminist icon, though easier as a symbol for mainstream Christianity, and as such her popularity has seen a rapid upsurge over the last two decades.

Her shrines, particularly Medjugorje, have become vast centres of pilgrimage; more people are reporting seeing her, and her messages are even being channelled in a best-selling book.[4] She is upheld as the spiritual mother of humanity and a paragon of Christian femininity: an example of perfect devotion, passive will submitting to divine authority: 'Let it be done to me according to thy word' (Luke 1:38). She therefore exemplifies the discipleship model of female spirituality, but may be found correspondingly unhelpful as a role model for feminists – some of whom find her cult sentimental and infantile. In Mary, Eve is redeemed – but at a price. In her theological isolation from the weakness of real woman, she is not only an impossible ideal but bears no relation to the actual status of real women within the church.

There is no incontrovertible evidence for the Goddess in the Judaeo-Christian tradition, either as part of God's oneness or as a consort, worshipped with him or separately. However, the possibilities so tantalizingly glimpsed in Hochmah–Sophia, in the Shekhinah, and to some extent in the figures of the Madonna and Magdalen, have inspired many spiritual feminists to a rediscovery of the divine feminine.

The concern of goddess spirituality is to put the Goddess back at the centre of existence and spiritual experience, with or without a male consort or equivalent. It is therefore a threat to the very foundations of Christianity, which has been male-created and male-dominated from its beginnings. Feminist theologians are therefore sometimes ambivalent or even hostile to such concerns. For example, Mary Grey points out the dangers of separatism, escapism and dualism, of indulgence in 'unhelpful nostalgia' (1989, 53), especially given the shaky evidence on which the mythology is constructed. Other feminist theologians are more welcoming of what they see as a positive and creative development, for example Rosemary Radford Ruether, Elisabeth Schussler Fiorenza and Ursula King. Others again move to the radical fringe, though sometimes retaining a link by labelling themselves post-Christian, such as Mary Daly. Carol Christ has become ever more deeply committed to goddess and nature spirituality, while retaining a toehold at least in the academic tradition as a thealogian. Thealogy is a corollary discipline that has grown out of the enormous increase in writing and debate on feminist theology and goddess spirituality.

Ursula King describes this approach as 'fundamentally different from traditional male-oriented and male-dominated theology. Thealogy gives primacy to symbols rather than to rational explanations which are so prevalent in theological thought' (1989, 131).

For many women this change is too little, too late. These have abandoned the uphill struggle to recreate a gender-balanced theology within the Judaeo-Christian tradition and have left the fold altogether to seek a more feminist and holistic kind of religion within the women's spirituality movement.

## The Women's Spirituality Movement

The Goddess is the central theme in the women's spirituality movement, also known as wimmins or womyns spirituality, feminist spirituality, womanspirit, and most specifically goddess spirituality. Charlene Spretnak emphasizes that 'Women's spirituality is not synonymous with Goddess spirituality', since 'some practitioners of the former are uncomfortable with any anthropomorphizing of the One', although in practice all these terms tend to be used loosely as synonyms.[5] Emily Culpepper is unhappy even about the term 'spiritual', perceiving it as carrying 'a heavy load of dualistic, anti-body associations behind it which feminists recognize as ultimately being a key component of the androcentric oppressive dichotomy between female and male' (1978, 232).

The women's spirituality movement arose partly out of feminist theology, partly in connection with Paganism, and was also strongly influenced by Jungian psychology. There is so much correlation between Jungian psychology and spirituality that there have been many practitioners with a foot in both camps as well as a specific interest in women's spirituality, ever since the books of Esther Harding first published in the 1920s. Well-known modern writers are Naomi Goldenberg, Demaris Wehr, and June Singer. Not all of these are goddess worshippers. For example, Marion Woodman is one of the leading figures in female psychology, who has written extensively on the birth of the conscious feminine, drawing on ideas about the Triple Goddess and the Great Goddess, but as inner archetypes rather than objects of devotion. *Descent to the Goddess* by the Jungian psychologist Sylvia Perera is one of the most influential books on the subject.[6] Male Jungian psychologists have also been highly influenced by goddess spirituality and written important books, particularly Edward Whitmont and Robert Johnson, and the Jungian-influenced mythologist Joseph Campbell.[7]

All the known ancient religions of the Middle East had a Great Goddess figure: Tiamat in Babylon, Inanna in Sumeria, Astarte in Canaan, Isis in Egypt. The goddesses of ancient Greece and Rome continued as sources of inspiration in literature and art, but were in no way incorporated into Christianity, unlike some other aspects of classical philosophy and spirituality. It is believed, however, that some attributes of these ancient goddesses, particularly Isis, have influenced concepts and images of the Virgin Mary as Mother of God, particularly as the Madonna with Child. The three main Western religions – Judaism, Christianity and Islam – are unusual in their complete lack of a Goddess. Indeed, their myths feature the conquest and slaying of the mother goddess by the heroic warrior gods of the new tradition. Merlin Stone (1976) has researched the anti-Goddess iconography of the Eden myth as well as the historical references throughout the Old Testament to the desecration of the altars and sacred places of the Canaanite goddesses. Even Sts Michael and George and their Dragons may be interpreted as variants of ancient myths of sun or sky gods conquering the mother goddess as serpent or dragon, for example the Babylonian creation epic in which the god Marduk defeats the serpent-dragon Tiamat.

Many of the goddesses from ancient and contemporary religion have been reclaimed and adopted by modern Western women as symbols of creativity and healing, liberation and empowerment. Celtic goddesses such as Brigit are particularly revered, as are the Greek goddesses, who are often linked with feminine archetypes.[8] Other ancient goddesses may resonate with some women, for example Inanna and the Egyptian goddesses Isis and Hathor. The goddess movement is still Eurocentric, rarely extending beyond the Near East, but African goddesses such as Oya are sometimes worshipped. Native American spirituality does not talk of goddesses, but spirit guides such as Buffalo Calf Woman are inspirational for many women and Grandmother Earth is probably the most important sacred presence in the tradition.

Eastern religions have retained their goddesses, who are still widely revered and worshipped. The Hindu goddesses provide the richest, most multi-dimensional symbolism of all, from the gentle sweetness of Uma and Parvati to the fearsome power of Kali and Durga, so their attributes are often internalized by goddess worshippers, though they rarely feature in Hindu-based NRMs. Tara is the pre-eminent goddess in Tibetan Buddhism, central in many Tantric rituals. The male bodhisattva Avalokitesvara was adopted by Chinese Buddhism, and in an unusual example of trans-sexuality became feminized into the goddess Kuan Yin, one of the most important deities throughout Chinese religions. She was also worshipped in Japan as Kannon.[9]

*The Divine Feminine and the Social Status of Women*
These examples, however, raise an important issue that is not often addressed in women's spirituality: the relationship between the divine feminine and the role and status of women in society. For example, although Kuan Yin is the Goddess of Mercy and Compassion, it was not she but the economic requirements of the communist regime that put an end to footbinding. Similarly, the manifold powers of the Hindu goddesses have not yet succeeded in eradicating female infanticide and dowry-burnings. Ursula King is one of the few writers to have tackled this contentious question, asking whether the Great Indian Goddess – perhaps the most ancient and venerable of still-current female deities – can be a source of empowerment for women. Devi (also known as Mahadevi and Shakti) is 'the supreme ruler of all earthly creatures and the entire universe . . . victorious over all adverse powers' (1993, 28), but she is also identified with *maya* (illusion) and *prakriti* (matter), hence may also be perceived as the force that keeps humanity bound to the illusory material world. Furthermore, despite the tremendous power of *shakti*, the female power and energy of the universe found in women as well as the goddess, Indian women are still subject to male power at all stages of their lives and highly restricted in their religious and social roles. This is enshrined in the law of Manu which dictates that women must be 'protected' by men throughout their lives 'in youth by their fathers, in married life by their husbands, and in old age by their sons. A woman is never fit for independence.' King

concludes that Hinduism 'provides exuberantly rich, but also very ambivalent, symbolic resources for contemporary women' (ibid., 34).

In another book, King poses the direct question: 'Is the worship of goddesses in ancient times – or in living religions today for that matter – in any way a proof for the existence of female power and the high status of women or does this worship ultimately rest on male projection?' (1989, 125). Male projection may superimpose divine beauty and grace on the seemingly most unworthy of mortal women, or may despise and denigrate women while worshipping the divine feminine. It is well known that a group of gay clergy were among the least supportive and even most hostile factions in the women's ordination campaign (although other gay priests were actively supportive). Yet gay priests are also at the forefront of the high Anglican movement of devotion to the Virgin Mary, which suggests some correlation between the rejection of female sexuality in real women and the idealization of the non-sexual mother goddess. Some of the men who have written most appreciatively and fervently about the need for a rebirth of goddess spirituality are gay or bisexual, whether covertly or openly. It seems significant that Andrew Harvey, while still promoting the Goddess, has publicly denounced his former female guru whom he formerly believed to embody the Shakti, since he claims she refused to bless his homosexual marriage (see p.186).

It is clear that the Goddess as a symbol has no innate meaning, value or predetermined social outcome. It is therefore important that in Western culture goddess worship should take place in a feminist context, in order to ground and integrate the spiritual with the social and political issues. There are examples of the divine feminine being incorporated in Western religion without this precondition with the same results, that is without raising the social and spiritual status of women. For example, the Mormons image the spiritual parents of humanity as a deity who is both male and female, but women cannot become bishops. There is a similar situation in the Unification Church, where the Reverend and Mrs Moon are widely believed to be the Heavenly Parents, yet women play a restricted and subordinate role in the movement.

*Goddess ontology*

Despite the centrality of the Goddess to the women's spirituality movement, there is no consensus as to her ontological status and meaning, whether she has an outer, independent reality, or is simply a symbol of inner potential. Carol Christ summarizes the main three definitions in a groundbreaking essay:

> 1) The Goddess is divine female, a personification who can be invoked in prayer and ritual; 2) The Goddess is symbol of the life, death, and rebirth energy in nature and culture, in personal and communal life and 3) the Goddess is symbol of the affirmation of the legitimacy and beauty of female power (made possible by the new becoming of women in the women's liberation movement). (1992, 278)

The Goddess is usually not anthropomorphized as a substitute for the male God, in hierarchical terms; an oft-heard cry is that 'We don't want Yahweh with a skirt'. On the other hand, she may be personalized as a Being with powers, with whom one can communicate. The crucial difference is that she is not seen as transcendental, separate from creation, but as immanent in the individual and nature. In Starhawk's splendid aphorism: 'The Goddess does not rule the world; She is the world' (1989, 23). Many women, especially those approaching the Goddess from a background of psychology and personal development, which are still so heavily influenced by Jung, see the Goddess in symbolic or archetypal terms as a consciousness-raising principle or role model. As such, she is equivalent to the god within of Eastern-based and New Age NRMs: the Goddess Within. She may also be a symbol for healing, and such women often identify with the healers and midwives of the Middle Ages, and may themselves be practising healers. As well as self-healing, as Gaia she is the most significant symbol of planetary healing (see below). She is also an important symbol of female empowerment, legitimating women's own power and independence, and inspiring them to formulate and realize their own potential and goals. As Creatrix, she inspires and channels women's creativity.

The Goddess is also an important source of inspiration to men. For example Tony Grist, an Anglican vicar, recently left the church to become a Pagan largely on account of his objections to Christian patriarchy: 'I am allergic to heavy fathers.' He has chosen instead to express his 'devotion to the Feminine Principles, the Mother Goddess, whom I choose to personalise as Isis'.[10] Druidry is also criticized as patriarchal, but the Goddess is central for the Druid priest Philip Shallcrass: 'Over the years I have come to reverence the Goddess as a being external to myself. I am persuaded of Her reality by the fact that She speaks to me, gives me visions, shows me signs through the natural world and awakens power within me; the power I need to act as a Druid and as a Priest' (1996, 15).

Starhawk originally came to the Goddess in this more psychological and rational way but, as happens with many people, deepening experience changed these perceptions and concepts into a more animistic spirituality. She told a gathering in London that

> At first I believed the Goddess was simply an archetypal energy, until I noticed that she seems to work for real. Now I believe she is not just a psychological reality but has her own energies. . . . Everything is alive and full of spirit and intelligence, and can communicate. The old powers are reawakening and returning, and can reconnect us. They give vitality to the physical world, flowing back and forth between the seen and unseen worlds.[11]

Starhawk is a feminist witch and Pagan. In Paganism, the Goddess is welcomed and finds a natural home at the centre of existence and spiritual experience, with or without a male consort.

## Paganism

The meaning of Paganism has changed from its origins as a state-endorsed religion to a pejorative term applied both to polytheistic tribal religions and to anti-religious hedonists; later, less judgmentally, it described the pre-Christian vestiges of Celtic folk religions in Europe. Now Paganism is an umbrella label, encompassing a congeries of magical, ecospiritual and goddess-worshipping individuals, groups and networks. It includes a number of recognizable traditions, some of which can trace a separate history. For example, Druidry goes back to at least the eighteenth century, though it claims roots back to the ancient world. Another movement popular in northern Europe, though less so in America, is Asatru or Odinism, based on the Norse tradition. The largest and most predominant group in Europe and America is Wicca. In addition, Paganism may be globalized to cover traditional shamanic and/or polytheistic religions such as Taoism, Shinto, Santería, Candomblé and tribal religions. Hinduism is sometimes claimed as Pagan on account of its polytheistic tendencies, though this is disputed. Also included are groups based on earth mysteries, ritual magic and chaos magic. To give some idea of the range, the Internet currently lists 40 British Pagan groups, including the Association of Hedgewitches, Scarlet Tantric Pagan Centre, Dragon Environmental Group, Fellowship of Isis, Northern Earth Mysteries Group, Order of Bards, Ovates and Druids, Pagan Animal Rights, and Robin's Greenwood Gang.

Numbers of Pagans are impossible to estimate accurately, given the diversity, fragmentation, privacy and lack of formal organization, but it is clear that it is a rapidly growing movement throughout Europe and America, both in terms of numbers and public prominence.[12] Those who join come from all backgrounds though generally conform to the profile of the counter-cultural seeker: white, middle-class, well-educated, but slightly more likely than the average NRM member to come from an unconventional religious background (Kelly 1992). There are signs of some difference of opinion and orientation between the more respectable wing of professional householders and the radical fringe of 'ecowarriors' and 'crusties' (aka New Age travellers), debated in *The Wiccan* (now *Pagan Dawn*). But at the moment there is not a public rift, and the different factions sometimes do rituals together.

*Mythology and History*
There is an ongoing debate, sometimes fierce, as to the provenance and lineage of the present Pagan revival, especially the extent of an ongoing tradition. Pagans usually believe that the roots of their religion lie far back in a prehistoric, prepatriarchal, prelapsarian golden age when the Great Goddess ruled supreme, and women and men lived together peacefully in small matriarchal communities. The mythology is partly based on historical and textual research, particularly by Merlin Stone (1976), and partly on the archaeological work of Marija

Gimbutas (1982). Gimbutas contrasts the Old European and Indo-European civilizations: 'The first was matrifocal, sedentary, peaceful, art-loving, earth- and sea-bound; the second was patrifocal, mobile, warlike, ideologically sky oriented, and indifferent to art' (in Christ and Plaskow 1989, 63). This idyll was rudely interrupted around 4500 BCE by the invasion of Indo-European tribes from the north, fierce male warriors with swords on horseback who worshipped male gods of storm and battle. They overthrew the matriarchy, imposing a new patriarchal order with all its attendant evils, including religions that excluded the Goddess and her priestesses, and subjugated women to male gods, priests, rulers and husbands. There is a lively ongoing debate as to the existence and extent of matriarchy and goddess worship, focused particularly on the sacred significance of the abundance of female figurines.[13]

Whatever the historical truth of these beliefs, they form a coherent mythology that gives a quasi-theological underpinning to most pagan and goddess-worshipping traditions and constitute part of its appeal. There is an ongoing debate as to the relative merits of mythological truth versus hard historical fact. As Ursula King expresses it: 'women do not really need history to justify their religion, for whether there was a religion of the Great Goddess in ancient times or not, there certainly exists one today' (1989, 144). On the other hand, some witches themselves are unhappy about the blurring of boundaries. One radical feature of the women's spirituality movement is the honouring of people's own experience as legitimate revelation, rather than relying on male priesthoods to monopolize and mediate divine revelation. Carol Christ (1992) notes the spontaneous emergence of the goddess symbol in the dreams, fantasies and thoughts of women. Naomi Goldenberg (1992) argues that these are valid sources of revelation, making the comparison with the basis of Jung's theories in personal revelation.

Yet at the same time there is a concern for lineage and continuity, roots in nature and tradition, a bulwark against the shifting uncertainties and fragmentation of the post-modern world. For example, Wiccans call their path the Old Religion, although followers of indigenous traditions such as Native American spirituality sometimes disparage Wicca as invented or constructed. Pagans who claim continuity tend to reject classification as an NRM, including the label neo-Pagan, although some Pagans themselves adopt this term which is more accurate.[14]

Mythological history traces a continuity of Paganism through the vicissitudes of the ancient world, despite Aryan depredations, up to the era of early Christianity. It is the missionary zeal of the church that is held responsible for virtually eradicating Paganism – which was now seen not as a religion but as primitive, intellectually contemptible superstition – in a violent revolution in which temples were looted and destroyed, books burned, ceremonies banned, participants massacred, and the entire culture of the Graeco-Roman world wiped out in iconoclastic madness: a repeat performance of the destruction of Canaanite religion carried out by Judaism and a precursor of the ravages of the Protestant Reformation. This violence reached its murderous crescendo in the 'Burning Times': the European witch-hunts of the Middle Ages.[15] The witch-hunts are clearly a complex socio-religious phenomenon, but one probable trigger is the rise of the male medical profession campaigning against the predominance of women as midwives and healers, particularly in the villages. It is believed that vestiges of Paganism continued as an oral tradition and may be found in folklore and customs, agricultural ceremonies such as the green man processions that still take place in Britain and Germany, songs, myths and fairy tales. There is no evidence for the survival of witchcraft into the Middle Ages and even the present century in organized covens or as an underground feminist spirituality movement, but the myth is captured in this verse from a modern folk song:

And the Pope declared the Inquisition
it was a war against the women whose power they feared.
In this holocaust against the nature people,
nine million European women died.
And the tale is told of those, who by the hundred,
holding together, chose their deaths in the sea,
while chanting the praises of the Mother Goddess,
a refusal of betrayal, women were dying to be free.[16]

A more probable provenance for modern Paganism is in the hermetic tradition that flourished during the Renaissance, in occultism, gnosticism, alchemy and Kabbala.[17] The rise of science in the seventeenth century relegated Pagan beliefs and rituals to the realm of primitive superstition, but interest reawakened in association with the poetry and nature worship of the Romantic movement. The nineteenth century witnessed the rise of various occult movements, such as Freemasonry and Druidry. The Western Mystery Tradition has held an appeal for people since the end of the nineteenth century, particularly on account of its Celtic trappings which ensured its popularity in Ireland. The Order of the Golden Dawn was a highly influential esoteric society, attracting such luminaries as the poet William Butler Yeats. Most of the well-known magicians served an apprenticeship in it, including Aleister Crowley who became its leader, and later joined another influential occult group, the Ordo Templi Orientis.

In its present form, Paganism is predominantly an outgrowth of the 1960s occult revival, which has culminated in the New Age, although there is much disagreement over the relationship. Some see Paganism as a movement within the broader field of the New Age, perhaps its ecospiritual wing. In support of this argument, the two movements share many common beliefs and most Pagans see themselves as part of a wider movement of consciousness and planetary healing. Others see the New Age and Paganism in more dichotomous terms, either complementary or opposed. There is increasing dislike of the term New Age; for example, in a survey of goddessworshippers, Jo Pearson found that 74 per cent felt no connection with the New Age. So-called New Agers themselves often reject this label on account of its negative, 'flaky' image, and its association with the New Age travellers – although others see the travellers as the most worthwhile, 'grounded' wing of the movement. So far no appropriate alternative term has been found, so most people continue to use 'New Age'.[18] The Pagan priestess Monica Sjoo is vehemently opposed to the New Age as irredeemably patriarchal, hierarchical and oppressive – all the accusations which feminists levy against the Judaeo-Christian tradition. Yet some of her language and beliefs are quintessentially New Age. She denounces channelling, while practising her own form of channelling and communication with spirits and retaining a 'soft spot' for the entity Seth. So the boundaries are permeable.

The differences in values and attitudes could be summarized as follows:

| New Age | Pagan |
|---|---|
| Aquarius | Gaia |
| Transcendence | Immanence |
| Mind and spirit | Body and soul |
| God | Nature |
| Light | Dark |
| High | Grounded |
| Innovation | Tradition |
| Guru devotion | Empowerment |
| Masculine | Feminine |
| Prosperity consciousness | Simple living |
| Meditation | Magic |
| Channelling spirits from the astral plane | Journeying into the lower world |
| Enlightenment | Harmony with nature |
| Creating a new heaven and earth | Saving the planet |

*Beliefs and Practices*
There are no formal creeds or dogmas in Paganism, and this is part of the appeal in contrast to organized religion:

> Modern Neo-Paganism and Witchcraft . . . [is] a surprising and amazing attempt by Westerners in the heart of our industrial society to create non-authoritarian and non-dogmatic religions. . . . What's unusual about modern Pagans is that they remain anti-authoritarian while retaining rituals and ecstatic techniques that, in our culture, are used only by dogmatic religions or are the province of small and forgotten tribal groups.[19]

Diversity of doctrine and praxis is part of its strength and appeal, though it may lead to confusion. For example, although traditional Pagan societies are polytheistic, and some Pagans see polytheism as a defining characteristics, others see the minor deities and particular forms as being subsumed into the one Great Goddess and/or God, of which they are simply personifications. An oft-repeated maxim is: All the Gods are one God, and all the Goddesses are one Goddess. This belief could be termed a variation on monotheism (see meanings of the Goddess above), but choice is fundamental.

There are a few beliefs common to most if not all Pagan groups. In summary: whether deity is conceived as polytheistic or monistic (and the two categories may be overlapping or interchangeable), s/he is immanent in creation. The Goddess is pre-eminent, sometimes as an archetype but often as a deity, being worshipped with or without a male consort. God/dess has different names and forms in different traditions, but the Triple Goddess predominates. Creation is a unity in which all life forms are interconnected and of equal value. Paganism is often described as an earth-based spirituality in which the seasonal festivals are celebrated and the human body is sacred. Paganism is highly ritualistic, and magic is widely practised. Some of these beliefs and practices are examined in more detail above and below.

### The Appeal of Paganism to Women

As we have seen, Eastern-based NRMs had a strong appeal among women of the 1960s counter-culture, and many Pagans began their alternative spiritual quest by exploring Eastern traditions. Yet sexism is rife, particularly in the more conservative NRMs. Even in NRMs where women are encouraged to attain positions of power, to become enlightened, to be leaders and teachers, there is usually not a corresponding emphasis on the Goddess. Furthermore, many women wish to find or construct a Western form of spirituality. The main criticism of the turn East made by even sympathetic theologians and philosophers such as Harvey Cox (1979) and Jacob Needleman (1977) is that Westerners will not flourish if they uproot themselves and try to take on another culture, although this is countered by Westerners who claim to feel more at home in Eastern religions, sometimes supported by past-life memories.

Starhawk's main criticism of these religions is that the emphasis on dropping the ego is dangerous for most women, who have not yet developed a strong sense of self, a position very close to the Christian feminist critique of the doctrine of sinful pride (see pp.87–8). Starhawk does not believe women receive anything in return for their surrender; rather, that they are in bondage, however ecstatic. Such a path may be helpful for men to contact their 'feminine' side, but women cannot become whole by exaggerating these already over-emphasized qualities. 'We become whole through knowing our strength and creativity, our aggression, our sexuality, by affirming the Self, not by denying it' (1989, 205). Vivianne Crowley also criticizes the attraction to Eastern-based NRMs, particularly in terms of the master–disciple relationship, believing that 'The Western mind is not truly guru-oriented'. In an interview she explained why although many of her friends were getting involved in the Osho movement, she herself had not joined:

> I felt it was a cult based on worship of a human being. I found people wearing the guru's portrait round their necks bizarre and worrying. It seemed to be giving up one's own will. I certainly couldn't have joined something that was guru-oriented, I valued my independence. Particularly as a woman, it was very important to me to be in control of my own life.

Vivianne Crowley is a Wiccan high priestess. Wicca is the largest and predominant Pagan tradition. Since women are in the majority, particularly in the US but also in Britain,[20] whereas Druidry and Asatru are male-dominated,[21] I shall describe Wicca in more detail.

## Wicca

The term Paganism is provocative enough, but witchcraft evokes even stronger protest, although contemporary witches carefully distinguish their craft from satanism, which they see as a Christian heresy constructed to legitimate the medieval witch-hunts. Wicca (sometimes known as white witchcraft or simply as the Craft) is the largest and best known of the Pagan movements. Indeed, in America the terms Wicca and Paganism are sometimes used interchangeably.

Wicca was invented by Gerald Gardner in the 1940s, drawing extensively on the 1920s' writings of Margaret Murray and purportedly based on the remnants of neolithic fertility cults, although his claims of continuity are now largely discredited.[22] Its development coincided with the repeal of the Witchcraft Act (which made witchcraft illegal) in 1951 and its replacement by the Fraudulent Mediums Act. In the early 1960s two of Gardner's initiates, Raymond and Rosemary Buckland, brought Wicca to the US and founded the first American coven in New York. Since then American Wicca has become open and syncretistic with a less rigorous initiation process. It is sometimes referred to as Wiccan or Goddess-centred Paganism. The second main influence on Wicca is the Alexandrian tradition founded by Alex and Maxine Sanders. In 1971 one of their initiates, Stewart Farrar, published *What Witches Do*, the first book to publicly describe Wiccan ritual, thus bringing it to much wider knowledge and triggering its growth and a plethora of other books, particularly by Starhawk, Vivianne Crowley and Marian Green.

*Magic and Gender Polarity*
The practice of magic is fundamental to Wicca, as in many other Pagan groups, and is one of the main elements in its appeal. Most initiates have former experience of New Age divination systems, particularly astrology and Tarot, while runes are central to the northern European traditions and dowsing is increasingly popular. Nowadays there is an increasing emphasis on shamanic technique, particularly the induction of trance states.

As discussed in Chapter 8, women have always been pre-eminent in esoteric traditions, and most of the major shapers of the current revival have been women, such as Helena Blavatsky, Alice Bailey and Dion Fortune. There is an esoteric tradition, particularly adhered to in Wicca but upheld by earlier magicians such as Dion Fortune, that feminine qualities are in the ascendent in the inner world where magic takes place. Jung was an important influence on Dion Fortune, and the Jungian psychologist Vivianne Crowley has had a shaping influence on Wicca. Thus women are seen as intuitive, feeling, relating, nurturing; men are strong, decisive, active in the world. But there is also a concept of female strength as earth-based, regenerative, 'a strong and powerful woman who's very independent, and comes into interaction with the god of her own free will'. Furthermore, the emphasis is on achieving balance between one's inner masculine and feminine attributes in order to become an integrated whole person. This process enables women who have previously been passive, underachieving, or concentrated on motherhood, to develop their minds and careers. One woman had become a management consultant as a result of the confidence gained through her spiritual practice.

On the other hand, women and men who have previously been overly intellectual or business-oriented might have a child or develop their creative side. Wicca provides opportunities for rebalancing through developing new skills: developing the intellectual faculty through teaching, lecturing, writing; the feeling side through becoming a counsellor, healer, spellmaker; and the intuitive side through creating artefacts, statues, altars.

The anthropologist Susan Greenwood describes magic as 'one form of rebellion from a patriarchal rationalist culture, the return of the romantic feminine being a gateway to the otherworld'. The magical will is a central concept, and it is clearly important for women to know and believe in their will as valid and capable of achieving their goals – in contrast to the emphasis in Christianity and the master–disciple relationship on submission. But Greenwood sees the development of will in magical practice as being along the lines of a specifically masculine model, closely allied to the Nietzschean will to power in its emphasis on power and control over the self, and ultimately the universe. This contrasts with the feminist witchcraft model. Starhawk has written extensively on power, contrasting the patriarchal ideal of power-over (hierarchical, dominant, top-down) with the feminist/spiritual ideal of power-from-within as interconnected, egalitarian and immanent: 'power-from-within *is* the power of the low, the dark, the earth; the power that arises from our blood, and our lives, and our passionate desire for each other's living flesh' (1990, 4).[23]

Whatever its literal efficacy, magic can be an important means of personal development and empowerment for women. Some women enter Wicca feeling quite disempowered, and the effect of performing magical rituals seems similar to the positive thinking and affirmation that are so widely used in the New Age. The main purpose of magic is generally agreed to be multi-purpose: for insight, personal growth, spirituality and power, but more inner- than outer-directed; concerned more with producing confidence and creativity than cars and wealth. In this respect it is clearly influenced by the HPM and positive thinking. Some Wiccans tend to the view that psychology and magic 'should walk hand in hand', but others believe that 'the forces are more than archetypes'. Essentially the aim is self-healing, which is connected with the broader aim of planetary healing.

## Social Organization: The Coven

The coven is the form of social organization and community in Wicca. Covens meet regularly to celebrate the Sabbats or seasonal festivals such as the equinoxes and solstices, and the esbats or full moons. They perform magical spells and other rituals, meditations and visualizations, and may also serve a therapeutic function for those going through emotional difficulties. As Starhawk expresses it: 'The coven is a Witch's support group, consciousness-raising group, psychic study centre, clergy-training program, College of Mysteries, surrogate clan, and religious congregation all rolled into one' (1979, 49).

The degree of structure and formality varies. Some groups are more open or even leaderless and members can join and leave at will, particularly in America, although mainstream Gardnerian and Alexandrian Wicca is more authoritarian. Each coven is autonomous, run by its elders, though connected with the parent covens through which the elders were initiated and sometimes to larger networks such as the Pagan Federation and Fellowship of Isis in Britain, and the Circle Network in America. Vivianne Crowley describes the structure as 'more like a loose net than a hierarchical pyramid' (1994, 102). Although in practice the high priest and priestess hold ultimate authority, all initiates are nominally priests and priestesses, so in this respect it is egalitarian compared to the master–disciple relationship. Crowley described the difference in an interview: 'I suppose the difference from a cult with a guru is that the assumption in Wicca is that people will progress through the three levels and emerge at the same level as the leader, so the emphasis is on training people up to the same level as oneself, though it's recognized that when they come in there's a difference of experience.'

Despite this relative democracy, the hierarchical structure of the coven is still open to abuse – as is spiritual authority of any kind. There have been rumours of the abuse of power in some covens, but no evidence. Greenwood argues that the charisma bestowed upon the high priestess through her transformation into Goddess in the Drawing Down the Moon ritual creates a dualism in which the priestess may become 'a matriarch of the otherworld' as against the patriarchy of this world. She cites fieldwork experiences of rituals where participants 'were put in a position of extreme powerlessness', one initiate was 'confirmed in his child-like, novice status', the high priest was 'absolutely drained and exhausted', but the high priestess was 'glowing, radiant and at that point definitely charismatic'. She writes of this high priestess that 'her control is absolute, stifling alternative views and ideas', also mentioning another coven in which the power of the priestess was considered problematic.

Shelley Rabinovitch has done extensive demographic research on Paganism in Canada and the USA, which reveals that an overwhelming majority had experience of severe childhood trauma and abuse. They came to Paganism seeking healing, but might be subject to repetition syndrome. She has come across some examples of the abuse of power in covens, including sexual exploitation, by women as well as men. She knows of one temple-based group where 'it's a long-standing joke that you only get your first degree if you sleep with the high priestess and/or the high priest.' The initiates did not necessarily take it as abuse but as an expression of Pagan morals as well as a prerequisite for getting initiated, and for some it was also an act of hero/ine worship – though both priests now have 'feet of clay'. In her opinion these incidents are 'more indicative of dysfunctional upbringing than anything specifically wrong with the religion or its morals/ethics. We have individual instances of abuse, but none that seem to be systemic' (personal communication).

### The Role of the Priestess in the Wiccan Coven

Many Wiccans, particularly women but also men, describe the appeal of a doctrine 'where the feminine is held in high esteem'. The high status of women as priestesses in Wicca derives from Gardner, who was initiated by a woman, Dorothy Clutterbuck, worked closely with Doreen Valiente, and was influenced by Leland's research into Italian witchcraft which reveres the divine feminine. He therefore emphasized goddess worship and the predominant role of the priestess in the coven. In Wicca, as with high or ritual magic, sexual polarity is seen as vital, and covens must usually contain even numbers of men and women, preferably heterosexual. As with the New Age and many NRMs, ideas of gender are Jungian and gender roles are traditional but complementary: women mediate the Goddess, men mediate the God; women initiate men, and vice versa.

Covens are usually led by a priest and priestess, who function nominally as equals, but it appears that in most covens the priestess takes precedence. This status derives from the pre-eminence of the Goddess over the God, *prima inter pares*, and reflects the prevailing belief in matriarchy. One Wiccan said that even when the priest was the more powerful and assertive personality, he would tend to stand back and defer to his priestess. The high priestess is in charge of the rituals and the magic circle, which can only be cast by a woman. In hereditary Wicca lineage is matrilineal, the most powerful inheritor being the seventh daughter of a seventh daughter (although to continue this tradition nowadays might be considered non-environmentally friendly). Women also play the major role in ritual; only the Goddess speaks the message or charge, through the priestess. This information is given by Vivianne Crowley (1993) in an article on the power of women in modern Paganism. She continues by interpreting the symbolism in the high priestess's initiation ritual:

> The sword and crown are seen as symbols of power and legitimate authority, and are given by the God to the Goddess. Power and legitimate authority therefore belong to her, not him. This symbolic gesture recognizes the underlying reality of male–female relations: the greater physical strength of the male. The woman can only rule because the man permits her to do so. In Wicca, he does. (1993, 135)

This passage seems to undermine the basis of the female power so persuasively described and advocated previously, by defining its conditions as not 'natural' and intrinsic but social – a precarious authority granted by men, which can therefore be abrogated by men. The belief is interpreted by feminists as heterosexist and anti-feminist, and has led to a schism and the creation of a new 'sect' of Wicca: feminist witchcraft.

## Feminist Witchcraft

The attraction of feminists to goddess spirituality is a recent phenomenon. In the 1970s the women's movement was hostile to goddess spirituality, which they saw as a distraction from the real, political work. Even some feminist theologians joined the attack; for example, Mary Daly pinpointed what she called 'spiritualization' as a device enabling women to refuse to see 'the problem of sexual caste'.[24] Other spiritual feminists saw this split as an unnatural divorce, an unnecessary and destructive chasm, as expressed by Hallie Igglehart:

> We are saying the same things about the abuse of power-over relationships, the right to physical and mental health, the destruction of the environment, the importance of the personal and the political, the individual and the collective, and the necessity of the overthrow of the patriarchy on all levels. We have the same goals and values, but sometimes use different words to describe them or tools to actualize them. (1982, 404–5)

In the late 1970s, feminists started getting interested in Paganism, partly through a politically motivated search for a more egalitarian religion, partly through having psychic and 'energy' experiences that could not be explained in terms of politics or science. They took Wiccan beliefs and practices, such as goddess worship and circle-working, but 'turned them into something completely different'. Two books were particularly influential: *The Holy Book of Women's Mysteries* by the Hungarian-born American witch Zsuzsanna Budapest, which contains detailed descriptions of the seasonal festivals and other rituals; and *When God Was a Woman* by Merlin Stone, which popularized research on ancient matriarchal societies and goddess worship. Liaison between Pagan and feminist groups began to take place through study groups, circles and festivals. Feminist magazines carried features and debates on women's spirituality, and *WomanSpirit* magazine was also read by feminists. Feminist theologians started to move closer to goddess worshippers in their explorations of the divine feminine (see above). Even the redoubtable Mary Daly now approves of witchcraft as 'an Otherworld journey in feminist time/space', describing the witch as 'one who is in harmony with the universe; wisewoman, healer; one who exercises transformative powers'.[25] Feminists are more likely than Wiccans to use the word witch, reclaiming it for its associations with healing and female power.

There is some disagreement as to whether or how far this breach has been healed. For example, Neitz (1990) believes the tensions have abated and that there is far more sympathy, tolerance and sometimes co-operation. There is certainly co-operation on the Internet, where the Virtual Sisterhood exchange news and views on political and spiritual issues. Yet Jo Pearson found that 90 per cent of her goddess-worshipper sample were not feminist. Greenwood argues that political feminism has brought dissent into the occult subculture, since high magicians see politics and patriarchy as irrelevant to spiritual growth and that even planetary destruction is unimportant so long as knowlege is retained.

> This attitude takes the urgency out of any politics for change. By contrast feminist witchcraft by its very nature is a challenge to the political social system of patriarchy. Engaging in feminist ritual therefore becomes a political act. This is based on the central tenet of magical practice – that the microcosm (the individual) is a part of the macrocosm, and that work on the microcosm will have an effect on the macrocosm. Feminist witchcraft is a practical politics, it is about making changes from the inside. (1996, 122)

Some women feel that women flourish best in a segregated spiritual community. The debate between single- and mixed-sex communities continues in all fields of human development, including education, and there are arguments on both sides. In schools the evidence suggests that girls perform better academically in single-sex schools but that there are other developmental and social advantages to mixed schools. The arguments are similar in religion. Traditionally nuns have had separate communities from the monks and in Christianity achieved a degree of power and independence during the Middle Ages that led to their being swiftly subordinated to the authority of their abbots and bishops. In other religions, such as Buddhism, their status has been so low as to lead to their complete disappearance in some traditions. The FWBO have experimented with mixed and single-sex retreats and communities and have come to favour the single-sex solution. Women as well as men tend to claim that thereby they are less distracted and can make greater spiritual progress.

Feminists wanting a women-centred, women-only movement in Paganism were attracted to Dianic witchcraft, which is devoted to Diana, the virgin huntress who was served only by women. Some but not all of these groups are lesbian, although some lesbians and gay men prefer to work in a mixed group, whether heterosexual or homosexual. It is significant that both witches and lesbians use the term 'coming out' to describe going public with their identity. Dianic witchcraft began within American Wicca, attracting some censure for disregarding the balancing of male and female energies through polarity that is central in Gardnerian Wicca. Zsuzsanna Budapest's coven, founded in 1970, took Dianic witchcraft in even more radical directions, rejecting the Wiccan traditions of hierarchy, initiation and sexual polarity and becoming the model for this trend.

In the late 1970s there was some hostility and tension between Wicca and feminist witchcraft: 'Some neopagans were angry about feminist disregard for their traditions (that is, initiation, hierarchy, and the importance of balancing male and female energy). What neopagans called "their traditions", feminists sometimes called "sexist" and "homophobic"' (Neitz 1990, 368–9). The hostility continues between some groups and individuals, although in practice the boundaries are hard to draw, especially in America where they are more fluid anyway. For example, Starhawk calls herself a Wiccan and a feminist witch, although her British following is virtually entirely drawn from feminist witchcraft.

There are three main areas of difference between the two groups: gender and sexuality; authority; class. Feminists see the Wiccan emphasis on gender polarity as heterosexist and unnecessary. Wiccans claim these are used for wholeness, but feminists reject the Jungian-based concept of male and female sides, focusing on their humanity as ungendered. Although there is a growing acceptance of homosexuality within Wicca, some lesbians are sceptical as to its depth, believing it is on the lines of 'Some of my best friends are gay, but we wouldn't want them in our group'. Feminists prefer to experiment with different combinations: lesbian-only, women-only but including heterosexuals, and mixed gender and sexual orientations. A few have experimented with drawing down the God as well as the Goddess, though tend to feel uncomfortable with the inherent gender issues.

Paganism attracts rebels, but some groups are more ordered and authoritarian, including Wicca. Although the structures are relatively democratic compared with most Christian and Eastern-based NRMs, the high priest and priestess still have great power over their coven and its offshoots. Feminist witches favour much looser, more open structures, many choosing leaderless groups. As one explained, 'My feminism has led me to the idea that I don't need a leader, my spirituality to the idea that I can find my own path.' Some work alone, coming together for sabbats and other group rituals. Feminist witches are less tied to tradition and more eclectic than Wiccans, particularly in Britain, even drawing from yoga and Buddhism: 'I pick things up as I go along if they seem useful.'

Class is another area of difference and conflict. Wicca is perceived as predominantly middle-class, even upper-class, derived from the English aristocratic tradition of high magic. Wiccans are mainly professionals with families and mortgages, whereas working-class rebels are more likely to be attracted to anarchist and feminist groups such as chaos magic, the New Age travellers, and feminist witchcraft. One witch described this tendency as in line with the history of the women's movement, whereby 'ideas were put up by white, middle-class women, criticized by lesbian, working-class and black women, and so got very diverse.' Class, understandably, is less of an issue in America, where both movements are now more tolerant and mutually co-operative.

Starhawk emphasizes the need for multiple options:

> I distinguish between separation and separatism. Women need women's spaces, especially at this point in history when many of us are recovering from hurts inflicted by men. There is a special intensity in women's mysteries and an unequaled intimacy in women's covens. Women who love other women, or who live Virgin, belonging to themselves alone, attain a very special power. But it is not the only form of power inherent in feminist spirituality, nor is it the best form for everyone. The Goddess is Mother, Crone, Lover, as well as Virgin; She is bound up with the birth, love, and death of men as well as of women. If She is immanent in women, and in the world, then She is also immanent in men. (1989, 201)

Starhawk has been the single most influential figure in drawing feminists and social and environmental activists into Paganism, through her writing,[26] and her spiritual and political activities. She even turns the tables, subsuming feminism into a spiritual vision:

The feminist movement is a magicospiritual movement as well as a political movement. It is spiritual because it is addressed to the liberation of the human spirit, to healing our fragmentation, to becoming whole. It is magical because it changes consciousness, it expands our awareness and gives us a new vision. It is also magic by another definition: 'the art of causing change in accordance with will'. (ibid., 208)

Nature religion (also known as deep ecology and ecospirituality) is the most vital, dynamic, cutting-edge trend throughout Western religion at this time. The mainstream churches as well as most of the NRMs are beginning to take the environment seriously and polishing up their green credentials, even where there is little support from scripture and tradition for this position.[27] Paganism defines itself first and foremost as a nature religion, and sees itself as holding the moral high ground here, with its history and/or mythology of animism, reverence for nature and nature spirits, emphasis on immanence and deep connection with the land and the seasonal rhythms.

## Shamanism and Native American Spirituality

Native American spirituality and other tribal and/or shamanistic traditions have a particularly strong appeal in this respect, as having an ancient, unbroken relationship of harmony with the earth. Although not all Native Americans accept the label shamanism, there is a connection with the original shamanic religions of Siberia, which spread across Asia and the then land-bridge to Alaska, down the American continent, becoming the basis of present-day Native American spirituality. Shamanism could be termed dualistic, in that it believes in two distinct worlds, material and spiritual, though they co-exist in harmony. The shaman acts as an intermediary, communicating between worlds; the priest for his tribe, using spirit guides and power animals for healing and soul retrieval. The Native American medicine man or woman does similar work, while newer Pagan groups have adapted the techniques into a reconstructed neo-shamanism. The main difference from traditional shamanism is that practitioners are also trainee shamans, undergoing journeys and other processes, and learning to heal themselves.

In Native American spirituality magical ritual is less important, though the induction of altered states of consciousness
is central. Its appeal lies more in its balanced way of living,
through honouring the earth and the interconnectedness of
all living beings. This includes balance in male–female relations, and between the masculine and feminine attributes of
the individual (though these qualities are not necessarily seen
in gender terms). Women are, however, seen as superior, as
having a stronger connection with the earth through their
wombs, though motherhood is not their only path of development (except in more conservative tribes). The Navajos have
a matrilineal society. Land is controlled by women and passed
on from mother to daughter. Women can divorce their husband simply by placing his saddle outside the door, and they
have responsibility for the children and future generations. Men
and women have separate religious rituals, but come together
for some ceremonies. There are few women leading tribes, but
one exceptional example is Wilma Mankiller, Cherokee chief,
warrioress and spiritual leader.

There are said to be links between Tibetan Buddhism and
the Hopis, and there have been meetings between the leaders,
although the two traditions have very different attitudes to
nature.[28] Buddhism prescribes love for all sentient beings but
excludes nature, which is seen as a resource to be utilized and
controlled. Native American spirituality includes plants and
even stones on equal status. As one follower expressed it: 'Stones
have a vibration, an essence, they're sentient beings. Everything has an energy and you interact. To speak with a stone,
a tree, you have to merge with that energy, consciousness,
which is sometimes difficult with the Western mind-set. We
naturally see ourselves as separate, whereas their world is a
fully integrated universe.' Practitioners learn to shift their
consciousness in order to perceive and relate in these radically
altered modes, in tune with nature and the environment.

Some Pagans speak of nature in similar terms, and several
described the importance of their experiences with nature as
children, sitting in trees and merging with the forest. In refu-
tation of accusations that in joining such traditions people are
denying their roots, Native American teachers encourage their
followers to use this knowledge to reconnect with their roots.
The tradition of sacred place has been largely lost in the West,

but can be recovered, as found by one person now using these techniques in Britain:

> If you get to the the bones of it, Native American spirituality correlates completely with what's held in this land in a sacred way, which we've got very out of step with. Walking the shamanic way is to go deeply within yourself, into remembering, dreaming – as with the Aboriginal dreamtracks – reawakening the dream of this land out of its slumber. It's there, this land has incredible richness.

## Ecofeminism

Ecospirituality is equal in importance to Goddess spirituality as a strand of Paganism, and even more important as a defining and unifying factor. The combination of these two concerns has produced a philosophy known as ecofeminism, which 'provides a distinctive framework both for reconceiving feminism and for developing an environmental ethic which takes seriously connections between the domination of women and the domination of nature'.[29] Ecofeminism is not synonymous with Paganism, transcending religious boundaries and being found within the world religions in the West and many traditional religions throughout the world. In traditional religion its beliefs may be taken for granted as natural rather than highlighted with a label, as in Native American spirituality. The leading spokesperson and writer for ecofeminism in Christianity is Rosemary Radford Ruether, who does call herself an ecofeminist. In Britain Mary Grey and Ursula King are working within this framework. On the radical margin where Christianity meets (or at least comes close to) Paganism are Carol Christ, and Mary Daly who punningly entitled one of her books *Gyn/Ecology*. A related trend in Christianity is creation spirituality, originated by Matthew Fox (1988; 1991), in which reverence for nature and the feminine are central doctrines.

In Buddhism, ecofeminism is rarely adopted as a term, but the philosophy is central to the reconstruction of Western Buddhism taking place at the moment. Joanna Macy (1991) is better known as an 'engaged' Buddhist, involved in a range of social and political issues, including the environment, though not overtly feminist. Stephanie Kaza is a Zen Buddhist who teaches feminist and environmentalist ethics at the University of Vermont, invoking female deities such as Kuan Yin and Green Tara. In Britain, Martine Batchelor (1996) is the most active spokesperson and writer on environmental and women's issues, though she rejects the label ecofeminist, pointing out that although there are many Buddhist women whose efforts have done much to improve the status of women in Buddhism, few of them are feminist-identified. Christina Feldman (1989; 1994) has also written extensively about women's spirituality in a way that could be called ecofeminist, although again without adopting the term: 'Learning to value everything about being a woman is the key to a connected spirituality. The reconciliation between our own body and spirit is the key to the reconciliation of humankind and nature' (1989, 62). Charlene Spretnak (1991) is an interfaith activist with Buddhist leanings, a *vipassana* practitioner and one of the most prominent ecofeminists.

### Gaia and Goddess

The favourite personification of the Goddess within Paganism and the women's spirituality movement is Gaia: a relatively minor deity in the Olympian pantheon who has come to symbolize the entire environmental movement in its ecospiritual dimensions. This identification takes off from James Lovelock's Gaia Hypothesis, which seeks to demonstrate scientifically that the earth is a unified living organism in which all other life-forms are interdependent. Given the primacy of ecospirituality in all contemporary Western religions, Gaia may be seen as the most paradigmatic ecofeminist symbol. She stands for the Great Goddess in her roles as Earth Mother and Creatrix. These are seen as her most important functions in nature religion at this time of planetary crisis. Correspondingly, within feminist spirituality 'Nature and the Goddess become symbolic of an essential femininity, the antithesis of patriarchal society' (Greenwood 1996, 114).

The roots of ecofeminism are in the ancient association of women with the earth, in contrast to a male identification with the sky, heaven and spirit. As we have seen, this association is the basis of a cluster of beliefs which portrays women as more sensual, fleshly, and materialistic – hence lower, inferior, less spiritual, more fallen and sinful. Goddess spirituality and nature religion have reclaimed the belief but reversed the value judgements. Ecofeminists such as Starhawk advocate an earth-based, immanent spirituality in which Earth as Goddess is the repository of ancient wisdom and healing strength. Jocelyn Chaplin perceives the Goddess as 'a kind of ecological balancing process, the rhythm of life that works within the material world. . . . She could be described as a very earthy (I do dislike the world "feminine") kind of wisdom that we can all hear if we listen to ourselves properly.'[30] Therefore, in being more 'natural', women are also more spiritual.

### The Spiritualization of the Female Body
Early feminists from Mary Wollstonecraft to Simone de Beauvoir decisively rejected the identification of women with their bodily processes and with nature, believing that women's liberation lay in transcendence of nature. Contemporary feminist theologians have pointed out the dangers of even a positive reclamation of the concept, in particular the risk of bringing back biological determinism through the back door. This conservative naturalism is clearly seen, for example, in the current backlash against career women in favour of motherhood as women's 'natural' role.[31] Feminist witches are also wary of being constrained by symbolism:

> I'm quite happy personally with the association [between women and nature], but I also have a brain, I can talk and be logical, very assertive, even aggressive. I can be very organizing and get things done. I can detach myself from what's happening. I can take charge in emergencies, sort things out – and then come back and be much more organic.

Some spiritual feminists also warn of the dangers of too literal a genderization of nature, pointing out that in other cultures these values have been reversed. For example, in ancient Egypt the earth was male while the sky was female, and in ancient Crete the sun was a female symbol.[32]

Earth-based spirituality includes exaltation of the female body, whose rhythms parallel the rhythms of nature and the seasons. Pagans have created rituals to celebrate these significant turning points or 'gateways', particularly menstruation and childbirth. Menstruation has been written about extensively by women from various spiritual paths, who are attempting to transform it from curse to celebration, from agent of pollution to symbol of life and regeneration. In traditional religion, menstrual blood is perceived as profoundly ambivalent and taboo: 'Dangerous, impure, powerful, magic and sacred, it had to be shunned or surrounded by special rituals. It also often endowed women with a special sacral power from which men had to keep apart' (King 1989, 74). In Indian and Tibetan Tantra, this potent substance is valued as containing powerful magical properties and may be ritually drunk, sometimes as a cocktail mixed with semen. Susan Greenwood has found evidence of similar attitudes in Pagan magic where menstruation is seen to be the source of a woman's special shamanic powers, and the female body is exalted:

> Bodily experience is the very essence of feminist spirituality and is seen as the locus of women's power. The body is thus the source of self-affirmation and identity. Female bodies are seen to be the repository of special magical powers associated with the menstrual cycle. The womb is a mystical holy grail and cauldron of rebirth. (Greenwood 1996, 114)

## The Triple Goddess and Ageing

NRMs in general do not have much to say about ageing, particularly for women. In some, women are valued as *gopis, dakinis*, sex goddesses, but discarded when they age as in secular society. The rarity of older women and men in the NRMs of the 1970s gave them a certain status and valuation as substitute parents and grandparents. Nowadays, those members who have devoted their prime to their religion and are now middle-aged are beginning to worry about their lack of pension plans and whether they will be looked after in their old age.

One of the most important symbols in Paganism is the Triple Goddess: maiden, mother and crone. This is an alternative female Trinity that rebalances the Western over-emphasis on female youth and beauty, which has even permeated some sectors of Paganism. Neitz depicts the stereotypical neo-pagan goddess as perennially young, thin and beautiful, with delicate Caucasian features, long wavy hair and pre-Raphaelite clothing (1990, 353), although this portrayal may well reflect American cultural preoccupations and is less common in European symbolism. Feminists challenge this over-emphasis of the Goddess as Maiden – a celebration of the female body limited to the nymphet. Reclaiming the mother–daughter bond is an important element of the matrilineal doctrine, and a popular and powerful ritual for women is to recite the names of their foremothers as far back as they can remember – which rarely extends beyond two generations. The myth of Demeter and Kore is important for this purpose.

What to call the third aspect of the Goddess is certainly an issue. Mary Daly has tried to revive the words hag and crone as labels that women may wear proudly, but so far without much success. Barbara Walker's book *The Crone* has been considerably less successful than some of her other titles. Even feminist witches are not overly enthusiastic about the usage of this symbol:

> I think as an image and spiritual entity to work with the crone is very powerful. I think there's a real problem when you start trying to correlate human reality with it, trying to see the crone in ordinary women. It's quite daunting when you're still trying to work out your childhood problems to have the crone thrust upon you. It's OK to embody her for a ritual if you're old, but to have to do it in daily life, be wise and sensible, may be difficult.

Vivianne Crowley defines the third aspect of the Goddess not as crone but as Wise Woman and Woman of Power: 'Women are enjoined not to be passive vessels at the disposal of men, but women in control of their own destiny' (1996, 151). It seems likely that the more positive-sounding term 'wise woman' will gain wider currency as an important symbol in the endeavour to restore dignity, function and status to postmenopausal women. Native American society, with its honouring of the Grandmothers as tribal leaders and counsellors, is a model of this possibility. Wiccans and feminist witches contact the appropriate goddesses, who may also be connected with death, such as Hecate who understands the secrets of life and death:

> Hecate is the most difficult aspect of the Goddess for both men and women to understand. It is easy to love what is beautiful like the Virgin Kore. It is easy to love what is

powerful and strong like Maeve the Queen. It is not so easy to love what is old and weak, a woman no longer fertile, who has given over her worldly dominance to others. Hecate teaches us an important lesson: that the feminine should be valued for itself. This is not because it brings sexuality or power, but because deep within the feminine there is an eternal wisdom; for Hecate is also the High Priestess, the keeper of the Mysteries. (Crowley 1996, 150)

### Ecospirituality, Feminism and Social Justice

One of the main criticisms of the HPM was its narcissism, an emphasis on the self at the expense of society.[33] As a generalization it may be claimed that NRMs have tended to concentrate more on spiritual growth than social justice, though there is also evidence that interest in growth and mysticism may lead to political activism (Wuthnow 1976). The criticism partly reflects the puritanism of a society that favours repression of personal needs in the service of more productive external goals, a religion that values sacrifice over self-development – particularly for women. Meditation has often been condemned in Western society as navel-gazing, lotus-eating, while its positive benefits have been ignored, including the need for clear insight and developed consciousness to guide effective action. The widespread shift in the 1960s and 1970s from an ethic of self-discipline to self-development was perhaps a natural rebalancing, and this process may now be almost complete. Certainly the pendulum is swinging back again, and alternative spirituality is moving back to an outer focus with a more comprehensive vision: from healing the self to healing others, to healing and saving the entire planet. Wiccans and other Pagans have sometimes been drawn into social action from a more purely spiritual focus out of their experiences of harassment, loss of jobs and homes, custody cases and, particularly in America, the struggle for their constitutional rights. There seems to be more fear in America of the consequences of holding such contentious beliefs, whereas in Britain there is more tolerance, as a result of which Pagans are both more integrated into society and more open about their beliefs. However, there is also a movement the other way: Starhawk and other spiritual leaders are attracting more and more feminists and social activists, particularly following the collapse of the left. One of the favourite adages of holistic spirituality is adapted from the feminist slogan: the personal is political is spiritual.

Of the many current causes and protest movements, Pagans are most drawn to the peace and environmental movements, though feminist witches are also involved in gender issues and gay/lesbian rights. Starhawk has been at the forefront of many nuclear protests in America. In Britain, with its long-established socialist tradition, there is a greater tendency for spiritual feminists to be also involved in broader social and political issues. The Greenham Common peace camp in the 1980s was a largely feminist demonstration, which drew in many Pagans. Nowadays Pagans are at the forefront of the road protest movement, pressure groups for access to sacred sites, and animal rights; they are also involved in campaigns on pollution, deforestation and conservation. They may use magic for these purposes, group rituals for planetary healing.

The environment is now almost universally admitted to be the most important and urgent issue of the time. Any religion that can convincingly claim to be a nature religion is therefore both at the centre and the leading edge of current concerns. All religions offer scope for environmental and social action, but Paganism currently seems to offer the most coherent combination of ecospirituality, psychospiritual development, and reverence for the divine feminine. The main emphasis is currently on ritual, but the spotlight is on environmental action, and the perceived heroes of Paganism are the ecowarriors on the front lines of the peace movement and road protest movement. In Britain this is the site of one of the most fascinating if somewhat bizarre alliances, where landowners, academics, New Age travellers and ecospiritualists stand shoulder to shoulder in a common cause, as in the recent Twyford Down and Newbury bypass protests. The current (1996) occupation of Wandsworth Common in London is organized by an Oxford academic, George Monbiot, with a group of 'drop-outs, druggies, aesthetic idealists, anarchist activists and political reformers'.[34] How long such an alliance can last and whether it will issue in effective action remain to be tested.

Whether Paganism will take off as the leading movement in alternative spirituality, or even grow to the point where it seriously challenges organized religion, remains to be seen. In the meantime, it certainly comprises the most vital and interesting group of NRMs in the West. In her introduction to the tenth anniversary edition of *Spiral Dance*, Starhawk proclaimed:

> The renewal of the Goddess religion and other earth-based spiritual traditions will continue to grow over the next decade. As the community grows, our spirituality becomes more embedded in every aspect of our lives. As more children are born and grow up in the Goddess tradition, we will develop more materials for them and more rituals rooted in life cycles and transitions. . . .
>
> The next decade will see crucial decisions made about the future of the environment, the social structure, and the health of the world we leave to the generations that follow. With courage, vision, humor, and creativity, we can use our values to reinstate the living web of all interconnected life as the measure by which all choices are judged. (1989, 12)

# 10 A New Model of Spiritual Needs and Values

This book has focused on women in the more counter-cultural NRMs, but within the broader context of gender issues, religion and society. It has attempted to throw some light on why women are drawn into these movements and what they get out of them. Some of their choices might appear misguided, deluded or masochistic to others, though rational, valid and empowering to themselves. Some have suffered in the process, casualties of aggressive recruitment tactics or the self-aggrandizing addictions of power-hungry leaders, but these problems are not unique to NRMs. Women are as likely to be abused by their psychotherapist, priest, professor or professional advisor as by the leader of an NRM. Some members of NRMs have suffered mental illness or committed suicide, but there is no evidence that the rates are any higher than for any other walk of life, that it happened on account of the religion, or that it would not have happened anyway. Conversely, it may be that other members were saved from mental breakdown or suicide by finding a spiritual path, as is sometimes claimed. The majority are not lost souls, 'flakes', failures or *dharma* junkies but relatively 'normal' people seeking alternatives to the social, ethical and spiritual solutions offered by mainstream religion and society. They include celebrities, socialites and high-ranking professionals, which is partly why so much media and academic attention has been paid to the phenomenon.[1]

Most people who join NRMs claim to have benefited thereby, in terms of spiritual, social, sexual and even professional development. It appears that NRMs meet and fulfil important needs, that motivations are matched with choices. Accordingly, I have developed a typology of spiritual needs and values, which can also be correlated with broader spiritual and cultural trends.

## Typologizing Religion

There are various ways of classifying religions and religiosity, but they are mostly descriptive rather than analytical. They

232

therefore fail to explain the most important questions, such as why people join a particular religious group. Psychology is more concerned with motivation than sociology, and has produced a number of typologies, but these focus on religiosity – the religious experience – rather than the differences between religions. Most typologies of religiosity are based on the contrast between external observance and inner experience, function and faith. Hence we have James's distinction between institutional and personal religion; Allport's concept of extrinsic versus intrinsic religion; Spilka's consensual versus committed; Fromm's authoritarian versus humanistic.

Batson and Ventis (1982) have developed the most comprehensive and sophisticated version of this model, based on social psychology, complete with empirical measurement scales. They added a third dimension on the basis that previous analyses had ignored important distinctions in the inner dimension, between the fundamentalist experience of faith based on certainty and the open-ended, flexible, self-critical experience of the seeker. They described their model religion as means, end, and quest. They contrast the 'it's good for business' attitude of the pragmatic, means-oriented churchgoer with the 'I've found it!' triumphalism of the end-oriented fundamentalist, and the quest approach typified by mystics such as Buddha, Malcolm X and Mahatma Gandhi. Batson and Ventis's theory also correlates with Troeltsch's sociological model of church, sect and mystical religion. Troeltsch had predicted in 1931 that mystical religion would flourish in the modern world.

NRMs are usually typed according to provenance, a non-contentious but unilluminating approach. We may talk, for example, about Christian-based, Eastern-based, Western occult and New Age movements, which tells us little beyond the obvious and fails to highlight either the significant differences between these groups or the similarities between movements in different groupings. The most widely used analytical typology is Roy Wallis's distinction between world-rejecting and world-affirming NRMs, to which he later added the third dimension of world-accommodating. This is useful for interpreting group dynamics and the resulting social structures, but still does not explain why people join certain groups and what they hope to gain.

The dangers of charismatic leadership, coupled with concern

for the wellbeing of members, have inspired a detailed and comprehensive model of NRMs for the purpose of distinguishing an authentic spiritual guide from a charlatan: the Anthony model (Anthony *et al.* 1987). It assesses NRMs along three dimensions, each with two polarities: its metaphysics (monism versus dualism); its central mode of practice (charismatic versus technical); and its interpretive sensibility (unilevel versus multilevel). It is a sophisticated ideal type construct but hard to apply, as their classifications demonstrate. For example, the Osho movement is grouped with the Manson Family under the heading of 'unilevel charismatic monism', making no distinctions between the very different operations and outcome of charismatic authority in these movements They aim to provide criteria whereby one can 'test' a master to discover if he or she is '*completely* plausible, a living embodiment of ultimate spiritual truth, love, being' (88) but admit that 'The annals of all the great spiritual traditions include many examples of masters who outraged conventional morality with behavior designed to awaken people to a deeper truth', including Jesus and St Francis (298). It is an impressive model but complicated, non-empirical and subjective, and therefore of limited utility.

## A New Model of Spiritual Needs and Values

A more useful model, conveying more insights into these issues, may be gained by adapting Maslow's theory of human motivation (1943; 1970), popularly known as the 'hierarchy of needs'. It is a synthesis of approaches, human- rather than animal-centred and based on clinical experience, which he called a 'holistic–dynamic theory'. He distinguished five levels of need that must be satisfied to produce a healthy, fully functioning human being. If one or more of these needs is not satisfied, the individual will tend to be arrested at that developmental stage, unable to progress to further stages until that need is met. Maslow labelled these needs: 1) **physiological; 2) safety; 3) belongingness and love; 4) esteem; 5) self-actualization.**

Maslow's hierarchy of needs is well known and highly regarded, and has been widely adopted as a model in psychology, education and human resource management. However, although it has an immediate strong impact as a clear and almost self-evident truth, and is often quoted, it has seldom been applied beyond the basic psychological model. Yet it can be adapted into a sociological classification of religion and religious motives, with particular reference to NRMs. It can thus help analyse and answer the most significant and fundamental questions: a) what are the differences between NRMs and between their memberships; b) why people join – and leave – particular NRMs; c) why such categories as fundamentalists, liberals and mystics in all religions tend to feel greater affinity with each other than with other categories in their own tradition; d) how sects form from churches and other large groups.

For the purposes of this book, with its focus on gender and its theme of contrast between counter-cultural and conservative NRMs, I have simplified the model to reflect this broad dichotomy by combining the five levels into two main groupings. I call these **Traditionalism** and **Personal Development**. This works because the first two levels are closely related in various respects, and because survival is rare as a life-need in the relatively affluent West, particularly as applied to religious choices. The last three needs are also closely interrelated and may be understood as a spectrum of personal development from simple self-improvement to spirituality; the stages of the ego's individuation, ripening, expansion and dissolution into a larger whole.

I have also reversed the third and fourth need. Maslow found this to be the most common reversal in the hierarchy, and I would suspect a gender bias at work here: whether for psychobiological or social reasons, esteem-needs tend to be valued higher than love-needs by men, vice versa for women. Psychospiritual approaches demonstrate that love-needs can only be fulfilled once the ego-needs for success are satisfied, so it makes sense to put these first.

Each need can also be related to gender issues, except the first which is pre-gender and the last which is beyond gender. If needs are met, people tend to 'graduate' from an NRM back to society or to another NRM that fulfils a 'higher' need. If needs are not met, people will tend to either leave or form a breakaway sect within the larger movement to meet these needs.

## A) Traditionalism

### 1. Survival Needs
I have renamed Maslow's physiological need 'survival', since this is the requirement underlying the needs for food, sleep,

shelter, sex and so on. He called them 'prepotent', meaning that 'in the human being who is missing everything in life in an extreme fashion, it is most likely that the major motivation would be the physiological needs rather than any others. A person who is lacking food, safety, love, and esteem would most probably hunger for food more strongly than for any- thing else' (1970, 36–7). At this level of need, gender issues have low priority. In societies and human groups where sur- vival is continually under threat by famine and other hazards, religions such as fertility cults will cater predominantly for these needs. Such religions are usually animistic or polytheistic, and the aim is to appease the gods or spirits. Cargo cults are a modern example. Groups who are persecuted or enslaved and have no political or military recourses will tend to develop 'black magic' rituals to protect themselves and harm their enemies, such as Voodoo.[2] There are few if any Western NRMs at this level, since these needs are either better met or catered for by secular means. However some movements such as the Jesus Army recruit among street people, for whom survival is the primary issue.

## 2. Safety Needs

Maslow summarized this level as a person's preference for 'a safe, orderly, predictable, lawful, organized world, which he can count on and in which unexpected, unmanageable, cha- otic, or other dangerous things do not happen' (1970, 41). It also provokes a need for powerful parent figures or protectors and under extreme threat encourages the acceptance of dic- tatorship. Applied to religions, what is at stake is not so much the literal threat of attack as a perceived threat, usually in a non-physical or supernatural form. The danger may be per- ceived in secular or spiritual terms, as arising from the break- down of society and its institutions; hedonism and materialism; or from satanic forces, perhaps in the form of a rival religious group or leader – who is more likely to be condemned to hellfire than attacked with spells at this level. Gender issues present at this level as willingness to submit to an authoritar- ian male such as husband or religious leader to fulfil a need for clearly demarcated roles, family values and obedient chil- dren. Religions at level two will be conservative, patriarchal, even misogynistic; suppressive of female sexuality as a threat to

family stability. Fundamentalism is a more aggressively proselytizing expression of these needs, probably in an attempt to
increase safety by eliminating the threat of competing creeds
or converting the 'other' to 'our' side. Examples are evangelical sects and NRMs such as the Jesus movement, Lubavich
Hasidism, and the Islamic Revolutionary Guards, the Unification Church and ISKCON. These last two NRMs also have
elements of level three and even level four, so may be termed
transitional movements.

## B) Personal Development

### 3. Esteem Needs

Self-respect and self-esteem are needs of the ego that arise
when the previous two levels of need are satisfied. Maslow
subdivided these into inner and outer needs: inner needs include achievement, mastery, confidence, independence; outer
needs include reputation, prestige, status, fame, dominance.
At one end this level is about power, at the other end about
empowerment. Religions at level three will be hierarchical,
with demarcated priesthoods and levels of initiation or advancement, sometimes within a pyramid structure. They are
usually led and dominated by men, but women will challenge
prescribed gender roles and experiment with sexual, social,
professional and religious alternatives. Women and men will
be drawn to groups and techniques that promise wealth, health,
happiness and success such as *est*, Silva Mind Control,
Scientology, assertiveness training, and positive thinking. Movements that draw on prosperity consciousness, such as the Way
International will appeal, as well as Eastern-based groups like
TM and Soka Gakkai whose methodologies combine material
and spiritual reward. Those that have ultimate spiritual goals
tend to promote them either in terms of 'instant enlightenment' or as a guaranteed outcome after successfully completing
the many (usually expensive) stages or courses of an extensive
programme. Personal development comprises a spectrum from
self-improvement to self-realization in which the boundaries
are not clearly demarcated. Accordingly, level-three techniques
may contain potential for higher levels of meditation and
psychospiritual growth, which could take practitioners to the
fourth or even fifth level. For example, many people join TM

for a 'quick fix' style of meditation and then discover its deeper potential, though others move on to a level-four NRM.

## 4. Love Needs

Once the basic individuation needs for mastery of the external world, achievement and success are met, the needs of the affective domain for love, acceptance and relationship arise. Interest in the wider group, community or society emerges, rather than the level-two identification of self with family or society against the 'other'. It could also be described as a higher development of love: from eros to agape. Equality and partnership become important here, and service becomes spiritualized and compassionate, rather than the duty-bound activity of level-two religions. Maslow argues that 'the tremendous and rapid increase in T-groups and other personal growth groups and intentional communities may in part be motivated by this unsatisfied hunger for contact, for intimacy, for belongingness and by the need to overcome the widespread feelings of alienation, aloneness, strangeness, and loneliness' (1970, 44). Since women are generally perceived as better at these skills, more loving, open and intuitive, they will tend to be drawn to this type of religion in larger numbers and attain high status, even leadership positions. The style of leadership is less authoritarian and hierarchical than in previous levels; more democratic, egalitarian and focused on human values. In these religions personal development is the predominant goal, sometimes called personal or spiritual growth – as compared with the self-improvement of level-three groups. Examples are the Human Potential Movement, Gurdjieffian groups, the Osho movement, New Age and Pagan groups. Most of the Eastern, meditation-based groups can be located here, such as Elan Vital, Siddha Yoga and Sahaja Yoga, as well as Westernized Buddhist groups with charismatic leaders such as the FWBO. In practice, level four overlaps considerably with level five, which the leader claims to exemplify. However, the needs of the followers often remain at level four.

## 5. Self-Actualization Needs

Maslow's term 'self-actualization' could be used in the broader sense of a process of personal development covering levels three to five. It begins with the basic ego needs for esteem, developing through relationship and affectivity to a strong, integrated sense of self, at which point a more mystical approach to spirituality emerges, culminating in ego-transcendence. At the fifth level self-actualization extends beyond the humanistic to the trans-personal dimension. This was indicated by Maslow, who believed that mystics were the most likely group to be self-actualized and have 'peak experiences' of ecstasy and union. This approach was more fully developed by later transpersonal psychologists such as Assagioli and Charles Tart. Maslow wrote extensively about self-actualization, which was his main contribution to psychology. He equated it with self-fulfilment but also with the desire to 'become everything that one is capable of becoming' (1970, 46), which points to the self-realization concept of Eastern mysticism. This is also the point at which dualism, including the duality of gender, begins to be transcended into union or unity with a greater whole. In a true level-five group there will therefore be no restrictions on female leadership, unless it is operating within a highly misogynistic society. However, women attracted to such movements will be more concerned with spiritual growth than gender issues, and may also be uninterested in sexual and family relationships. Religions at this stage are monistic and mystical, including the mystical and esoteric traditions of all religions, such as Zen Buddhism, Dzogchen, Sufism and Kabbala.

*Advantages and Limits of the Model*
Sociological explanations are hampered by the scientific requirement of value neutrality, which proscribes any classification using distinctions between higher and lower, better and worse. While morally commendable and helping to avoid bias, the effect is to impoverish interpretations of values-based phenomena such as religious belief. Maslow criticized psychology for this tendency, as reflecting a lack of value for what is important in people's lives. Applied to religion, it makes it difficult to highlight either the psychospiritual benefits or the abuses.

Like any typology, this one is approximate in its placement of particular movements within the hierarchy. In practice, an individual human being may appear arrested at a certain stage but will usually have elements of all the stages, and the order of importance may change over time or even from moment to moment. This will be even more the case with groups of people. Hence NRMs, particularly the older and larger ones, will display elements of more than one need. Even the more consistent movements will have a bell curve formation, with members at either end displaying the characteristics of the levels on either side. The order may well change as the group becomes more established and successful – or less so, even persecuted; as the leadership and/or socio-economic conditions change, attracting a different type of membership. Some groups transform their character fast, or may contain two quite different tendencies containing internal tensions, creating interesting classificatory questions, and these are discussed below. The main limitation is that it cannot be applied wholesale to the world religions, since these depend for their success on catering for multi-level needs and therefore contain all five levels, though not within the same group. It can, however, apply to sects and other groups within larger denominations.

The main criticism that could be levelled at this model is moral rather than academic, that it is overly élitist. In a sense this is the case, but in a descriptive-analytical rather than value-judgemental way. It highlights values as the basis of religion and society, which is being increasingly recognized in the public and professional arenas. But the application is non-élitist and flexible, in that people may subscribe to all these values but choose a religion that caters for the level they are currently most identified with, which is not fixed but changeable. Furthermore, spirituality is perceived as existing at all levels of human need, not just at the final level of self-actualization.

## Spiritual Trends in Western Society

The British ruled India for 300 years, but failed to penetrate the mysteries of Eastern spirituality. This happened as the third stage of a colonization process that began with a political empire, continued with the 'coca-colonization' of economic development, and ended with the quest to extract the secrets of enlightenment from the yogis, sadhus and gurus. There was an element of aggression in this quest; the phrase 'hunting guru' was sometimes used. Enlightenment was the aspiration of the counter-culture, but the Western mind lacked the confidence and skill to undertake the quest for ultimate truth unaided. In these circumstances it could be argued that charismatic authority was needed; that it was a reasonable, practical decision for seekers to choose a guru – an adept – to guide them into the uncharted terrain of mysticism.

The master–disciple relationship provides a time-honoured structure and methodology for spiritual growth, for which thousands of seekers renounced families and careers, and endured the hardships of India. Western education had overemphasized 'left-brained' intellectual functioning; meditation and *bhakti* developed the 'right-brained' faculties of intuition and receptivity, which are required for attuning to the more subtle realms of spiritual experience. To a sociologist, discipleship is a socialization process; to a practitioner it is an initiation into an expanded domain of consciousness. Undoubtedly many gurus abused their authority, provoking a strong reaction against spiritual authority and towards more democratic, egalitarian structures. Feeling exploited but having learned meditation, Westerners are rejecting the guru model and setting up as teachers and authorities in their own right. Some of the best known, most influential teachers and leaders in the alternative spiritual world are now speaking out against the guru model including Jack Kornfield, Andrew Harvey and Ram Dass – all former pioneers and promoters of Eastern mysticism.[3]

The last 30 years have seen many changes in religion and society, and the position of women in both. There has been a trend, which is still continuing, towards polarization into what may be broadly termed the old and new paradigms. This is sometimes viewed as a sharply demarcated opposition between the millennialist optimism of the New Age and the apocalyptic gloom of the Fundamentalists: the angels of light against the forces of darkness, except that nobody agrees on who is which. Both types of religiosity are known to be growing fast, while the middle ground loses ground, but their growth is happening in different ways. The evangelical movements are becoming more restrictive, more patriarchal, resisting the influence of feminism with 'real man' religion. The evangelical groups actively proselytize, while the influence of the New Age is more subtle and pervasive.

The HPM has sometimes been classified as an NRM, but at most it was a quasi-religion: a kindergarten and recruitment ground for NRMs proper, its identity now diffused within the broader New Age movement. Both the HPM and New Age are precluded from full religious status by their lack of formal doctrines and rituals, loose organization as a congeries of centres and courses run by individual teachers, therapists and entrepreneurs rather than a priesthood. However, the influence of both is stronger and more widespread than ever through the primacy given to personal development in mainstream society and business. Other New Age ideas and practices have affected the lives of many of us. We are now more likely to eat whole grains and have a vegetarian in the family; have an aromatherapy massage; visit a homoeopath; consult a psychic; go on a self-improvement course; think positively and repeat affirmations of our worthiness; hug trees, love dolphins and save rainforests; believe in reincarnation; disclose our feelings and 'grow' from our relationships; practise yoga and meditation.

There are three major contenders for spiritual hegemony in the West: Christianity, Buddhism and Paganism. There are also three major trends within the new paradigm that particularly affect women in NRMs, but also women and men in all religions and to some extent the whole of society. These are: 1) spirituality; 2) feminism; 3) environmentalism. I shall discuss these in terms of the three front-runner religions, in conjunction with concerns about power and authority.

*Spirituality*
In the 1970s Christianity was almost universally rejected by members of non-Christian NRMs, often with some vehemence, as outdated, sterile, authoritarian, hierarchical, misogynistic, fear-based, sin-obsessed, lacking wisdom, compassion and spirituality. Some of these criticisms are still voiced, and Christianity is still in decline, particularly among the intelligentsia who are mostly either entrenched in scientific rationalism, or moving into religions based on personal development and Eastern philosophy. But there has also been a revival of a mystical Christianity closer to the experiences discovered in NRMs: a more spiritual, androgynous, environmentally friendly version than is found in most mainstream churches. Buddhism is the

fastest growing of the world religions in the West and, in so far as it may be classified as an NRM, the most respected and admired. Over the course of its long history it has developed perhaps the most sophisticated philosophy and praxis of any religion. Buddhism, like all religions, has suffered from scandals and abuses of power linked to its authoritarian structure, but it also has an impeccable, highly revered world leader in the Dalai Lama, as well as many other influential teachers. Paganism has the edge regarding its more democratic structures, although it also contains hierarchical groups that are more open to abuse. But compared to the authority of a guru or pope, the high priest and priestess have less power and less of a gap between them and the coven members.

The spirituality of the 1990s has learned and absorbed much from the counter-culture of the 1970s. In many ways it is a revival of the experimental idealism of that period, but is creating a more integrated, feminized, politicized and Westernized spirituality. Whereas the 1970s saw a move away from ritual, tradition and social action to an inner-directed search free from all accretions, the pendulum has swung back again but with a difference. The emphasis is more on functionalist syncretism: pick and mix your own ritual, which is legitimated by whether it works. The New Age is still influenced by Eastern mysticism but also more now by Celtic spirituality, which is even more influential on Paganism and Christianity. There is a return to ritual but within the more 'natural' context of a return to our roots: to mark and celebrate seasonal rhythms and festivals, life changes and transitions such as birth, marriage and death, but also physiological stages such as menstruation and menopause. Compared to Buddhist meditation, however, the status of magic is still low in Western society, perceived as less sophisticated and effective if not primitive superstition. It has an exotic appeal but it is unlikely to gain greater acceptance without modernizing, for example through psychology or positive thinking. Shamanism, with its range of techniques for healing and for attaining altered states of consciousness, probably has greater potential as a praxis. Pagan doctrine is also somewhat underdeveloped and incoherent compared to Buddhist philosophy and meditation, which provide an ancient yet advanced and relevant spiritual methodology in tune with philosophy, psychology and new science.

*Feminism*

It is clear that women do not necessarily choose a spiritual path on account of gender issues. Gender is relevant in traditionalist movements, where women willingly sacrifice freedom and independence for the security of a stable family life and distinct gender roles. It is relevant for some women on a path of personal development who are in active rebellion against patriarchal religion and in active search of feminist or matriarchal alternatives. But other women are uninterested in gender issues, being intent on growth as a whole person or human being, as a soul or spiritual being. Such women will tend to reject groups that are hostile or oppressive towards women, but will not necessarily be looking for a female, feminine or feminist path. Some women attracted to a path of non-dogma see feminism as itself a dogma, despite its libertarian aims. For example, one woman who had left the Rigpa Foundation on account of the 'abusive behaviour' of Sogyal Rinpoche, calls herself a feminist but has no interest in goddess spirituality or any 'separatist aspirations'. There is agreement among women on the need for 'wholeness' but not on whether wholeness as a woman requires a specifically feminist spiritual path (with or without political activism), a Jungian-based exploration and integration of anima and animus, or whether gender is largely irrelevant on the spiritual path.

Despite these provisos, women's spirituality is one of the most significant religious trends. The 1990s have moved on from the benevolent paternalism of the master–disciple relationship, which worked in the 1970s but is found less appropriate for current needs. Even the few Eastern-based NRMs still led by their founders have become less authoritarian, and this is even more the case where the founder has died. Women are endeavouring to make these movements more self-determining and egalitarian, which is resisted by some men but supported by others. The failures of female leadership in the Osho movement at Rajneeshpuram can be ascribed to the dangers of male charismatic authority supported by female unquestioning devotion, although Osho gave women many opportunities for empowerment and spiritual growth, beyond the limits of most other religions or even the Western workplace of the 1970s. BK women lead the movement and are effective in the world and as exemplars of spiritual purity. But the conditions – renunciation of the body, sexuality, sensual pleasure and family life – make this movement unlikely to appeal as a full-time religion on a wide scale. Buddhism, like most Eastern-based NRMs, has suffered setbacks in the feminist cause from the misdemeanours of male teachers and gurus. It is beginning to address these issues openly and seriously, and there are many highly talented and respected women in the leadership of most groups. It is therefore recovering ground, though not yet as advanced as Paganism in its advocation and support of female spirituality and leadership. Paganism is the only religion to have a developed thealogy that not only perceives the Goddess as equal or superior to the God, but follows through by giving women equal or superior spiritual status. It is also the only religion that contains a specifically, consciously feminist branch: feminist witchcraft.

*Environmentalism*
The one point all religions are agreed on is the need for an environmental awareness or dimension within spirituality. Both Buddhism and Christianity have records of domination and exploitation of the environment legitimated by their theologies but are now compensating for their pasts, particularly through the work of ecofeminists in both religions. Paganism has embraced ecospirituality more wholeheartedly and convincingly than any other religion, with its claimed history or mythology evolved from ancient fertility cults and nature religions, its theology based on seasonal ritual and nature worship, and its activism at the forefront of environmental action and protest groups. The failure of the counter-culture to develop into a religion is partly a consequence of its lack of 'groundedness' in a practical, social cause. The grounding of Paganism and other NRMs in environmentalism, integrated with other social and gender issues as well as spirituality, could well become an important factor in their survival and growth into the next millennium.

**The Future of Religion**

The future of religion clearly lies with the choices of young people. Christianity in particular has the problem of an ageing, declining membership, so needs to attract young people in order to both enliven and swell its ranks. Buddhism has its main membership from the 1970s counter-culture, which means the average age is mid-40s with a decreasing rate of entry among young people, perhaps partly owing to its greater respectability. The dilemma of counter-cultural or antinomian NRMs is that when new – in a state of 'pure' charisma – they are highly attractive to young people. As they grow, they want to appeal to a wider spectrum of people, but in the process tend to become routinized, respectable – and less fun. Hence they lose their younger membership. Chris Brain's 9 O'Clock Service, like many NRMs, was very successful in attracting younger people, which may have been the main reason for the support from the church, but it swung too far into anti-nomianism, leading to abuse and disrepute. Finding the golden mean between wildness and respectability to attract the energy of youth and the resources of older professionals is the challenge and aim for most religions.

The young people who in the 1970s would have joined Buddhism, the Osho movement, or another of the more counter-cultural NRMs, are now tending to join Paganism instead. There are three interconnected routes of entry. The primary route is through 'techno-shamanism', a development of the Rave/Acid House dance culture that emerged in Britain in the late 1980s to become an oppositional subculture for rebellious youth. The combination of Ecstasy and music, including Pagan bands such as Succubus Incubus, produces altered states of consciousness, which people then become interested in reproducing through non-drug means: shamanic drumming, chant and magical ritual. Some Pagan groups such as the Society of Druids do rituals at raves as well as at rock festivals, particularly Glastonbury. These are well attended by Pagans, providing another route of entry. Whereas older people are likely to become interested through reading books, younger people are more likely to search the Internet, where Paganism is well represented on the home pages and in newsgroups. A third route of entry is environmental activism, particularly the road protest movement, thus attracting people to Paganism who might previously have joined a left-wing party or cause.

One non-politically correct but fundamental question is: Who will win? Whether the New Age and evangelical movements will clash in a final Armageddon that leads to apocalypse, the return of the Dark Ages, or a New Age of sweetness and light, is hard to predict. For the foreseeable future the likeliest outcome is the continued growth of both, accompanied by the continued decline of mainstream Christianity. It may be that there will be no outright winners, but increasing overlap and globalization especially among the most popular religions, caught between deconstructive post-modernism and holistic syncretism. Syncretism has traditionally been condemned by theologians as transient, superficial and vulgar, although Christianity has survived partly through its skills in absorbing, borrowing and adapting from other religions and social trends. The New Age and Paganism make a virtue of syncretism, which is the leading mode for the appropriation and development of ideas in our post-modern age.

There are certainly many signs of formal and informal interfaith interaction, including Buddhist–Christian dialogues, a certain amount of Buddhist–Pagan overlap,[4] and even Pagan–Christian merging. As one neo-shaman expressed it, 'Christ was a great shaman, healer and teacher, connected with spirits, possessing extraordinary powers. So I see no contradiction between Christ as avatar and the shamanic tradition.' If a new world religion were to emerge from this new religious consciousness, it would be likely to contain elements of all these strands in a synthesis akin to creation spirituality, whether Christianity, Buddhism or Paganism were its main identity. It would certainly need to feature Christian mysticism, shamanic technique, social activism, Goddess spirituality and ecospirituality. Yet just as nations refuse to surrender their identity in a greater confederation, so more likely than a grand syncretism of religions is a continuing, increasing diversity. In religion as in nature, diversity is strength.

# Notes

## Introduction

1   I am adopting the sociological term for such movements: '"NRM" is an entirely appropriate, value-free term to be used at a time when there is a strong tendency to regard virtually all expressions of religion as equally valid' (Beckford 1985, 15). I sometimes use the term 'new religion' for variety.

2   Counting movements is notoriously difficult, but most assessments agree that there are upwards of 500 NRMs in Britain, 2000 in America. Counting members is even harder, given the levels of commitment, fast turnover, and tendency for NRMs to over-estimate their membership. There are probably around one million people who have had at least minimal involvement in an NRM in Britain in the last 30 years, but far fewer who have become full-time members. It is unlikely that even the largest movements have had more than about 1000 members at any time, though the worldwide membership may be far higher (Barker 1989).

3   The model also applies more clearly to the more 'world-rejecting', communal NRMs with charismatic leaders. The more world-accepting or -accommodating movements are less sharply demarcated from society, hence display these characteristics less clearly.

4   There does appear to be a certain amount of professional bias at work in the choice of positions. Psychologists have a professional interest in emphasizing the biological and psychological bases of gender, which they tend to do, although humanistic and transpersonal psychologists are more flexible. On the other hand, sociologists and feminist researchers from all disciplines are professionally and ideologically drawn to social explanations.

5   For example, Rosemary Ruether: 'There is no necessary (biological) connection between reproductive complementarity and either psychological or social role differentiation' (1983, 111).

6   The authors of one of the most authoritative textbooks on gender conclude: 'In the absence of clearly specified theories, ambiguities in defining our variables and in describing our results lead us to fall back on our intuitive, commonsense understanding of men and women' (Archer & Lloyd 1985, 47).

7   For detailed discussions of feminist methodology see Roberts 1981; Bowles 1983; Gorelick 1991; Lorber & Farrell 1991; Lather 1991. In addition, the *Journal of Feminist Studies on Religion* continuously features articles and discussions on methodology, particularly by Elisabeth Fiorenza.

8   Cited by Lather 1991, 121.

## 1 New Religions and the Counter-Culture

1 Cited in the report of the 1995 State of the World Forum, held in San Francisco.

2 The term was invented by the historian and philosopher of science Thomas Kuhn in 1962, and popularized by various New Age writers, particularly Marilyn Ferguson 1989, whose book provides the best overview of the ideas and interests. New Paradigm is also sometimes used by the more intellectual wing of this movement, in distinction from what they see as the 'flakier' New Age end.

3 See Campbell 1995, Hutton 1996 for, respectively, the influence of Romanticism on the New Age and Paganism.

4 For more detailed accounts of the counter-culture see Roszak 1968; 1970; Wuthnow 1976; Bellah 1970; Glock & Bellah 1976; Ferguson 1989. Schur 1976 and Lasch 1978 give more critical accounts.

5 See Rowan (1976) on the development of humanistic psychology and the HPM. See also Anthony *et al.* 1978; Claxton 1981; Stone 1981.

6 Reich proposed this argument in *The Function of the Orgasm* and developed it in his later book *The Mass Psychology of Fascism.*

7 *Bertrand Russell: The Spirit of Solitude* by Ray Monk (London: Cape 1996).

8 Interview with Lynda Lee-Potter, *Daily Mail,* 25 May 1996.

9 Review by Nicholas Lezard in *The Guardian,* 9 February 1996.

10 This trend is partly evidenced by the steady fall in belief in God since the Second World War recorded by the Gallup polls, and its replacement by belief in spirit or life force. See Campbell 1995 for further discussion, and chapter 10 of this book.

11 Peter Berger saw this as an inherent problem of modern social life: 'The paradox of techniques . . . applied to the attainment of nonfunctional relations with other people points to the inherent difficulty of the de-modernizing impulse: one wants to be sensitive to others in the manner of a poet, and one is trained for what purports to be such sensitivity in situations that are planned and manipulated in readymade packages' (1977, 186).

12 See for example Conze 1951; Bellah 1970; Wuthnow 1976; Cox 1979; Ellwood 1979; Glock & Bellah 1976; Needleman 1977; Hardy 1984; Oliver 1979; Tipton 1982.

13 Koestler (1960) has noted that Jung has no following in India and is disliked for his perceived misinterpretations of Indian religion and philosophy. Jones (1979) shows how they were based on unqualified, unproven assumptions of correlations between Western psychology and Eastern religion.

14 See Tonkinson's 1996 anthology of the Beats' writing on Buddhism, with an introduction analysing its appeal and influence. See also Tomory (1996) for a colourful eye-witness chronicle of counter-cultural India.

15 Glock and Bellah (1976, 1). It was also noted with some misgivings and cynicism by the theologian Harvey Cox: 'It could be said . . . of many of the current Eastern masters that they came teaching enlightenment but what happened was yet another spate of American self-

improvement sects' (1979, 136). However, Sharma argues that it fulfilled a real need: 'Meditation thus may be seen as compensating for ... the spiritual emptiness of the Protestant Ethic' (1985, 123). John Crook sees it as a positive and successful trend: 'In the West today there are numerous centres providing instruction in Eastern "ways". Many of these are excellent and do good work. This is especially true of those that stick closely to the simplicities of a basic psychological practice and teach the elements of meditation, be it *vipassana, zazen,* Tibetan, or the tantric bioenergetics of Bhagwan Shree Rajneesh' (1980, 375).

16    For example, Sangharakshita realized aged 15 that 'I was not a Christian and never had been'. When he read some Buddhist scriptures a year later, he 'knew that I was a Buddhist and always had been' (1976, 15).

17    His birth-name was Rajneesh Chandra Mohan, but he later gave himself the title Bhagwan (see below). On his return to India in 1986 after being deported from America, he changed his title to Osho.

18    The most comprehensive and detailed analysis of the Rajneeshpuram phase is given by Carter (1990).

## 2   The Making of the Master–Disciple Relationship

1     The most significant work on charismatic authority is by Bryan Wilson and Roy Wallis (see bibliography).

2     See Wuthnow (1976); Wallis 1979; Stark & Bainbridge 1985.

3     There is a strong correlation between Richardson's (1978) active convert paradigm, Volinn's (1985) spiritual journey, and Batson & Ventis's (1982) 'quest' dimension of religous experience. Batson & Ventis developed questonnaire scales to empirically detect this approach, and provide some evidence of a correlation with mental health.

4     Mullan 1983, 51. There is broad consensus on this profile among researchers; see also Belfrage 1981; Thompson & Heelas 1986; Milne 1986; Fitzgerald 1986; Gordon 1987. In terms of personality type, both Krishna Deva's (1981) and Latkin's (1987) personality testings show that sannyasins tend to be well balanced but individualistic, even rebellious.

5     See Batson & Ventis 1982, drawing on Gallup polls and other surveys.

6     See Chapter 9 for a discussion of the relations between the women's movement and feminist witchcraft.

7     The following section is based on Lofland & Skonovd's 1981 typology of 'conversion motifs'. They distinguished six motifs: intellectual, mystical, experimental, affectional, revivalist and coercive. Lofland later criticized the model as deterministic, but it is useful if applied flexibly. See also Barker 1989 for a chapter discussing different theories and processes of conversion.

8     Cited in the official biography by Joshi (1982, 15). Lewis Carter criticized it as 'a collection of images selected for public projection of an enlightened master' (1990, 42), but his own rational language of 'vertically integrated new spiritual business' and 'product testing' (46–7) is equally tendentious, alien to the world of spirituality.

9     Hardy (1988) has noted that the Jains were the great tellers of religious stories in India.

### 3   Abuse of Power: The Shadow Side of Charismatic Authority

1     See Koestler 1960; Brent 1972; Mangalwadi 1977.

2     This problem is explored in depth by Leonard (1982) and Secunda (1992), who describe the devastating effects on women's self-esteem and ability to love and be loved stemming from inadequate fathering.

3     As this book goes to press (1996), public concern in Britain over sexual misconduct in the priesthood has come to a head following another major scandal in the Catholic church: the resignation of Bishop Roderick Wright (aka the 'bonking bishop' and the Bishop of Muck) after running off with a female parishioner. It was then revealed that he was also the father of an unacknowledged son by another woman. There has been extensive media coverage of similar stories over the last few years, including an article based on research on 50 women who had had relationships with Catholic priests (Clare Jenkins, *Guardian*, 3 January 1994). Wright was widely viewed as compounding his misdemeanours by selling the story to Britain's most scurrilous and disreputable tabloid newspaper, the *News of the World*. The evidence suggests that about 50 per cent of the Catholic priesthood in the developed world are involved in sexual relationships, and that the numbers are higher elsewhere. It is also known that compulsory celibacy is a major factor in the loss of over 100 000 priests since the Second Vatican Council ended in 1965. A number of support groups have been set up to deal with the predicament of the women and children involved in these relationships, including Seven-Eleven and Sonflowers in Britain. The problem of the sexual abuse of children has reached the point where the Catholic Church has taken out an insurance policy to deal with legal cases.

4     These quotations are taken from the words of Brain's female parishioners on a BBC1 television documentary (*Heart of the Matter*, 26 November 1995) and as reported in the press at the time of the events.

5     'Mo letter' written in 1978 and cited in Melton 1994, who gives the fullest account of sexual practice in the Family. See also Wallis 1986; Davis 1984 for an insider's account by Mo's daughter.

6     This is recognized in professional training: 'The most complex form of learning takes place when training is concerned with the values and attitudes of people and groups. This is not only the most complex area, but also the most difficult and dangerous': Michael Armstrong, *Handbook of Personnel Management Practice* (London: Kogan Page, 1991) p. 427.

7     Campbell (1996, 99). See also Smith 1987, another feminist researcher who reached similar conclusions regarding the position of women in Tantra. Geoffrey Samuel also disputes Shaw's interpretation on the basis that women teachers in Tibet were a very small minority, and only four or five out of 84 Mahasiddhas were women; also that the

relationship between Padmasambhava and his consorts was not equal (personal communication).

8     The main source for these unsubstantiated rumours is an ex-sannyasin Hugh Milne (1986).

9     Merging is a common metaphor applied to the master–disciple relationship in Eastern religion and NRMs, including Elan Vital (Dupertuis 1986) and the Osho movement.

10    As Anne Wilson Schaef, one of the foremost therapists of the Recovery movement explains it: 'We have long wondered why persons in destructive, battering relationships do not just get out. The more we understand the powerlessness of addiction . . . and addictions as an addictive disease that is progressive and fatal, the more we understand the stranglehold of dependency and addiction. Addictive relating erodes the psyche and the being so much that often those in addictive relationships are too battered and bewildered to quit or get out' (1992). The point is also made strongly in such bestsellers of popular psychology as *Women Who Love Too Much* by Robin Norwood, and *Men Who Hate Women and the Women Who Love Them* by Susan Forward. Butterfield notes the same pattern of 'inner circle secrecy' in Trungpa's organization, again making the comparison with dysfunctional families.

11    See for example Boucher 1988, Butterfield 1994 on Buddhism; Webster 1990 on Swami Rama; Goldman 1988 on the Osho movement; Finnigan (forthcoming 1997).

12    Cited in the *Guardian* 1994, see note 4.

13    The ritual is described in her book *Daughters of Eve* (London: Aquarian 1992).

14    In Tibet 'it was, and still is felt by some women that having sex with an advanced Tantric adept will bring physical and spiritual benefit' (Stevens 1990, 79). This observation has been made by several Buddhists who have lived in Tibetan monasteries, including Stephen Batchelor.

## 4   Devotion: The Path of Feminine Spirituality?

1     On gender roles and spirituality in Indian religions see Gupta 1986; Young 1987; Leslie 1989; Gombrich 1990.

2     'In its highest form [*bhakti*] becomes "love", and that as a mutual relationship between Krsna and the devotee' (Hardy 1988, 624).

3     See Batey 1971 on Gnosticism; Bolle 1987 chronicles the *hieros gamos* in ancient religions and its influence on love poetry.

4     'Physical sexual imagery was used of mystical religions, and men and women spoke of raptures or being rapt, which comes from the same root as raped. But the difference was in the willing consent of abandonment to God' (Parrinder 1980, 218).

5     John Donne, Holy Sonnet, in *The Metaphysical Poets*, Helen Gardner (ed.), (Harmondsworth: Penguin, 1968).

6     This view is of course increasingly common among feminist theologians and others. See for example Munro 1992; Sharma 1985.

7     Esther Harding (1970; 1971) developed his ideas on femininity extensively, romantically and mythologically in the 1930s, and is still widely

read. Among contemporary psychologists Marion Woodman is the most highly regarded with her theory of the 'conscious feminine'. Linda Leonard (1982) focuses on the father–daughter relationship. Jean Bolen applies Jungian archetypes in creating a goddess typology for women. Sylvia Perera in her classic book *Descent to the Goddess* retells the Sumerian myth of Inanna as an initiation ritual for women. June Singer seeks the Divine Feminine in the Judaeo-Christian tradition, and has also written on androgyny (see below). Some male Jungian psychologists have developed these ideas influentially, particularly Robert Johnson (1989), and Edward Whitmont (1982), who has criticized the sexism in Jung and his female collaborator Toni Wolff. The main feminist theologians who have criticized Jung are Naomi Goldenberg, Charlene Spretnak (1982), and Carol Christ (1979).

8   Gurdjieff also held this traditional view: 'Nature of woman is very different from that of man. Woman is from ground, and only hope for her to arise to another stage of development . . . is with man. Woman already know everything, but such knowledge is of no use to her . . . unless have man with her. Man have one thing that not exist in woman ever; what you call "aspiration"' (Peters 1980, 124).

9   The above quotes are cited from three separate lectures reprinted in another women's issue of the *OTI* (16 May 1992).

10  A special 'women's issue' of the *OTI* (16 August 1991) was dedicated to women's issues and lists some of their criticisms.

11  The landmark work was Valerie Saiving's 1960 essay 'The human situation: a feminine view' reprinted in Christ & Plaskow 1992. This position is now held by many feminist theologians.

12  Kraemer (1980) describes ecstatic ritual in the cult of Dionysus in ancient Greece; Lewis (1971) writes extensively on ecstatic elements in traditional possession cults; Knox (1950) describes the manifestations of 'enthusiasm' in Christianity.

13  The Toronto Blessing is explored by a member of the Toronto Airport Vineyard in *Catch the Fire* by Guy Chevreau (London: HarperCollins 1994).

14  Extracts from a 1979 *darshan* diary reprinted in Osho 1984.

15  On the psychological definition and measurement of androgyny see Bem (1974; 1979) who created the Bem Sex-Role Inventory, and argued that 'a mixed, or androgynous, self-concept might allow an individual to freely engage in both "masculine" and "feminine" behaviors' (1974, 155).

    Whitmont uses Jung's terms animus and anima to 'denote archetypal masculinity and femininity respectively', preferring to use 'indigenous Western words for psychological dynamics and leave the Chinese Yang–Yin for the cosmic and biological principles which they were intended to denote' (1982, 40). Rowan (1981) also objects to the loose use of yin and yang in the HPM and New Age, but they remain popular with participants.

16  Spretnak 1982; King 1987; 1989.

17  For example, Carmelite friars find it hard to describe the physiological symptoms of mystical experiences because of the association of eroticism

with masculine concepts of God and Christ, whereas Carmelite nuns as 'Brides of Christ' have no problem. There is a theory that St John of the Cross's theology attempted to 'feminize the soul' for union with a masculine God (Hood & Hall 1980).

18 In Hindu mythology the *gopis* are the cowgirls who became Krishna's girlfriends and devotees.

## 5 Sexuality: Union or Opposition of Body and Spirit?

1 US figures based on Wuthnow 1976 and Aidala 1985. British figures based on figures from the Office of Population Censuses and Surveys (OPCS). The most relevant statistics show that following a sharp rise in marriage during the 1950s–1960s, there has been an ever-sharpening fall since 1971, culminating in a 7 per cent drop in 1990/1 (latest available figures). Among first-time marriage partners 1985–8, 58 per cent had cohabited, compared to 33 per cent 1975–9 and 6 per cent in the late 1960s. The age of first marriages has increased by about 2 years in the last 20 years. Divorces have increased from 2.1 per thousand in 1961 to 13 per 1000 in 1990, and are happening sooner, from a rate of 10 per cent divorces after 25 years in 1951 (1 in 80) to 10 per cent after 4.5 years in 1981 (1 in 9). Figures for adultery are more contentious, showing enormous variation. *Relate*'s figures of 60–70 per cent men, 40 per cent women have been widely contested, and other evidence varies from 5–25 per cent or even lower. A European-wide survey in 1990 showed 19 per cent of British people found marriage outdated, supported by a 1993 Mori poll showing 16 per cent agree that marriage is dead. The information is supplemented by a 1994 survey of nearly 20 000 people, *Sexual Behaviour in Britain* by Kaye Wellings *et al.* (Penguin 1994).

2 A 1993 book, *Women, Celibacy and Passion* by Sally Cline, was the impetus for a spate of publicity on this phenomenon. See also Hodgkinson (1986).

3 Ruether 1987, 218; see also Ruether 1990; King 1989; Bednarowski 1992. For general accounts of sexuality and religion see Goldberg 1931; Parrinder 1980.

4 Judaism is often regarded as accepting, even affirmative of sex, but historically it has regarded women as profane and polluted. Archer 1990 ascribed Jewish misogyny to an ancient blood taboo, in which male blood was positively valued and female blood negatively valued. See also Plaskow 1989; Long 1992.

5 Donnelly 1982; Hurcombe 1987; Fischer 1988; Grey 1989; Ruether 1990. Fox 1988 bases his sexual mysticism on the Song of Songs, interpreting its imagery wholly in terms of the Cosmic Christ.

6 Young (1987, 70). See also Marglin 1987; Gombrich 1990. Koestler described the Indian attitude to sex as 'more ambivalent and paradoxical than any other nation's' in its combination of asceticism and eroticism (1960, 136–8).

7 Allione 1984; Boucher 1985; Friedman 1987; Stevens 1990; Shaw 1994.

8 'Women's Role in World Peace', address to launch British chapter of the Women's Federation for World Peace, November 1992.

9 Cited in ISKCON's official magazine *Back to Godhead* 1991, issues 1 and 2, in which a selection of women devotees express their views. See Knott 1987; 1995 for a full account of women in ISKCON. These attitudes and practices were also confirmed in my own fieldwork.

10 The following quotations are taken from a BK pamphlet *Purity and Brahmacharya: A Solution of Our Problems*, privately published in Delhi (1976) and not generally available outside India.

11 Skultans 1993, 53. See also Babb 1986. Newby made the same point regarding the Shakers: 'Inherent in celibacy, moreover, was the negation of the institution of marriage. Thus, no woman was the legal "property" of any man, and Shaker women were certainly not "dead to the law"' (1990, 98).

12 Berger 1974, 181; see also Luckmann 1967, 111–12.

13 For example, Margharita Laski in her book *Ecstasy* found that 33 per cent mystical experiences in her survey had been triggered by sexual love.

14 Osho's line on homosexuality was inconsistent, as with most of his teaching. Mostly he opposed it, but from a psychological rather than moral perspective, seeing it as an arrested stage of development, encouraged by repression, hence 'born as a religious phenomenon in the monasteries'. He argued that homosexual relationships were dull and one-dimensional, lacking spark and adventure, for which the 'polar opposites' of male and female were needed. He suggested that homosexuals should try to 'progress' to the third, heterosexual stage in order to attain the ultimate goal of transcendence. In practice, homosexuality was tolerated for men and women.

15 See Mullan 1983; Thompson & Heelas 1986; Palmer 1987.

16 *OTI* 1991, 4(22), 11; 4(24), 12.

17 The US immigration service got evidence that many of the marriages contracted at Rajneeshpuram were arranged for the purpose of obtaining permanent residency visas (Mann 1991, 74; Carter 1990, 151). However, Fitzgerald observed that some at least appeared to be genuine (1986, 313).

18 Geoffrey Samuel discusses the possible influences of Tantra on Crowley and Wicca in a paper comparing Paganism and Tibetan Buddhism (in preparation).

19 For academic accounts see Christ & Plaskow 1979; Neitz 1990. A good practitioner's account is Noble 1991.

20 This trend has attracted media attention in national newspapers and magazines, for example 'Pagans of Suburbia' in *Elle*, February 1994, and articles on alternative weddings in the *Independent* 13 February 1995 and 24 December 1995. Even *Hello!* magazine has featured a celebrity handfasting. Graham Harvey has written a chapter on Handfastings in Druidry in *The Druid Renaissance* (Thorsons 1996).

21 See Kanter 1972 on social control of relationship in nineteenth–century groups. Aidala 1985 discusses these trends with regard to contemporary communes.

22  Cited in Mann 1992, 159. See also Milne 1986, 143 and Carter 1990, 60 on this point.
23  The most balanced, comprehensive account of Family sexuality is by Melton 1994. Father David's daughter's book is an informative insider's account but coloured by the bitterness of an abused ex-member (Davis 1984).

## 6  Motherhood and Community: Beyond the Nuclear Family

1  For the anti-cultist view see Rudin 1984; Ritchie 1991. For sociological discussion see Barker 1989; Wilson 1990. Robbins & Anthony discuss the issue in the first edn of *In Gods We Trust* (Transaction, 1981) in the context of 'brainwashing', viewing 'cultism' more as the consequence than cause of dissolution.
2  See Thorne 1982; Berger & Berger 1983; Baker 1990. Fletcher gives a conservative defence of the nuclear family as universal, even divinely appointed, but still sees the liberation of women as 'the one factor most radically changing the nature of familial relationships, [which] may yet prove to be the most significant of all revolutions in the modern world' (1988, 149).
3  See Hall 1978 for the history of utopian communes.
4  Wuthnow 1976; Ferguson 1980.
5  The Fellowship for Intentional Community, which has its own Internet site, lists over 500 US communities in its 1994 Directory, around 50 of which have been founded in the last five years.
6  See Aidala 1985; Boucher 1988; Rose 1990; Davidman 1990; Goldman 1991; Greenwood forthcoming.
7  See Brigitte & Peter Berger 1983 for a fuller account of the influence of feminism on family life.
8  This position is partly based on the Hindu doctrine that the goal of the religious life is to become *dwija*, twice-born, a rebirth into the spiritual Self.
9  Goldman (1991) argues that many sannyasins had dysfunctional childhoods but admits that their interpretations were probably influenced by the movement's psychology-based belief that families are the root cause of all emotional dysfunction. Latkin's (1987) widescale psychometric testing found that they were a mentally healthy and well-balanced group.
10  Barker makes this point, citing scriptural references to Jesus's and Buddha's exhortations to their disciples (1989, 87).
11  See Kanter 1972; Kern 1981 on Oneida.
12  See Barker 1989; Jacobs 1989; Hardman 1992. Rudin 1984 gives the ACM view.
13  For the anthropological view see Thorne 1982; for the feminist spiritual view see Stone 1976; Sjoo & Mor 1987. Leonard 1982 and Secunda 1993 argue that girls are psychologically damaged by lack of a father.
14  See Osho 1991 for a fuller account of his philosophy of education.
15  The New Man was a key concept in Osho's teaching, first expressed in a message to the World Symposium on Humanity: 'I teach a new man, a new humanity, a new concept of being in the world. I proclaim

Homo novus. . . . My sannyasins, my people, are the first rays of that new man. . . . The new man embodies a more viable, mutant image of man, a new way of being in the cosmos, a qualitatively different way of perceiving and experiencing reality. So please don't mourn the passing of the old. Rejoice that the old is dying, the night is dying, and the dawn is on the horizon' (1987, 89–94).

Osho's (1991) teachings on the 'new child' are compiled into a book distributed by Osho Ko Hsuan School.

16    Gordon 1987; Mullan 1983.

## 7  Gender Roles, Work and Power

1    Pavlos 1982, 132; see also Rudin 1984.

2    *Back to Godhead*, 1, Jan./Feb. 1991; 2, Mar./Apr. 1991.

3    Cited in the official FWBO magazine *The Golden Drum* (Nov. 1989–Jan. 1990), an issue devoted to the discussion of women's issues.

4    Thomas Robbins, *Cults, Converts and Charisma* (London: Sage, 1988), p. 51. On gender roles in women's spirituality see King 1989; Neitz 1990; Finley 1991; Bednarowski 1992.

5    Ferguson 1982, 355; see also Berger 1974; Roszak 1968.

6    This proclamation was originally made in a 1978 discourse and was printed on the back cover of the compilation of Osho's teachings on women's liberation (1987).

7    Braun 1984; Palmer 1987; Latkin 1987; Goldman 1988.

8    Cited by Thompson & Heelas 1986, 93. They appear to endorse this statement, quoting a Medina sannyasin in support.

9    1983b, 155. Buddha actually claimed the commune's life would be reduced from 1000 to 500 years.

10    See Munro 1992, who argues that not only did Jesus choose women as his close disciples but they chose him as God's agent of redemption. Mann 1991 notes the importance of women in launching the careers of Sri Aurobindo, Krishnamurti and Maharishi Mahesh Yogi as well as Osho. See Herrera's 1992 autobiographical account of her role in the Maharishi's career. It is also noteworthy, remembering that Osho was born into a Jain family, that Mahavir's first disciple was a woman, Arya Chandana, whom he later appointed as head of his order of nuns.

11    Joshi 1982, 100. Milne notes that 'It was mostly Laxmi who spread the idea that Bhagwan was a Godlike person who could influence events – the weather, financial matters, relationships, trouble with the police. . . . She would say, "He will take care of it, don't worry"' (1986, 71).

12    See Gordon (1986, 160, 222–3) for an account of her treatment, which she also gave me in her final interview. Gordon also describes a personal interview he had with Osho in which he questioned Sheela's appointment, but Osho refused to admit any misjudgment or exploitation.

13    See also Mullan 1983; Thompson & Heelas 1986.

## 8  Female Spiritual Leadership in NRMs

1    Feminist scholarship has done much to rediscover and revive these forgotten figures. The most comprehensive anthology of writings across

the traditions is *An Anthology of Sacred Texts by and about Women* by Serinity Young (London: Pandora, 1993). Torjesen 1993 researched women's leadership in early Christianity. Tharu & Lalita 1991 produced a comprehensive collection of Indian women writers. Allione 1984 and Shaw 1994 have resuscitated many Tibetan and Tantric women writers and mystics.

2   A favourite device was to sit people in front of Osho's picture while in a heightened emotional state, often triggering strong conversion experiences. There were mixed responses to the priest–therapists, some reverential, some critical: 'They'd walk around with halos, and I always found that nauseating, sickening, a manipulative trick, a hierarchical way of being with people.' One therapist bluntly admitted: 'It was a religion, and I became a priest.' See Puttick 1994 for a chapter on Rajneesh therapy. See also Claxton 1981; Heelas & Kohn 1986 on HPM therapy. Palmer & Bird 1992 discuss therapy as socialization.

3   There was a contest for leadership between Gurumayi and her brother Nityananda, which she won. There are allegations of organized harassment against him by ashram staff, bugging and surveillance, environmental damage, and various other ethical concerns. Research on Siddha Yoga was carried out by Catherine Wessinger in 1990 and is cited in Jacobs 1991. Accounts of these episodes and the characters involved vary considerably.

4   Martine Batchelor has 'abbreviated' the relative status of Buddhist nuns to monks thus: 'Korean nuns are 90 per cent equal to monks, Japanese nuns 60 per cent, Taiwanese nuns 85 per cent, Thai nuns 15 per cent, Tibetan nuns 45 per cent' (1996, xiii).

5   Friedman (1987) and Boucher (1993) interviewed a number of these teachers, demonstrating the rich variety of their approaches. Some of these are named and discussed below; other renowned teachers include Toni Packer, Ruth Denison, Yvonne Rand, Aya Khema, Tsultrim Allione, Ria Gross, Pema Chodron, Charlene Spretnak, and Gesshin Prabhasa Dharma.

6   Friedman 1987; Boucher 1993.

7   Ellwood presents an alternative interpretation of her approach as a magus or trickster: 'that figure in many mythologies who cleverly outwits both gods and men and manages to establish a precarious immortality for himself on the tenuous boundary between heaven and human society' (1979, 56).

8   The only published research on Chrisemma is a chapter in Shaw (1994).

9   For a personal account of a visit to Ammachi see Housden 1996.

10  Quotations from his book 1991, 33, 36, 130. Interview in *Yoga Journal* Sept/Oct 1991. Harvey also provided the questions for Mother Meera's own book *Answers* (London: Rider, 1992).

11  Research for a PhD on Sahaja Yoga is currently being undertaken by Judith Coney at SOAS, University of London.

12  For a challenging, in-depth account of the role of women in early Christianity, see Torjesen 1993.

13  See Mary Greer's article 'Women of the Golden Dawn' in *Gnosis*, Fall 1991, 56–63 for their influence on this society. Ironically, two of them

are best known for their association with more famous men, Mathers as brother of the French philosopher Henri Bergson, Gonne as muse to W.B. Yeats.

14   'Pelagia of Antioch, a dancing girl and prostitute who was converted to Christianity, lived in male garb until her true sex was discovered after her death. Another devout woman, Margarita, fled the bridal chamber to become Pelagius the monk and eventually the prior of a monastery. Expelled for allegedly fathering the doorkeeper's child, she kept secret her true identity and died alone as a hermit, at which time her innocence was recognized. A similar accusation of alleged paternity, followed by later reinstatement to holiness, befell the female ascetic monk Marina (Marinus)' (Linn 1987, 497).

15   Jungian psychology also makes this distinction, criticizing the imma-ture or 'puella' woman whose 'shadow... is tied up with power – a power which she has not truly and responsibily accepted' (Leonard 1982, 58) as well as her opposite, the 'armoured Amazon' who is instructed to 'free herself of the idea she must be like a man to have power' and 'soften her armor' (84).

## 9   Goddess Spirituality: The Feminist Alternative?

1   The reformist v revolutionary argument was developed by Christ and Plaskow in the first (1979) edition of *Womanspirit Rising*, but modified in the revised (1992) edition as well as in their subsequent book *Weaving the Visions* (Plaskow & Christ, 1989).

2   Two detailed and fascinating studies of the Goddess of Wisdom are a closely argued work of painstaking scholarship focused mainly on the Judaeo-Christian tradition by Long (1992) and a more inspirational though also well researched book focused more on the Western mys-tery traditions by Matthews (1991). There is also a chapter on Sophia in Baring & Cashford (1993).

3   The source for this belief is Hippolytus, cited by Pagels in Christ & Plaskow 1992. See also Haskins 1993 for a popular, iconographic history of changing fashions in devotion to Mary Magdalen. Most feminist theologians deal with the Virgin Mary in their writings, but the most challenging and stimulating account, again largely iconographic, is by Warner 1976.

4   *Messages from Mary* by Annie Kirkwood, a Texan medium who claims a direct connection with Mary.

5   Spretnak (1982, xix). See below for discussion of different meanings of the Goddess.

6   While on the subject of psychology, it may be worth noting the diffi-culty in choosing an appropriate adjective to describe important books by women; there is no female equivalent to 'seminal'.

7   See Whitmont 1982. Johnson has written various books on the subject of femininity and masculinity, of which the best known are *She* and *He*. Devotion to the goddess is implicit in Campbell's writings, but his most extensive essay is in a compilation on the divine feminine, *In All Her Names*, edited by himself and Charles Muses.

8    The most popular goddesses in this respect are Artemis, Athena, Aphrodite and Hera. Jean Shinoda Bolen has added Hestia, Demeter and Persephone, and these seven archetypes are the subject of her best-selling book *Goddesses in Everywoman* (New York: Harper & Row, 1984). See also *Odyssey with the Goddess: a spiritual quest in Crete* by Carol Christ (New York: Continuum, 1995).

9    See Campbell 1996 for a full account of the origins and significance of Kuan Yin.

10   Grist explained his position in uncompromisingly trenchant terms in an article in the *Guardian* (15 April 1991), an English national newspaper to which he is a regular contributor.

11   Extract from a talk given at St James's Church, London, 30 April 1996.

12   Adler, a practitioner, estimated that there were only around 10 000 American Pagans, whereas Kelly (1992) has come up with a figure of 300 000, growing rapidly, based on a range of methods and sources. In Britain estimates vary wildly – between 2000 and over a million – but 10–30 000 seems a more likely estimate, again accompanied by rapid growth and diversity. Tanya Luhrman (1989) estimated 2000 organized practitioners of magic, which seems a conservative figure but was based on extensive research. Clan Mother Shan tells the press there are over a million Pagans, but this does seem somewhat exaggerated. The *World Christian Encyclopaedia* lists 30 000 witches. Beth Gurevitch has a database of 100 000 people interested in the New Age and Paganism, including 11 000 witches. Around 2000 people attended the first Pagan festival in London in 1988. Michael York has done extensive research and gives a conservative estimate of around 10 000 British Pagans, 40 000 in America (personal communication).

13   Most spiritual feminists and Pagans accept that they are representations of the sacred female or goddesses, and two of the most important books popularizing this mythology are *The Great Cosmic Mother* by Monica Sjoo and Barbara Mor (San Francisco: Harper & Row, 1987), and *The Myth of the Goddess* by Anne Baring and Jules Cashford (London: Viking, 1991). But even in this camp there is dispute. For example, Lucy Goodison (1994) has done extensive research on ancient Crete and finds little evidence for a goddess-worshipping matriarchy. Gimbutas's theories were partly based on unacknowledged anthropological sources, particularly the writings of Jacob Bachofen. For a fuller account of the literature and its influences on theories of matriarchy, see Morris 1994, who also exposes the Eurocentric bias of much feminist mythology.

14   Margot Adler uses the term neo-Pagan, as does Michael York. Reluctance to be classified as an NRM is common among movements so termed by sociologists, particularly those that claim ancient lineage, such as ISKCON.

15   The height of the witch-hunts was actually during the early modern period. Historians have estimated 300 000 deaths, but feminist researchers suggest a much higher toll, estimates varying between three and nine million, of which around 85 per cent were women. On the other hand, two Pagan historians give a much lower figure of 40–100 000

(Jones & Pennick 1995). For a full account of the witch-hunt see Barstow 1994. For a fuller discussion on roots, see York 1991; Jones & Pennick 1995.

16  From *The Burning Times* by Charlie Murphy, often sung in Pagan gatherings; cited by Crowley 1993.

17  This is the opinion of Susan Greenwood (in preparation), based on extensive anthropological research.

18  The relationship between Paganism and the New Age is an important but complex issue, beyond the scope of this book. It is clear that many beliefs and practices are common to both, although meanings and significance may differ considerably. For example, belief in karma and reincarnation is common to both but usually emphasized more in the New Age, particularly in conjunction with Eastern teachings. Practitioners themselves tend to be unconcerned with classification, and may identify with either, neither or both camps, while being given a different label by a sociological observer. Michael York (1991) has made an in-depth comparison between the two movements and finds much convergence but also significant contrast in values.

19  Margot Adler, cited by Gadon 1989, 237.

20  In the US women have always predominated, partly because it has become a more loosely defined religion, and many non-aligned Pagans identify themselves as Wiccans. In Britain the ratio of women to men has changed dramatically from around 30:70 to 55:45 (figures from the Pagan Federation).

21  York (1991) suggests that the Asatru Free Assembly is patriarchal and conservative, while the Odinist Fellowship is neo-Nazi, although they deny this allegation. Crowley (1993) points out that the role of the *volva* (seeress) is important, one of the most prominent being Freya Aswynn. Although Druidry in general is male-dominated, one of the fastest growing groups within it is Pagan Druidry, which is less patriarchal and contains many goddess followers; see Shallcrass 1986.

22  See for example Kelly 1992. The most comprehensive insider account of Wicca is *Wicca* by Vivianne Crowley (1996).

23  Some feminist theologians have developed similar models of female/feminist power, for example Elizabeth Fiorenza, Mary Daly, Ursula King, Mary Grey.

24  In *Beyond God the Father*, first published in 1973 (1985, 5).

25  Cited by Neitz 1990, 358.

26  *The Spiral Dance*, first published in 1979, is considered by American booksellers to be one of the 20 most influential women's books of the last 20 years (*Publisher's Weekly*, 5 November 1992).

27  It is significant that in Britain there are 5 million members of environmental groups, as compared with 3.7 million churchgoers. David Starkey at the London School of Economics has described ecology as having 'replaced Christianity as the religion of our age' (*Independent*, 27 May 1996).

28  Geoffrey Samuel (1996) gives an extensive comparison between Paganism and Buddhism, particularly *qua* nature religions.

29  Karen J. Warren, quoted on the Internet.

30  Interview with Brenda Polan, the *Guardian*, 15 November 1988.
31  This issue is discussed in detail by Ursula King (1989). As Christ and Plaskow express it: 'A fully adequate feminist theology must express the combination of rootedness in nature and freedom that feminists experience in their lives' (1992, 12).
32  It is interesting that it is mainly Christian or Christian-based theologians who are sounding the alarm, for example King 1989, Grey 1989, Christ & Plaskow 1989. Although their warnings contain an important point, they may also reflect the difficulty of overcoming millennia of body-negative dualism and the Christian denigration of immanence in favour of transcendence See Goodison (1992) on gender and symbol.
33  See in particular Lasch 1979; Schur 1976.
34  Paul Vallely, *Independent*, 27 May 1996.

## 10  A New Model of Spiritual Needs and Values

1  See Barker 1989 for discussion on madness and suicide rates in NRMs and other areas of public concern such as crime, violence, finances and drugs. Research suggests that having a religious belief tends to result in improved mental health.

Barker also concluded from extensive research on the Unification Church, one of the most controversial NRMs, that 'while a small proportion of Moonies could be classified as inadequate, and a slightly larger (but still small) proportion could be classified as slightly sad or pathetic, most Moonies do not differ signify from their peers with respect to characterisitics which could form independent criteria for assessing whether or not a person could be classified as prone to "passive suggestibility"' (1984, 203).
2  Voodoo, along with some other Afro-Brazilian movements, has developed a more 'sophisticated' psychospiritual dimension in its post-slavery forms, under leaders such as Luisah Teish in America.
3  A recent book denouncing gurus, *The Guru Papers: Masks of Authoritarian Power* by Joel Kramer and Diana Alstad, has also influenced this swing of opinion.
4  The forthcoming issue of the American Pagan magazine *Green Egg* will be devoted to 'Buddheo–Paganism' (winter 1996). One woman who bridges Buddhism with shamanism, particularly Native American spirituality, is Joan Halifax (1993).

# Bibliography

Aidala, Angela (1985) Social change, gender roles, and new religious movements, *Sociological Analysis*, 46(3), 287–314

Allione, Tsultrim (1984) *Women of Wisdom*, London: Routledge

Amrito, Swami Prem (1989 unpublished) *The Choice is Ours: the Key to the Future – a Contribution to the International Scientific Revolutionary party, a Grand Synthesis of Communism, Meditation and Anarchism, inspired by the Enlightened Mystic Osho Rajneesh*

Anand, Margo (1989) *The Art of Sexual Ecstasy*, Los Angeles: Tarcher

Anthony, Dick, Ecker Bruce, & Wilber, Ken (1987) *Spiritual Choices: The Problem of Recognizing Authentic Paths to Inner Transformation*, New York: Paragon House

Archer, John & Lloyd, Barbara (1985) *Sex and Gender*, Cambridge: Cambridge University Press

Archer, Leonie J (1990) 'In thy blood live': gender and ritual in the Judaeo-Christian tradition, in Joseph (ed.)

Ardener, Shirley (ed.) (1975) *Perceiving Women*, London: Dent

Atkinson Clarissa *et al.* (eds) (1987) *Immaculate and Powerful: The Female in Sacred Imagery and Social Reality*, Wellingborough: Crucible

Babb, Lawrence A. (1986) *Redemptive Encounters: Three Modern Styles in the Hindu Tradition*, Berkeley: University of California Press

Baker, Adrienne D. (1990) Role expectations of Anglo-Jewish Wives at Midlife, unpublished PhD thesis, University of London

Bancroft, Anne (1989) *Weavers of Wisdom*, London: Arkana

Baring, Anne & Cashford, Jules (1993) *The Myth of the Goddess*, London: Arkana

Barker, Eileen (1984) *The Making of a Moonie*, Oxford: Blackwell

Barker, Eileen (1989) *New religious movements: A Practical Introduction*, London: HMSO

Barnes, Douglas F. (1978) Charisma and religious leadership: an historical analysis, *Journal for the Scientific Study of Religion*, 17(1), 1–18

Barnes, Michael (1990) The guru in Hinduism, in L. Byrne (ed.), *Traditions of Spiritual Guidance*, London: Chapman

Barstow, Anne (1994) *Witchcraze*, London: Pandora

Batchelor, Martine (1992) *Women and Ecology*, London: Cassells

Batchelor, Martine (1996) *Walking on Lotus Flowers*, London: Thorsons

Batchelor, Stephen (1994) *The Awakening of the West: The Encounter of Buddhism and Western Culture*, London: Aquarian

Batey, R.A. (1971) *New Testament Nuptial Imagery*, Leiden: E.J. Brill

Batson C. Daniel & Ventis, W. Larry (1982) *The Religious Experience: A Social Psychological Perspective*, New York & Oxford: Oxford University Press

Bednarowski, Mary (1992) The New Age and Feminist Spirituality: Overlapping Conversations at the End of the Century, in James Lewis & J. Gordon Melton (eds), *Perspectives on the New Age*, New York: SUNY

Belfrage, Sally (1981) *Flowers of Emptiness*, London: Women's Press

263

Bellah, Robert N. (1970) *Beyond Belief*, New York: Harper & Row

Bem, Sandra (1974) The measurement of psychological androgyny, *Journal of Consulting and Clinical Psychology*, 42(2), 155–62

Bem, Sandra (1979) The theory and measurement of androgyny: a reply to the Pedhezur-Tettenbaum and Locksley-Collen critiques, *Journal of Personality and Social Psychology*, 37(6), 1047–54

Berger, Brigitte & Peter L. (1983) *The War over the Family: Capturing the Middle Ground*, London: Hutchinson

Berger, Peter L. & Kellner, Hansfried (1974) *The Homeless Mind: Modernization and Consciousness*, Harmondsworth: Penguin

Bharti, Ma Satya (1980) *The Ultimate Risk*, London: Wildwood House

Bharti, Ma Satya (1981) *Death Comes Dancing: Celebrating Life with Bhagwan Shree Rajneesh*, London: Routledge

Boadella, David (1987) The fall of the light-bearer, *Self & Society*, 15(5), 229–32

Bolen, Jean Shinoda (1984) *Goddesses in Everywoman*, New York: Harper & Row

Bolle, Kees (1987) Hieros Gamos, in *Encyclopedia of Religion*, vol. 6, 317–21

Boucher, Sandy (1988) *Turning the Wheel: American Women Creating the New Buddhism*, Boston: Beacon Press

Bowles, Gloria & Klein, Renate (1983) *Theories of Women's Studies*, London: RKP

Brahma Kumaris (1976) *Purity and Brahmacharya: A Solution of our Problems*, Delhi

Butterfield, Stephen (1992) Accusing the tiger: sexual ethics and Buddhist teachers, *Tricycle*, Summer, 46–51

Butterfield, Stephen (1994) *The Double Mirror*, Berkeley, CA: North Atlantic Books

Camic, Charles (1987) Charisma: its varieties, preconditions, and consequences, in J. Rabow *et al.* (eds), *Advances in Psychoanalytic Sociology*, Malabar, FL: E. Krieger Publishing Co, 238–76

Campbell, Colin (1995) The easternization of the west, paper presented at the symposium 'NRMs: Challenge and Response'

Campbell, June (1996) *Traveller in Space: In Search of Female Identity in Tibetan Buddhism*, London: Athlone Press

Carey, Sean (1987) The indianization of the Hare Krishna movement in Britain, in Richard Burghert (ed.), *Hinduism in Great Britain*, London: Tavistock, 81–99

Carter, Lewis F. (1990) *Charisma and Control in Rajneeshpuram: The Role of Shared Values in the Creation of a Community*, Cambridge: Cambridge University Press

Christ, Carol P. & Plaskow, Judith (1992) *Womanspirit Rising: A Feminist Reader in Religion*, San Francisco: HarperSanFrancisco, 2nd edn

Clarke, Peter B. (1993) Why women are priests and teachers in Bahian Candomblé, in Puttick & Clarke (eds), 97–113

Claxton, Guy (1981) *Wholly Human: Western and Eastern Visions of the Self and Its Perfection*, London: RKP

Collin-Smith, Joyce (1988) *Call No Man Master*, Bath: Gateway

Cooey, Paula (1985) The power of transformation and the transformation of power, *Journal of Feminist Studies in Religion*, 1(1), 23–36

Cox, Harvey (1979) *Turning East: The Promise and Peril of the New Orientalism*, London: Allen Lane

Crawford, C. (ed.) (1986) *In Search of Hindduism*, New York: Unification Theological Seminary

Crowley, Vivianne (1993) Women and Power in Modern Paganism, in Puttick & Clarke (eds), 125–40

Crowley, Vivianne (1994) *Phoenix from the Flame*, London: Aquarian

Crowley, Vivianne (1996) *Wicca*, London: Thorsons, 2nd edn

Culpepper, Emily F. (1978) The spiritual movement of radical feminist consciousness, in Jacob Needleman & George Baker (eds), *Understanding the New Religions*, New York: Seabury Press, 220–34

Daly, Mary (1979) *Gyn/Ecology: The Metaethics of Radical Feminism*, London: Women's Press

Daly, Mary (1985) *Beyond God the Father: Towards a Philosophy of Women's Liberation*, Boston: Beacon Press, 2nd edn

Davidman, Lynn (1990) Women's search for family and roots: a Jewish solution to a modern dilemma, in Robbins & Anthony (eds), 385–407

Davis, Deborah (1984) *The Children of God: The Inside Story*, Basingstoke: Marshalls

Donnelly, Dorothy H. (1982) The sexual mystic: embodied sexuality, in Giles (ed), 120–41

Dowell, Susan & Hurcombe, Linda (1981) *Dispossessed Daughters of Eve: Faith and Feminism*, London: SCM Press

DuPertuis, Lucy (1986) How people recognize charisma: the case of *darshan* in *Radhasoami* and Divine Light Mission, *Sociological Analysis*, 47(2), 111–24

Eisler, Riane (1990) *The Chalice and the Blade*, London: Mandala

Ellwood, Robert (1979) *Alternative Altars: Unconventional and Eastern Spirituality in America*, Chicago: University of Chicago Press

*Encyclopedia of Religion* (1987), Mircea Eliade (ed.), New York: Macmillan Publishing Co.

Estes, Clarissa (1993) *Women Who Run with the Wolves*, London: Rider

Falk, Nancy & Gross, Rita (eds) (1980) *Unspoken Worlds: Women's Lives in Non-Western Cultures*, San Francisco: Harper & Row

Falk, Nancy (1987) Feminine sacrality, *Encyclopedia of Religion*, 302–12

Farrant, Sheila (1989) *Symbols for Women*, London: Mandala

Feldman, Christina (1989) *Woman Awake: A Celebration of Women's Wisdom*, London: Arkana

Feldman, Christina (1994) *Quest of the Warrior Woman*, London: Thorsons

Fell, Alison (1977) All a Girl Needs Is a Guru, *Spare Rib*, 59, 6–10

Ferguson, Marilyn (1989) *The Aquarian Conspiracy: Personal and Social Transformation in the 1980s*, London: RKP: 1981

Finley, Nancy J. (1991) Political activism and feminist spirituality, *Sociological Analysis*, 52(4), 349–62

Finnigan, Mary (1997) *The Iron Bird Flies*, London: Thorsons

Fischer, Kathleen (1988) *Women at the Well: Feminist Perspectives on Spiritual Direction*, London: SPCK

Fitzgerald, Frances (1986) *Cities on a Hill: A Journey through American Subcultures*, New York: Simon & Schuster

Fletcher, Ronald (1988) *The Shaking of the Foundations: family and society*, London: Routledge

Fox, Matthew (1988) *The Coming of the Cosmic Christ*, San Francisco: Harper & Row

Fox, Matthew (1991) *Creation Spirituality*, San Francisco: HarperSanFrancisco

Franklin, Satya Bharti (1992) *The Promise of Paradise: a Woman's Intimate Story of the Perils of Life with Rajneesh*, New York: Station Hill

Friedman, Lenore (1987) *Meetings with Remarkable Women*, Boston: Shambhala

Fromm, Erich (1950) *Psychoanalysis and Religion*, New Haven & London: Yale University Press

Fromm, Erich (1960), *Psychoanalysis and Zen Buddhism*, London: Unwin

Gadon, Elinor W. (1989) *The Once and Future Goddess*, San Francisco: HarperSanFrancisco

Gidley, Mick (ed.) (1990) *Locating the Shakers*, Exeter: University of Exeter Press

Giles, Mary E. (ed.) (1982) *The Feminist Mystic and Other Essays on Women and Spirituality*, New York: Crossroad

Gimbutas, Marija (1982) *The Goddesses and Gods of Old Europe 6500–3500 BC: Myths and Cult Images*, London: Thames & Hudson, 2nd edn

Glock, Charles Y. & Bellah, Robert N. (1976) *The New Religious Consciousness*, Berkeley: University of California Press

Goldberg, B.Z. (1931) *The Sacred Fire: The Story of Sex in Religion*, London: Jarrolds

Goldman, Marion S. (1988) The Women of Rajneeshpuram, *SCWS Review*, University of Oregon, 18–21

Goldman, Marion S. (1991) Experiencing Rajneesh: Transference, Gender and the Seeking Self, unpublished paper presented at the London School of Economics, 20 November 1991

Gombrich, Sanjukta Gupta (1990) Divine mother or cosmic destroyer: the paradox at the heart of the ritual life of Hindu women, in Joseph (ed.), 50–9

Goodison, Lucy (1992) *Moving Heaven and Earth*, London: Pandora

Gordon, James S. (1987) *The Golden Guru: The Strange Journey of Bhagwan Shree Rajneesh*, Lexington, MA: Stephen Greene Press

Gorelick, Sherry (1991) Contradictions of feminist methodology, *Gender and Society*, 5(4), 459–77

Goswell, Marilyn (1989) Motivational Factors in the Life of a Religious Community and Related Changes in the Experience of Self, unpublished PhD thesis, University of Bath

Grant, Linda (1993) *Sexing the Millennium: A Political History of the Sexual Revolution*, London: HarperCollins

Greene, Liz (1986) *Relating*, London: Aquarian

Greenwood, Susan (1995) Feminist Witchcraft, in Hughes-Freeland & Charles (eds), *Practising Feminism*, London: Routledge

Greer, Germaine (1984) *Sex and Destiny: The Politics of Human Fertility*, London: Secker & Warburg

Grey, Mary (1989) *Redeeming the Dream: Feminism, Redemption, and Christian Tradition*, London: SPCK

Griffin, Wendy (1995) The embodied goddess: feminist witchcraft and female divinity, *Sociology of Religion*, 56(1), 35–48

Gupta, Bina (1986) Role and status of Indian women: a comparison of contemporary Indian and American professional women, in Crawford (ed.), 165–82

Halifax, Joan (1993) *The Fruitful Darkness*, San Francisco: HarperSan-Francisco

Hall, John R. (1978) *The Ways Out: Utopian Communal Groups in an Age of Babylon*, London: RKP

Harder, Mary W. (1974) Sex Roles in the Jesus Movement, *Social Compass*, 21(3), 345–53

Harder, Mary W. *et al.* (1976) Lifestyle: courtship, marriage and family in a changing Jesus Movement organization, *International Review of Modern Society*, 6, 155–72

Harding, M. Esther (1970) *The Way of All Women: A Psychological Interpretation*, New York: C.G. Jung Foundation

Harding, M. Esther (1971) *Woman's Mysteries: Ancient and Modern*, London: Longmans, revised edn

Hardman, Charlotte (1992) Children in new religious movements: abused, captive or free? paper presented to the SSSR, Washington, November 1992

Hardy, Friedhelm (1988) The Classical Religions of India, in Sutherland *et al.* (eds), 569–659

Harrison, Shirley (1990) 'Cults': *The Battle for God*, London: Christopher Helm

Harvey, Andrew (1991) *Hidden Journey*, London: Bloomsbury

Harvey, Graham & Hardman, Charlotte (eds) (1996) *Paganism Today*, London: Thorsons

Haskins, Susan (1993) *Mary Magdalen*, London: HarperCollins

Haywood, Carol Lois (1983) The authority and empowerment of women among spiritualist groups, *Journal for the Scientific Study of Religion*, 22(2), 157–66

Heelas, Paul & Kohn, Rachael (1986) Psychotherapy and techniques of transformation, in Guy Claxton (ed.), *Beyond Therapy*, London: Wisdom

Herrera, Nancy Cooke (1992) *Beyond Gurus*, Nevada City, CA: Blue Dolphin

Hodgkinson, Liz (1986) *Sex Is Not Compulsory*, London: Columbus

Holden, Pat (ed.) (1983) *Women's Religious Experience*, London: Croom Helm

Hood, R.W. & Hall, J.R. (1980) Gender differences in the description of erotic and mystical experiences, *Review of Religious Research*, 21(2), 195–207

Hounam, Peter & Hogg, Andrew (1984) *Secret Cult*, Tring: Lion

Housden, Roger (1996) *Sacred India*, London: Thorsons

Hurcombe, Linda (ed.) (1987) *Sex and God: Some Varieties of Women's Religious Experience*, London: Routledge

Hutch, Richard A. (1984) Types of women religious leaders, *Religion*, 14, 155–73

Hutton, Ronald (1996) The discovery of the modern Goddess, paper presented at Lancaster University

Igglehart, Hallie (1982) The unnatural divorce of spirituality and politics, in Spretnak (ed.), 404–14

Jacobs, Janet (1984) The Economy of Love in Religious Commitment: The Deconversion of Women from non-traditional religious movements, *Journal for the Scientific Study of Religion*, 23(2), 155–71

Jacobs, Janet (1987) Deconversion from religious movements: an analysis of charismatic bonding and spiritual commitment, *Journal for the Scientific Study of Religion*, 26(3), 294–308

Jacobs, Janet (1989) *Divine Disenchantment: Deconverting from New Religions*, Bloomington & Indianopolis: Indiana University Press

Jacobs, Janet (1991) Gender and power in new religious movements, *Religion*, 21, 345–56

Jamal, Michele (1987) *Shape Shifters: Shaman Women in Contemporary Society*, London: Arkana

James, William (1960) *The Varieties of Religious Experience*, London: Fontana

Jones, David (1987) Bhagwan and the Human Potential Movement, *Self & Society*, 15(5), 203–8

Jones, Prudence & Pennick, Nigel (1995) *A History of Pagan Europe*, London: Routledge

Jones, R.H. (1979) Jung and Eastern religious traditions, *Religion*, 9(2), 141–56

Joseph, Alison (ed.) (1990) *Through the Devil's Gateway: Women, Religion and Taboo*, London: SPCK/Channel 4

Joshi, Vasant (1982) *The Awakened One: The Life and Work of Bhagwan Shree Rajneesh*, San Francisco: Harper & Row

Jung, C.G. (1986) *Aspects of the Feminine*, London: Ark

Kanter, Rosabeth Moss (1972) *Commitment and Community: Communes and Utopias in Sociological Perspective*, Cambridge, MA: Harvard University Press

Kaplan, Alexandra G. & Bean, Joan P. (eds) (1976) *Beyond Sex-Role Stereotypes: Readings Towards a Psychology of Androgyny*, Boston: Little, Brown & Co

Kaslow, F. & Sussman, M.B. (eds) (1982) *Cults and the Family*, New York: Haworth Press

Kelly, Aidan (1992) An update on neopagan witchcraft in America, in James Lewis & Gordon Melton (eds), *Perspectives on the New Age*, New York: SUNY Press

Kern, Louis J. (1981) *An Ordered Love: Sex Roles and Sexuality in Victorian Utopias – the Shakers, the Mormons, and the Oneida Community*, Chapel Hill: University of North Carolina Press

Kern, Louis J. (1990) Maternal Paradigms, Erotic Strategies and Sororal Consciousness: Sexuality and Women's Experiences among the Shakers and in the Kerista commune, in Gidley (ed.), 127–45

King, Ursula (1987) Goddesses, witches, androgyny and beyond? Feminism and the transformation of religious consciousness, in King (ed.), 201–18

King, Ursula (1989) *Women and Spirituality: Voices of Protest and Promise*, London: Macmillan Education

King, Ursula (1993) The great Indian Goddess: a source of empowerment for women?, in Puttick & Clarke (eds), 25–38

King, Ursula (ed.) (1987) *Women in the World's Religions, Past and Present*, New York: Paragon House

Kinsley, David (1987) Devotion, in *Encyclopedia of Religion*, 4, 321–6

Knott, Kim (1987) Men and Women, or devotees? Krishna Consciousness and the Role of women, in King (ed.), 111–28

Knott, Kim (1995) The debate about women in the Hare Krishna movement, *Journal of Vaishnava Studies*, 3(4), 85–109

Koestler, Arthur (1960) *The Lotus and the Robot*, London: Hutchinson

Kornfield, Jack (1989) Even the best meditators have old wounds to heal, *Yoga Journal*

Kraemer, Ross (1980) Ecstasy and Possession: Women of Ancient Greece and the cult of Dionysus, in Falk & Gross (eds), 53–69

La Fontaine, J.S. (1994) *The Extent and Nature of Organised and Ritual Sexual Abuse of Children*, London: HMSO

Laing, R.D. (1971) *The Politics of the Family*, London: Tavistock

Landes, Ruth (1947), *The City of Women*, New York: Macmillan

van der Lans, Jan & Derks, Frans (1986) Premies versus sannyasins, *Update*, 10(2), 19–27

Lasch, Christopher (1978) *The Culture of Narcissism: American Life in an Age of Diminishing Expectations*, New York: W. Norton

Lather, Patti (1991) *Getting Smart*, New York: Routledge

Latkin, Carl A. (1987) Rajneeshpuram, Oregon: An Exploration of Gender and Work Roles, Self-Concept and Psychological Well-being in an Experimental Community, unpublished PhD thesis, University of Oregon

Latkin, Carl A. (1991) From device to vice: social control and intergroup conflict at Rajneeshpuram, *Sociological Analysis*, 52(4), 363–78

Latkin, Carl A. (1992) Seeing red: a social-psychological analysis of the Rajneeshpuram conflict, *Sociological Analysis*, 53(3), 257–71

Leonard, Linda S. (1982) *The Wounded Woman: Healing the Father–Daughter Relationship*, Athens, OH: Swallow Press

Leslie, Julia (1983) Essence and existence: women and religion in ancient Indian texts, in Holden (ed.), 89–112

Leslie, Julia (1989) Religion, gender and *dharma*: the case of the widow–ascetic, unpublished paper presented at BASR annual conference in Oxford, 22–24 September 1989

Lewis, I.M. (1971) *Ecstatic Religion: An Anthropological Study of Spiritual Possession and Shamanism*, Harmondsworth: Penguin

Linn, P.R. (1987) Gender roles, in *Encyclopedia of Religion*, vol. 5, 495–502

Lofland, John & Skonovd, Norman (1981) Conversion motifs, *Journal for the Scientific Study of Religion*, 20(4), 373–85

Long, Asphodel P. (1992) *In a Chariot Drawn by Lions*, London: Women's Press

Lorber, Judith & Farrell, Susan (1991) *The Social Construction of Gender*, Newbury Park: Sage

Luhrmann, Tanya M. (1989) *Persuasions of the Witch's Craft*, Oxford: Blackwell

Macy, Joanna (1991) *World as Lover, World as Self*, Berkeley, CA: Parallax Press

Maitland, Sara (1987) Passionate prayer: masochistic images in women's experiences, in Hurcombe (ed.), 125–40

Mangalwadi, Vishal (1977) *The World of Gurus*, New Delhi: Vikas

Mann, W.E. (1991) *The Quest for Total Bliss: A Psycho-social Perspective on the Rajneesh movement*, Toronto: Canadian Scholars' Press

Marglin, Frederique Apffel, Female Sexuality in the Hindu world, in Atkinson *et al.* (eds), 39–60

Maslow, Abraham (1943) A Theory of Human Motivation, *Psychological Review*, 50, 370–96

Maslow, Abraham (1970a) *Motivation and Personality*, New York: Harper & Row, 2nd edn

Maslow, Abraham (1970b) *Religions, Values and Peak Experiences*, Harmond-sworth: Penguin

Masson, Jeffrey (1990) *Against Therapy*, London: Fontana

Matthews, Caitlín (1991) *Sophia Goddess of Wisdom*, London: Mandala

Mehta, Gita (1980) *Karma Cola*, London: Cape

Melton, J. Gordon (1994) Sexuality and the maturation of 'The Family', unpublished paper presented at Federal University of Pernambuco, Brazil

Meredith, George (no date [1987]) *Bhagwan: The Most Godless Yet the Most Godly Man*, Poona: Rebel Press

Milne, Hugh (1986) *The God that Failed*, London: Caliban

Morris, Brian (1994) Matriliny and mother goddess religion, *Raven*, 25, 68–76

Mullan, Bob (1983) *Life as Laughter: Following Bhagwan Shree Rajneesh*, London: Routledge

Munro, Winsome (1992) Women disciples: Light from a secret Mark, *Journal of Feminist Studies in Religion*, 8(1), 47–64

Needleman, Jacob (1977) *The New Religions*, New York: Doubleday, 2nd edn

Neitz, Mary-Jo (1990) In Goddess We Trust, in Robbins & Anthony (eds), 353–72

Nizami, F.A. (1988) Islam in the Indian subcontinent, in Sutherland *et al.* (eds), 368–89

Noble, Vicki (1991) *Shakti Woman*, San Francisco: HarperSanFrancisco

Occhiogrosso, Peter (1994) *The Joy of Sects*, New York: Doubleday

O'Flaherty, Wendy Doniger (1980) *Women, Androgynes and Other Mythical Beasts*, Chicago: Chicago University Press

O'Flaherty, Wendy Doniger & Eliade, Mircea, Androgynes, in *Encyclopedia of Religion*, 276–81

Osho (1977) *The Tantra Vision*, vol. 1, Poona: Rajneesh Foundation

Osho (1978a) *The Path of Love*, Poona: Rajneesh Foundation

Osho (1978b) *Yoga: the Alpha and the Omega*, vol. 9, Poona: Rajneesh Foundation

Osho (1978c) *Zen: the Path of Paradox*, vol. 1, Poona: Rajneesh Foundation

Osho (1978d) *The Divine Melody*, Poona: Rajneesh Foundation

Osho (1979a) *From Sex to Superconsciousness*, Poona: Rajneesh Foundation

Osho (1979b) *The Diamond Sutra*, Poona: Rajneesh Foundation

Osho (1979c) *Zen: the Path of Paradox*, vol. 3, Poona: Rajneesh Foundation

Osho (1981) *Philosophia Perennis*, vols 1–2, Poona: Rajneesh Foundation

Osho (1982a) *The Book of the Books*, vol. 1, Rajneesh Foundation International

Osho (1982b) *Zen: Zest, Zip, Zap and Zing*, Rajneesh Foundation International

Osho (1983a) *Theologia Mystica*, Rajneesh Foundation International

Osho (1983b) *Philosophia Ultima*, Rajneesh Foundation International

Osho (1984) *The Book: An Introduction to the Teachings of Bhagwan Shree Rajneesh*, Rajneesh Foundation International

Osho (n.d. [1985a]) *From Bondage to Freedom*, Cologne: Rebel Press

Osho (n.d. [1985b]) *From the False to the True*, Cologne: Rebel Press

Osho (1987a) *The Messiah*, Cologne: Rebel Press

Osho (1987b) *A New Vision of Women's Liberation*, Cologne: Rebel Press

Osho (1991) *The New Child*, Amsterdam: Osho Publikaties Nederland

Palmer, Susan J. (1986a) Purity and Danger in the Rajneesh Foundation, *Update*, 10(3), 18–29

Palmer, Susan J. (1986b) Community and Commitment in the Rajneesh Foundation, *Update*, 10(4), 3–15

Palmer, Susan J. (1988) Charisma and abdication: a study of the leadership of Bhagwan Shree Rajneesh, *Sociological Analysis*, 49(2), 119–35

Palmer, Susan J. (1993) Rajneesh women: lovers and leaders in a utopian commune, in Palmer & Sharma (eds), 103–35

Palmer, Susan J. (1994) *Moon Sisters, Krishna Mothers, Rajneesh Lovers*, Syracuse, NY: Syracuse University Press

Palmer, Susan J. & Bird, Frederick (1992) Therapy, charisma and social control in the Rajneesh movement, *Sociological Analysis*, 53(S), 71–85

Palmer, Susan J. & Sharma, Arvind (1993) *The Rajneesh Papers: Studies in a new religious movement*, Delhi: Motilal Banarsidass

Parrinder, Geoffrey (1980) *Sex in the World's Religions*, London: Sheldon

Paul, Diana (1979) *Women in Buddhism: Images of the Feminine in Mahayana Tradition*, Berkeley: University of California Press

Peters, Fritz (1980) *My Journey with a Mystic*, Laguna Niguel, CA: Tale Weaver Publishing

Plaskow, Judith & Christ, Carol P. (eds) (1989) *Weaving the Visions: New Patterns in Feminist Spirituality*, San Francisco: Harper & Row

Puttick, Elizabeth (1990) The Rajneesh movement: an update, *Religion Today* 6(1), 13–14

Puttick, Elizabeth (1993) Devotees and Matriarchs: Women Sannyasins in the Rajneesh movement, in Puttick & Clarke (eds), 63–76

Puttick Elizabeth (1994) Gender, Discipleship and Charismatic Authority in the Rajneesh movement, unpublished PhD thesis, University of London

Puttick, Elizabeth (1995) Sexuality, gender and the abuse of power in the master–disciple relationship, *Journal of Contemporary Religion*, 10(1), 29–40

Puttick Elizabeth & Clarke, Peter B. (1993) *Women as Teachers and Disciples in Traditional and New Religions*, Lewiston, NY: The Edwin Mellen Press

*Rajneeshism: An Introduction to Bhagwan Shree Rajneesh and His Religion* (1983) Rajneesh Foundation International

Ranke-Heinemann, Uta (1990) *Eunuchs for Heaven: The Catholic Church and Sexuality*, London: Deutsch

Reich, Wilhelm (1968) *The Function of the Orgasm*, London: Granada

Richardson, James T. (1978) *Conversion Careers: In and Out of the New Religions*, London: Sage

Ritchie, Jean (1991) *The Secret World of Cults*, London: Angus & Robertson

Robbins, Thomas & Anthony, Dick (1990) (eds) *In Gods We Trust*, New Brunswick: Transaction Publishers, 2nd edn

Rose, Susan D. (1987) Women warriors: the negotiation of gender in a charismatic community, *Sociological Analysis*, 48(3), 245–58

Rose, Susan D. (1990) Gender, education and the New Christian Right, in Robbins & Anthony (eds), 99–117

Roszak, Theodore (1970) *The Making of a Counter Culture*, London: Faber

Rowan, John (1976) *Ordinary Ecstasy: Humanistic Psychology in Action*, London: RKP

Rowan, John (1981) Against Yin and Yang and androgyny, *Self & Society*, 9(4), 192–5

Ruether, Rosemary Radford (1983) *Sexism and God-talk: Towards a Feminist Theology*, London: SCM Press

Ruether, Rosemary Radford (1992) *Gaia and God*, San Francisco: HarperSanFrancisco

Rutter, Peter (1990) *Sex in the Forbidden Zone*, London: Mandala

Samuel, Geoffrey (1996) Paganism and Tibetan Buddhism: contemporary western religions and the question of nature, unpublished paper presented at Lancaster University

Sands, Kathleen M. (1992) Uses of the thea(o)logian: sex and theodicy in religious feminism, *Journal of Feminist Studies in Religion*, 8(1), 7–33

Schaef, Anne Wilson (1992) *Women's Reality*, San Francisco: HarperSanFrancisco

Schur, Edwin (1976) *The Awareness Trap: Self-absorption instead of Social Change*, New York: Quadrangle

Secunda, Victoria (1993) *Women and Their Fathers*, London: Cedar

Shallcrass, Philip (1996) A priest of the Goddess, *Druid's Voice*, 7, 9–18

Sharma, Arvind (1985) The Rajneesh movement, in Stark (ed.), *Genesis, Exodus and Numbers*, New York: Paragon House, 115–28

Sharma, Arvind (ed.) (1987) *Women in World Religions*, New York: State University of New York Press

Shaw, Miranda (1994) *Passionate Enlightenment*, Princeton, NJ: Princeton University Press

Shaw, William (1995) *Spying in Guru Land*, London: Fourth Estate

Sherfey, Mary Jane (1973) On the nature of female sexuality, in Miller (ed.), *Psychoanalysis and Women*, Harmondsworth: Penguin, 136–53

Shunyo, Ma Prem (1992) *Diamond Days with Osho*, Cologne: Rebel Press

Sjoo, Monica & Mor, Barbara (1987) *The Great Cosmic Mother*, San Francisco: Harper & Row

Skultans, Vieda (1983) Mediums, controls and eminent men, in Holden (ed.), 15–26

Skultans, Vieda (1993) The Brahma Kumaris and the role of women, in Puttick & Clarke (eds), 47–62

Smith, D. (1990) Religious orientation, sex-role traditionalism, and gender identity: contrasting male and female responses to socializing forces, *Sociological Analysis*, 51(4), 377–85

Spretnak, Charlene (1991) *States of Grace*, San Francisco: HarperSanFrancisco

Spretnak, Charlene (ed.) (1982) *The Politics of Women's Spirituality: Essays on the Rise of Spiritual Power within the Feminist Movement*, New York: Anchor Press

Starhawk (1989) *The Spiral Dance*, San Francisco: HarperSanFrancisco, 2nd edn

Stark, Rodney & Bainbridge, William S. (1985) *The Future of Religion*, Berkeley: University of California Press

Stevens, John (1990) *Lust for Enlightenment*, Boston, MA: Shambhala

Stone, Merlin (1976) *When God Was a Woman*, New York: Dial Press

Streitfeld, Harold (1981) *God's Plan: The Complete Guide to the Future*, Oakland: Raja Press

Strelley, Kate (1987) *The Ultimate Game: The Rise and Fall of Bhagwan Shree Rajneesh*, San Francisco: Harper & Row

Subhuti, Dharmachari (1985) *Buddhism for Today: A Portrait of a New Buddhist Movement*, Glasgow: Windhorse

Sudesh, Sister (1993) Women as Spiritual Leaders in the Brahma Kumaris, in Puttick & Clarke (eds), 39–45

Sutherland, Stewart *et al.* (eds) (1988) *The World's Religions*, London: Routledge

Sviri, Sara (1993) *'Daughter of Fire' by Irina Tweedie: Documentation and Experiences of a Modern Naqshbandi Sufi*, in Puttick & Clarke (eds), 77–90

Taylor, Donald (1987) Charismatic authority in the Sathya Sai Baba movement, in R. Burghert (ed.), *Hinduism in Great Britain*, London: Tavistock, 119–33

Thompson, Judith & Heelas, Paul (1986) *The Way of the Heart: The Rajneesh movement*, Wellingborough: Aquarian

Thorne, Barrie with Yalom, Marilyn (eds) (1982) *Rethinking the Family: Some Feminist Questions*, New York: Longman

Thouless, Robert (1971) *An Introduction to the Psychology of Religion*, Cambridge: Cambridge University Press

Tipton, Steven M. (1982) *Getting Saved from the Sixties: Moral Meaning in Conversion and Cultural Change*, Berkeley: University of California Press

Tomory, David (1996) *A Season in Heaven*, London: Thorsons

Tonkinson, Carole (ed.) (1996) *Big Sky Mind: Buddhism and the Beat Generation*, London: Thorsons

Torjesen, Karen (1993) *When Women Were Priests*, San Francisco: HarperSanFrancisco

Tweedie, Irina (1979) *The Chasm of Fire: A Woman's Experience of Liberation through the Teachings of a Sufi Master*, Shaftesbury: Element

Tweedie, Jill (1980) *In the Name of Love*, London: Granada

Upadhyaya, K.N. (1986) The nature and role of guru in Hinduism, in Crawford (ed.), 63–88

Vandana (1978) *Gurus, Ashrams and Christians*, London: Darton, Longman & Todd

Volinn, Ernst (1985) Eastern meditation groups: why join? *Sociological Analysis*, 46(2), 147–56

Walker, Benjamin (1982) *Tantrism: Its Sacred Principles and Practices*, Wellingborough: Aquarian

Wallis, Roy (1984) *The Elementary Forms of the New Religious Life*, London: Routledge

Wallis, Roy (1986) Religion as fun? The Rajneesh movement, in Wallis & Bruce (eds), 191–224

Wallis, Roy & Bruce, Steve (eds) (1986) *Sociological Theory, Religion and Collective Action*, Belfast: Queen's University Press

Warner, Marina (1976) *Alone of All her Sex: The Myth and Cult of the Virgin Mary*, London: Weidenfeld & Nicolson

Weber, Max (1964) *The Theory of Social and Economic Organization*, translated and edited with an introduction by Talcott Parsons, New York: Free Press

Webster, Katharine (1990) The Case Against Swami Rama of the Himalayas, *Yoga Journal*, 95

Wehr, Demaris S. (1988) *Jung and Feminism: Liberating Archetypes*, London: Routledge

Weinstein, Krystyna (1995) *Action Learning*, London: HarperCollins

White, Charles (1980) Mother Guru: Jnanananda of Madras, India, in Falk & Gross (eds), 22–37

Whitmont, Edward (1982) *The Return of the Goddess*, London: Routledge

Wilber, Ken (1982) *No Boundary*, Boston: Shambhala

Wilson, Bryan R. (1975) *The Noble Savages: The Primitive Origins of Charisma and Its Contemporary Survival*, Berkeley: University of California Press

Wilson, Bryan R. (1990) *The Social Dimensions of Sectarianism: Sects and New Religious Movements in Contemporary Society*, Oxford: Clarendon

Wolfe, Tom (1976) The Me Decade and the Third Great Awakening, in *Mauve Gloves and Madmen, Clutter and Vine*, New York: Farrar, Straus & Giroux

Wuthnow, Robert (1976) *The Consciousness Reformation*, Berkeley: University of California Press

York, Michael (1991) A Sociological Profile on the New Age and Neo-Pagan Movements, unpublished PhD thesis, University of London

Young, Katherine (1987) *Hinduism* in Sharma (ed.), 59–103

Young, Serinity (1993) *An Anthology of Sacred Texts by and about Women*, London: Pandora

Zaretsky, Eli (1982) The place of the family in the origins of the Welfare State, in Thorne (ed.), 188–224

# Internet (World Wide Web) Pages

These have been selected as being the most informative, interesting and representative pages currently available. There is much anti-cult material, some of it persuasive, much of it less so. Mostly, this has been omitted. Many web sites have an email contact point for enquiries or comments, and I have found that a quick response is the norm. In any case, these are only suggested jump points for the vast amount of material available on the web. Please also note that these sites are not fixed for all time, so if there are problems, try using a search engine such as Altavista. Comments and questions regarding this book are welcome, and may be addressed to the author by email at liz@puttick. com.

| | |
|---|---|
| Brahma Kumaris | http://www.cs.man.ac.uk/~wallm5/bk/factfile.html |
| Buddhism/women | http://www.sju.edu/~dcarpent/2161/BIBLIO/women.html |
| Channelling | http://falcon.cc.ukans.edu/~ranma/wotchan.html |
| Dragon Network | http://www.ecosaurus.co.uk/coventry/environ/espirit/dra1.html |
| Ecospirituality | http://www.femina.com/femina/religion |
| ISKCON | http://www-ece.rice.edu/~vijaypai/htindex |
| Jesus Army | http://maths.uwa.edu.aul/~hartley/jesus |
| Michael teaching | http://www.roadrunner.com/~pivotal |
| Mother Meera | http://www.msn.fullfeed.com/rschenk/dmarshall/malinks.html |
| Osho Movement | http://www.earth.path.net/osho/ |
| Pagan Federation | http://www.tardis.ed.ac.uk/%7Eipf/pf_pagan.html |
| Pagan Link | http://www.innotts.co.uk/~iainlowe/paganism.html |
| Pagan Women | http://sunacm.swan.ac.uk/~paganfed/pf_womens.html |
| Raelian Movement | http://www.rael.org/10h.html |
| Starhawk | http://recall.lib.indiana.edu/~corwin/authors/starhawk |
| Transcendental Meditation | http://192.103.45.2/TM_Public/TM_courses.html |
| Unification Church | http://www.ettl.co.at/uc/europe/hq_europe.htm |
| Virtual Sisterhood | http://www.igc.apc.org/vsister/fembub |
| Wicca | http://www.lib.ox.uk/internet/mews/faq/archive/religions.wicca/ |
| Witchcraft/women | http://www.jo.com/~cortese/spirituality/wicca.html |
| Women's spirituality | http://www.femina.com/femina/religion |

# Index